The Flexible SEL Clas

Social emotional learning is more than just helping students be social. In this co-publication from Routledge and AMLE, Amber Chandler shows how middle and high school educators can be intentional about seeing their students for who they are, growing relationships, and building community.

Grounded in classroom experience, Chandler's practical strategies can be adapted to suit different needs, so you can create a Flexible Classroom and reach all learners. Topics include encouraging academic risk-taking without fear of failure, helping students self-manage, teaching self-awareness, modeling responsible decision-making and empathy, building relationship skills, and emboldening students to become more socially aware.

This updated second edition features new chapters on running Restorative Circles and focusing on resilience instead of deficit analysis. There is also a special section with post-pandemic takeaways, as we learn new ways to help students thrive.

Amber Chandler is a National Board Certified middle school English language arts (ELA) teacher in Hamburg, New York, and an adjunct professor at Canisius College in Buffalo, New York. No matter which level Chandler is teaching, the goal is always the same: to enable students to take charge of their own learning. Chandler's website, flexibleclass.com, has many resources to support teachers, and she regularly updates lessons and provides links to her webinars. Follow her on Twitter @MsAmberChandler and check out over 300 of her free resources on ShareMyLesson.com.

Also Available from AMLE

Content Area Literacy Strategies That Work:
Do This, Not That!
Lori G. Wilfong

Our Diverse Middle School Students:
A Guide to Equitable and Responsive Teaching
Elizabeth D. Dore and Deborah H. McMurtrie

The Successful Middle School: This We Believe
Penny A. Bishop and Lisa M. Harrison

Middle School: A Place to Belong & Become
Laurie Barron and Patti Kinney

The Flexible SEL Classroom

Practical Ways to Build Social Emotional Learning

2nd edition

Amber Chandler

Routledge
Taylor & Francis Group

NEW YORK AND LONDON

Cover image: GettyImages-1203009027

Second edition published 2022
by Routledge
605 Third Avenue, New York, NY 10158

and by Routledge
4 Park Square, Milton Park, Abingdon, Oxon, OX14 4RN

Routledge is an imprint of the Taylor & Francis Group, an informa business

First edition published by Routledge 2017

Library of Congress Cataloging-in-Publication Data
A catalog record has been requested for this book

ISBN: 978-1-032-13653-0 (hbk)
ISBN: 978-1-032-12662-3 (pbk)
ISBN: 978-1-003-23031-1 (ebk)

DOI: 10.4324/9781003230311

Typeset in Palatino
by Deanta Global Publishing Services Chennai India

Access the Support Material: www.routledge.com/9781032126623

Contents

About the Author

Amber Chandler is a National Board Certified middle school English language arts (ELA) teacher in Hamburg, New York, who has a master's degree in literature, as well as a School District Leader certification. Chandler has enjoyed a wide variety of teaching opportunities. Chandler is an 8th grade middle school ELA teacher, as well as an adjunct professor at Canisius College in Buffalo, New York. No matter which level Chandler is teaching, the goal is always the same: engage students to take charge of their own learning.

Chandler's blogs and articles have appeared in MiddleWeb, Share My Lesson, Getting Smart, ASCD's "Ideas From the Field," MomsRising, The Edvocate, and *AMLE Magazine*, as well as *New York Teacher*. Chandler's blogs and webinars for Share My Lesson, created by the American Federation of Teachers (AFT), have repeatedly been the top of the year, and several in the top five of the decade. Chandler enjoys speaking about student engagement, Project Based Learning, and Social Emotional Learning (SEL), at AFT TEACH, the Association for Middle Level Education (AMLE) annual conference, and Learning and the Brain conferences.

Chandler was chosen from a nationwide search as one of a handful of panelists for the Thomas B. Fordham Institute's "Evaluating the Content and Quality of Next Generation Assessments" to evaluate how state assessments compare in their ability to assess Common Core Standards. She's also served as a School Review Team member, offering her observations and expertise, particularly in the area of Project Based Learning.

Chandler is an SEL Consultant for Capstone Publisher's "My Spectacular Self" series, as well as for the GoPebble! Division. She provides SEL questions for student engagement, as well as offers developmentally appropriate advice to parents.

Chandler is an active AFT member as a Share My Lesson Partner and participant in the Resource and Materials Development at the Summer Educators Academy. Chandler recently served on NYSUT's "Future Forward Taskforce" as a voice for SEL initiatives as schools return to in-person, post-pandemic instruction. She serves as the president for her local Frontier Central Teachers Association.

Chandler's website, flexibleclass.com, has many resources to support teachers, and she regularly updates lessons and provides links to her webinars. Follow her on Twitter @MsAmberChandler and check out over 300 of her free resources on ShareMyLesson.com.

Introduction

When I wrote the first edition of *The Flexible SEL Classroom*, I remember feeling glad that I was a part of a first wave of people in the mainstream talking about Social Emotional Learning, but I was also concerned that many people would never have heard of SEL. Now, several years and a pandemic later, I'm quite certain that everyone in education has heard of it, though I'm still not confident that many understand it. Contrary to a really surface-level understanding, it isn't about socializing children per se. I've heard a number of administrators say, "We have to get students back in school because of the social emotional." What they mean, I think, is that being in-person provides important opportunities for our students' social development. However, SEL is so much more than that, and it is certainly not achieved simply by being present in a school building. Rather, as educators, we must intentionally set about truly seeing our students, grow relationships, and build community. That message was in the first edition, but I'm doubling down in this new version.

I've added a section at the end of each chapter called "Post-Pandemic Principles." Each chapter is already aligned to the Center for Academic, Social, and Emotional Learning's Competencies, so the added "Post-Pandemic Principles" are aligned to CASEL as well. In March 2020, COVID-19 was declared a pandemic by the World Health Organization, forcing school closures, virtual/remote learning, and set in motion all kinds of hybrid experiences as well. While it has become abundantly clear that we are not through the COVID-19 pandemic, I still feel comfortable with "post-" as a part of these headings. Why? The lessons we can take from 2020 alone are worth exploring systematically. I also believe that decision-making must be made with that guidepost in mind. Further, I think we need to be ready to make clear, intentional decisions about education that are ready to be implemented right now. Waiting until a true "post-" pandemic plan is in place is irresponsible, as we just simply don't know when that will be.

New to this edition are two topics that are especially important. First, addressed in Chapter 7 is the very real need for restoration. Students have lost their way forward, their faith in themselves, and their faith in the adults in the world to make sure that everything is OK. I've provided a layman's guide to implementing Restorative Circles and "bubbles," as well as questions to get you started right away. It is not necessarily possible for everyone to use full Restorative Circles in their day-to-day, but the chapter will help everyone get started on the work of restoration, and it provides the justification and guidance to begin *seeing* our students, which is ultimately the point of SEL. "Bubbles," or small restorative groupings, are explained, and these can be used to supplement other SEL activities.

Chapter 8 explains the role we will play as educators in helping our students recognize and develop their resilience. This chapter allows readers a lens to view the experiences our students have lived during the pandemic, as well as practical advice about how to leverage pandemic gains and stop the deficit analysis of our students. The chapter will help educators navigate the "losses," while helping reframe thinking to focus on the gains. We all know that assessments aren't going anywhere, but in this chapter I'll suggest some ways that formative and summative assessments can help students gain resilience.

The pandemic has devastated so many, laid bare the inequities that already existed, and taken its toll on the emotional reserves we have as educators. It is no wonder that teachers are leaving the classroom. We are being tasked with the impossible. However, for those of us who are still here, we must make a way for our students and ourselves to heal, and it is my sincere hope that this book will provide some practical advice, some from-the-trenches wisdom, and some inspiration. We must rely on each other, and forge a new way forward. This way forward is not one of standardized testing, cookie-cutter compliance, and one-size-fits-all instruction; rather, this is the time to wildly differentiate, to see our students as the dazzling humans they are, and to make sure that "education" is personalized. Perhaps, this is a moment to realize that education should have been this way all along.

Support Material

The following handouts from the book are also available on the Routledge website as free downloads:

Figure 2.1   Student Learning Profile
Figure 2.5   Group Project Application
Figure 3.2   Say What?
Figure 3.3   Metacognitive Minute Recording Sheet
Figure 4.1   Claiming Your Non-Negotiables
Figure 4.4   Personal Priorities Thermometer
Figure 4.8   Class Constitution
Figure 5.4   Fishing for Compliments!
Figure 5.6   Upstander Go-to Guide
Figure 6.1   Film Basics
Figure 6.3   Film Review Grading Guide
Figure 6.5   Film Viewing Notesheet
Figure 6.10   Empathetic Listening
Figure 8.1   *Cruella* Pre-Viewing Sheet
Figure 8.2   *Cruella* Student Viewing Guide
Figure 8.3   *Cruella* Teacher Viewing Guide
Figure 8.4   *Cruella* Rotating Chair Questions
Figure 8.5   *Playlist* Assignment

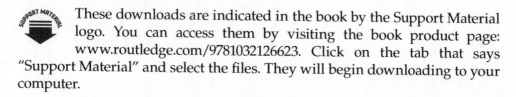 These downloads are indicated in the book by the Support Material logo. You can access them by visiting the book product page: www.routledge.com/9781032126623. Click on the tab that says "Support Material" and select the files. They will begin downloading to your computer.

1

The Truth about Grades and the Importance of Risk-Taking

Developed by Collaborative for Academic, Social, and Emotional Learning and used with permission.

Here's my dirty little secret. I have loved grades my entire life. That's because I get good ones. A nice, neat "A" at the top—no comments needed—would make my day. An "A+," and I was over the moon. It was validation of the most basic kind: you are smart, and you are doing well in school. Except, there's one little problem. Because I almost never received feedback, and I had been led to believe that I had this school thing covered, I never, and I do mean never, thought for a second about learning anything beyond what was

DOI: 10.4324/9781003230311-1

asked of me. It never occurred to me that there was more. Why? The teachers I respected were telling me this week after week. As a people pleaser, as long as they were proud of me, I was happy. It never entered my mind that I might receive less than an "A" in every college course I would take. Wow, was I in for a rude awakening when I sat in a room of students who had also received "A's" only to find out that they knew *way* more than I did about almost everything. Had my teachers been wrong?

They weren't wrong exactly, as I was really good at studying, and doing what they asked, which seemed to be monstrously important. Minus 2 points if your heading isn't correct. Minus 2 points if you failed to underline and highlight the vocabulary words you had to use in sentences. I owned those points. I was very good at following directions. However, as I quickly learned in college, I was clueless about what to do when I didn't understand something, which was a real and serious problem I had immediately. One day after I switched my major, I complained to my advisor, "I know I'll never use biology. Why do I have to take it?" His answer, I am sure, was meant to put me in my place, but it also spoke volumes about what was missing from my education. "Perhaps you will not use biology, but I assure you, in order to pass that class you will need to learn something more important. How to learn."

Trust me when I say this now, his words were crushing to my self-satisfied 18-year-old psyche. At first I was furious. Who was he to suggest that I didn't know how to learn? I had a full scholarship. What a jerk. Then, I was worried. What if he was right? What if my high school was really terrible, and I just got good grades because I was only good by comparison? Then, I was petrified. What was I going to do? This story has a happy ending, but it isn't one of smooth sailing. It is one of tears, nearly dropping out and returning home, and a "C" for the first time in my life.

I don't blame any of my teachers, but we know better now. We know about Growth Mindset. We know about the futility of standardized testing to measure the whole child. We know that students learn differently. The fact is, Social Emotional Learning (SEL) is exactly what was missing from my education, and perhaps that is why I am so interested in helping students *learn how to learn*, each and every one of them, in his or her particular set of circumstances.

You didn't hear about my parents in that story. Were they absent? Horrible? Nope. One of them had never graduated high school and the other had, but college wasn't even a possibility. They were thrilled that I got all "A's." Who were they to doubt a teacher? Now, imagine all the different family stories and life circumstances of the students in your room, and you'll realize why there must be more SEL in addition to the academic. Our students and their families have different belief systems about school, teachers, and grading. It is our job to teach students to learn, and the good grades will follow. Why do I care about grades? Because higher education still does, and as long as that is true, I will make it my goal for students to earn good grades and know what to do if they don't. In this book, I am going to address the social, emotional, and academic needs of students, but if you are anything like me, you might think that the academic should come first. Rather, I *thought* the academic should come first, until pretty recently.

Sneak Peek

In this chapter, we will

★ investigate the relationship between grades and GPA
★ consider the role of academic risk-taking in student success
★ recognize that students need more than academic learning

Following is the one major preconceived notion that needed to be dispelled for me to embrace SEL.

Are Grades and GPA the Most Important Predictors of Success?

In order for me to embrace SEL, I needed to dispel one major preconceived notion that had been driving my instruction for most of my career: grades and GPA are the most important predictors of success. Dr. Tim Elmore, the founder of Growing Leaders and author of 32 books on leadership, pinpoints "The Big Five" predictors of student success. "The Big Five" are derived from his expertise on the trends and needs of emerging generations. He writes:

> According to First Year Experience programs and our work with over 6,000 schools and organizations worldwide, we have reduced the list of highest predictors of student success (meaning engagement, excellent performance and satisfaction) to what we call the "Big Five." The "Big Five" are quite simple. When a student experiences these five realities they are most likely to graduate and excel in life:
>
> Getting connected to the right people.
> Possessing adaptability and resilience.
> Developing high emotional intelligence.
> Targeting a clear outcome.
> Making good decisions.

GPA and grades are stories about compliance and the ability to play the game of school. Don't get me wrong, compliance and playing the game of school are skills unto themselves—valuable ones at that—but they aren't the best indicators of success. Who amongst us hasn't known the "smart on paper" student who is completely helpless when they aren't simply responding to commands?

Converge this thinking to the middle grades, and it is clear that we need to take seriously the role we play in the social and emotional development of our students, because grades simply don't tell the whole story—or, lots of times, even the most important parts. The Association for Middle Level Education's foundational position paper, "This We Believe: Keys to Educating Young Adolescents," explains the paradigm we are working with as middle level educators when it comes to providing students with guidance and feedback: "Assessment should emphasize individual progress rather than comparison with other students and should not rely on extrinsic motivation. The goal is to help students discover and understand their own strengths, weaknesses, interests, and aptitudes" (26). AMLE's description of sound assessment techniques is especially relevant if a teacher is responsive and is moving away from traditional grading systems.

Academic Risk-Taking

One of the greatest goals I have in my classroom is to create an environment of academic and social risk-taking. This is carefully cultivated ground to be sure, but it is also a social/emotional need of students that is being met. Students don't want to be fed the material, but rather they learn best when they experience the learning. The difficulty with this approach is that students don't want to fail, particularly in front of their peers. However, I've found a way around this fear by incorporating the opportunity to make mistakes into my projects. "This We Believe" describes the type of academic risk-taking I'm referring to as a mode of exploration, and I love that! AMLE warns:

> If youth pass through early adolescence without broad, exploratory experiences, their future lives may be needlessly restricted. They deserve opportunities to ascertain their special interests and aptitudes, to engage in activities that will broaden their views of the world and themselves.
>
> (20)

As middle level educators, we should be jumping at the chance to impact students' lives so meaningfully through our teaching, and I for one feel privileged to be the tour guide for my students through the very bumpy terrain of middle school.

I knew there would be pushback. By 8th grade, students have already learned to choose projects that are safe, and they rarely challenge themselves to learn more because they are too programed to enjoy the grade and not the process. Ultimately, they are not comfortable with the inherent uneasiness involved with deeper learning. *My goal: normalize the uneasiness students feel when approaching challenges and alleviate the fear of failing to the point that students appreciate academic risk-taking.*

As I explained the parameters of the project, they were told they had to read 100 pages of nonfiction on the topic they chose, write a book review, and create and complete three activities which let them "show what they know" (Figure 1.1). The catch was this: one of the activities had to include academic risk-taking. They would not be penalized if they took a risk that resulted in an "epic fail." Instead, the fail was to be explained within their presentation, as well as what they learned, what they could do differently—reflections.

We brainstormed examples of what academic risk-taking would look like. Here are some great examples: trying a new kind of content delivery for their presentations (Powtoons, Canva, Haiku Deck, Piktochart, etc.); using a new (to them) way to complete a survey (SurveyMonkey, AllCounted, Typeform, Twitter polls); and contacting experts for their opinions (LinkedIn, email, phone interview, Google Hangouts, Twitter). To adults, these ideas might not be daunting, but to 13-year-olds there is nothing more nerve-racking than talking to an adult they do not know for an interview.

Some of my high-achievers were concerned, of course. Did they have to fail to do the project correctly? Would they lose points for succeeding? Of course not. But they needed for me to see their academic risk-taking to receive the points. For instance, if in the last two presentations a student did use Prezi, and they didn't choose something new, they'd not receive "risk-taking" points (I don't use a deficit grading model, but students still struggle with this). They were so used to complying and regurgitating that they weren't sure how to actually be creative and inventive—skills that are necessary for the 21st-century job market.

With freedom to fail, they were also free to seek out learning experiences instead of falling back on what they already knew. The best possible outcome happened: one of my high-achievers "failed" miserably with one of her tasks. She had researched animators, found the one she wanted to interview, and tried contacting him a few ways, to no avail. And then, she did the most wonderful thing: she learned from it and shared it with us in her presentation. Jessica's website explains what she attempted, what she learned, and what she'll do next time.

The most amazing conversations occurred around our reflection process because students were complimenting one another on risk-taking—an under-appreciated mindset. Until we recognize that academic risk-taking is, for the most part, discouraged, and until we intentionally normalize it, we will continue to create safe but stymied students. When grades are not the goal—but

---

When you were little did you ask a million questions about dinosaurs, space, germs, or some other topic, but no one really answered your questions? Ever wonder about something late into the night? Is there a burning question, searing your brain? If so, you are going to love this project. If not, then we're going to open your mind to new possibilities!

You are going to find your passion—something you want to read about, write about, take pictures of, share a story about, and even make a website to share your passion.

How It Works

First, we'll do some activities to help those who don't have a topic yet. You'll want to keep in mind that this is an individual project, and we'll be working on it for about a month and a half.

Next, after you have a topic, we'll formulate a "burning question." A **burning question** is something that you want to solve, discover, explore, or seek during your Passion Project journey. This question should be at the center of all you do. Your website will be designed to share the "answer" to your question. Don't worry. . . some questions lead to more questions, but you'll want to consider this carefully. You'll need to run it by me, since this part is such a big deal.

After you have a topic and a burning question, then you're going to find a non-fiction book on the topic. It has to be a *book*. I know. . . I know. . . there's this thing called the internet. Don't worry, you'll get to that. First though, you are going to read a book to gather background knowledge before your project really starts to take shape. When should you read this book? As soon as possible. You'll have reading time during class in the early part of the month, but you should carry this book with you to also read during study halls and free times.

Then, after you've read your book, the real fun begins! You'll need to design your **Project Parameters**. A Parameter is a rule or limit that controls what something is or how it should be done. Most of the time, I give you the parameters, but the beauty of this project is to find ways to chase your passion, and then, of course, "show what you know." I've italicized every graded part of the project (classwork or quiz grades).

FAQ (Frequently Asked Questions)

◆ How am I supposed to do this if I don't have the internet at home?
  – Study halls
  – Stay after school
  – We'll be working on this a substantial amount during class
◆ What if I don't know how to build a website?
  – I'll help
  – Your friends will help
  – The librarian will help
  – Watch the tutorials

Figure 1.1 Passion Project

◆ Why are the presentations timed?
  − Believe it or not, shorter presentations require more skill
  − We have lots of students
  − You have mastered the basics (loud, clear, prepared), so it is time to push ahead
◆ What is a Process Presentation?
  − It is the narrative of your journey
  − It will be told using the website you build
  − It is personal
◆ Can I invite people to the presentation?
  − Yes!
  − I will be inviting your parents and our administrators
◆ What happens if I am not taking the assessments?
  − You'll have even more time on the project
◆ What happens if I am taking the assessments?
  − You'll read when you have completed the assessment
◆ Can I do the same project as someone else?
  − Yes and No
  − Yes: you may have the same topic and even the same question
  − No: you are not creating a collaborative project, but you are encouraged to help each other out
◆ Do I have to use Wix?
  − No. It is just very easy to use, and I can give you the most guidance
◆ What if my parents don't want me to create a webpage?
  − You may do a Prezi
  − Please realize that we will keep these websites set to private if there is any concerns

Figure 1.1 Continued

learning and discovery—students will be far more successful in their futures when grades and gold stars aren't the norm.

Dr. Elmore's "Big Five" are realities experienced in a classroom with an emphasis on academic risk-taking. For example:

1. Getting connected to the right people.

    Jessica's attempts to connect with the animator led her to the conclusion that she shouldn't have simply given up after one person. Her final observation was that she could have researched someone else who would give her time. Her presentation also demonstrated for her classmates the appropriate channels by which to approach those who have knowledge they'd like to gain.

2. Possessing adaptability and resilience.

    When students are safe to make mistakes, they are then able to try new experiences, leading them to adapt to new situations, as well as be resilient when they aren't successful on their first attempt. Culturally, "failure" has many different interpretations, and we need to both value those interpretations as well as also offer our own acceptable ways to deal with situations that don't work out the way we planned.

3. Developing high emotional intelligence.

Students who are free to collaborate and not always compete are more likely to form better relationships. Project Based Learning such as this allows students to be in social situations in a safe and supportive environment, giving them practice for real-life scenarios.

4. Targeting a clear outcome.

When students are masters of their own fortune, they are able to goal-set more effectively. A by-product of a differentiated classroom is that allowing students to make their own decisions via choice-based activities teaches students to learn how to set goals for themselves and their work.

5. Making good decisions.

This one is particularly important for students. We often think of "good decisions" in school as code for good behavior, and it often is. However, there are also decisions that have weighty consequences that might not be noticeable right away. Should a student stay after and get extra help? Should a student try out for a team? Should a student ask for an extension? When we allow students to practice their own decision-making via a multitude of choices, they become more adept. Consider it rehearsal for the real-life decisions that they will all face, and any way we can help students learn to be their own advocates is helpful.

There are reputable studies that *do* link GPA and grades to academic success, such as the "Indicators of Success: GPA and Noncognitive Skills" put out by National Education Association (NEA) in the *Backgrounder*. However, when you examine what is being said, the non-cognitive skills are actually the glue that holds the sparkly accomplishments together. Here's an excerpt from NEA (I've emphasized the "glue" portions here):

GPA has proven successful at predicting future success because of its capacity to capture both cognitive skills and those critical to success (i.e. non-cognitive ability). GPA not only captures mastery of content knowledge, but also **skills not usually captured in tests—self-control**, for example. Self-control is an example of a non-cognitive skill. Non-cognitive skills—sometimes referred to as **"social and emotional learning," "soft skills," and/or "meta-cognitive learning skills"— consist of the skills not captured in cognitive tests such as aptitude tests, standardized tests, or course exams.** Nonetheless, these skills are critical to academic success: earning course credits, for example, requires a **set of behavioral skills, including self-regulation**. Mastery of such skills has proven predictive of future academic success, without such skills, changes in cognitive ability may be unlikely. Growth in non-cognitive skills has been tied to increases in course grades and future educational attainment. Non-cognitive skills—depending on the study one employs—**can include self-control, persistence, grit, optimism, curiosity, conscientiousness, social fluidity, and self-confidence—a range of personality and motivational habits.**

Truth be told, it is the set of skills that a student is able to employ that is the method by which the high GPA is earned, and thus the correlation to success is also dependent on SEL skill sets. Again, most teachers have stories about students who "just won't do the work" but are "so smart." We know that the knowledge and intelligence are inside, but are doubly discouraged when the child seems to be falling apart, never capable of what seems "normal" for school culture: handing in work, acting appropriate in different scenarios, getting along with peers, and understanding the hidden cues of school that so many other students seem to embrace without conscious effort.

More than Academic Learning

The sad fact is that "doing school" is socially and economically biased and doesn't take into consideration the students' abilities (and disabilities), talents, interests, cultural background, or the passions that would truly ignite learning for children. Shelly Wright's article "Academic Teaching Doesn't Prepare Students for Life" paints an especially ridiculous picture of what students are asked to learn:

> Today, I think most kids graduate only knowing if they're good at school or not. Often our students have many talents; they just don't fit in our current curriculum because their talents are likely not considered "real knowledge." And what is that? In the Biology curriculum that I've taught for the past several years, one of the objectives that my students need to know is earthworm reproduction. Really? Out of all the things we could be teaching a 17-year-old about biology, someone (a whole panel of someones, we can guess) decided earthworm reproduction was essential?

Additionally, for every student who achieves the meaningless "A's," there are also those who genuinely need more support and guidance, but take on a persona of someone who doesn't care because it is too demeaning to ask for the type of help that is needed. Schools too often silo children into groups based on flawed data, or even no data at all but rather character traits that have prevented them from being successful because they've never learned how to "do school." When the Common Core Standards caused nationwide panic, I was horrified to overhear two students talking about their classes, only to discuss themselves as "2's," referring to their English language arts (ELA) and math assessment scores. How horrible to think that these impressionable middle school students believed that those numbers precluded them from learning what others who did well should.

It is stories like these that make a Flexible Classroom crucial. In the following chapters you will find specific, reproducible, and targeted ways to create a Flexible Classroom. Each chapter will use the Collaborative for Academic, Social, and Emotional Learning (CASEL) Core SEL Competencies (Figure 1.2) as a lens by which we can view our students. As we focus our attention on a particular competency, we will examine the ways we can differentiate to meet those needs.

As educators, we simply can't believe that rote, one-size-fits-all, boring content is what is needed for our future. Rather, if teachers are willing to approach the classroom as a room full of individuals—not test scores, percentile ranks, demographics, or subgroups—we can impact students' entire lives by differentiating to meet their social, emotional, and academic needs.

Figure 1.2 Core SEL Competencies; Source ©CASEL 2017

Your Turn

How are you going to find the best ways to help your students become successful?

★ *Now, imagine all the different family stories and life circumstances of the students in your room, and you'll realize why there must be more SEL in addition to the academic.* How will you learn about your students' lives? What lessons can you incorporate into your curriculum to get students talking about their cultures?

★ *GPA and grades are stories about compliance and the ability to play the game of school.* What other measures can you find to assess your students' progress academically, as well as socially and emotionally?

Post-Pandemic Principles

In the summer of 2020, I was the director of our district's summer school. It was going to be virtual, of course, due to the Covid-19 pandemic, but that wasn't the most difficult part of my job. I was in the unique position of setting the policies for our summer school program, while my "normal" job during the school year is as a teacher in the district. I walked the line between administrator, president of our teachers' union, and a friend to most everyone who taught summer school. Teachers were ready for content. They were even ready with the technology. They were not, however, ready to deal with the question of the camera. Some believed we should adopt a "camera on" policy. Others thought that we should let students decide about their cameras, but give participation points for leaving them on. Some teachers didn't care much either way. We had a good discussion about what it meant for students to "participate" versus just sitting there with their cameras on. We had a decent amount of complaining about how difficult virtual learning was in the first place. Why did we think these kiddos were going to pass summer school, with the same exact format, with the same exact dynamic, as they had failed during the school year, with a very generous grading policy.

I made a radical decision. Cameras were not required to be turned on. Students could participate via audio or the chat box, or leave their cameras on. It would be up to the student. A teacher could make their preferences known, but participation points would not be used in any way as it related to the camera being on. If a teacher asked a question, students were expected to answer immediately, to assure everyone that they were indeed "there." Teachers should ask students questions and engage in the way the students feel comfortable. This is the same tactic I took with my own students when we were forced to be fully remote later in the school year.

You might be surprised to learn that teachers reported one of the best summer schools, with excellent results. Students and families were complimentary, and many claimed that their teachers' flexibility led to them feeling comfortable, something that most would never say about their regular school year. However, when I debriefed with the teachers at the end of the summer, we were surprised to figure out that *more* students participated and *more* students left their cameras on than during the regular school year.

What happened? Teachers had created a safe space for students who had previously not been successful by allowing them the opportunity to try in a different way, a way that made them feel more comfortable. Interestingly, students started the summer with their cameras off or just answering in chat, but once they were engaged in the class, and knew it was a safe environment to take risks, they would turn on their camera so they could communicate more efficiently. This was differentiation at its best, something we are going to need to embrace in the coming years.

The Post-Pandemic Principle we can apply as teachers is that at the heart of it, allowing students a choice—especially when they are "broken" or "damaged" as many students would describe themselves when it comes to school—is an act of goodwill that will show our students that we want them to be successful more than we want them to comply with what we want them to do.

2

Keeping All the Balls in the Air

The Importance of Self-Management

Developed by Collaborative for Academic, Social, and Emotional Learning and used with permission.

When I get anxious, I write things down. I make lists. I make lists to go with those lists. I make calendars on paper and electronically too. I send my husband those calendars. I have a copy for home and school. To me, organization is the key to my self-management—both in the "get things done" sort of way, but also emotionally, as I juggle the same types of lives many of you have. If I feel overwhelmed, it helps me keep all the balls in the air.

DOI: 10.4324/9781003230311-2

I don't know when this habit was formed exactly, but I remember folding a piece of notebook paper into quarters to plan out my week as early as middle school, which makes sense given the added responsibilities and activities that come with that territory. The simple act of writing down what I need to do releases endorphins that have gotten me through the rough patches. Lists, calendars, planners, and that very last-century act of "writing it down" are my ways to self-comfort when others can't possibly understand what I am feeling because, well, *they aren't me.*

It is so important for educators to acknowledge and honor the specific emotional situations that our students are facing, whether they are experiencing low-level test anxiety, peer pressure, or all the way to trauma. When my daughter was in 1st grade, she showed her first sign that she had inherited my condition of being a "mess in a dress" when I'm overwhelmed. There's nothing wrong exactly, no inciting incident or problem, but *everything is wrong.* You laugh, but then you cry, and the day seems to stretch into a perpetual roller-coaster road, both exciting and terrifying.

Like the heroic mom I am, to calm her nerves I bought her a little weekly planner where we could write things down together. As we filled in swim class, church, school, and a few birthday parties, I looked expectantly at her. Finally, I was going to use my intimate knowledge of handling stress for good, and my own problems were going to be cathartically transformed when my daughter is able to push away the panic with confidence! I could practically hear the triumphant music playing in the background. And then, she burst into tears. "This. Makes. It. Worse!" she said through sobs.

It had never occurred to me that my solution might actually, as she said, *make matters worse.* It was a turning point in my thinking as I realized that my solutions can actually be someone else's stressor. Imagine how often that translates into issues in the classroom! Immediately it occurred to me that I had scheduled, listed, and calendared (I've made that a verb—if you are an obsessive about planning, you'll get it) my students into anxiety on more than one occasion. Now, when I hand out the many calendars and organizational tools to my students, I'll tell them exactly what they need to look at (often, I bold it), versus what the planners amongst us need to know. One of my students who hated my calendars told me the same thing my young daughter was trying to: sometimes, too much information is paralyzing. I've started utilizing my website more, allowing students to click on what they want to see, versus what I think they should see. We might think we are doing the best thing for students, but if we don't seek their input and tend to their social and emotional needs, we might actually be contributing to our students' struggles.

Sneak Peek

In this chapter, we will

★ examine ways to facilitate students' ownership of behaviors and self-management
★ learn to integrate Google Calendar and wearable technology to help students self-regulate
★ create flexible due dates to encourage students to manage their own time
★ create interdependence through cooperative grouping and Resource Groups

---

Facilitating Students' Ownership of Behaviors and Self-Management

So, now you have the story about my daughter. There's also a story about my husband, who is a huge procrastinator, yet never misses a deadline and actually thrives under the pressure. Obviously, it gives me hives to think that there are hours (or even minutes!) until a deadline, and there's my husband—sweating, drinking too many Diet Cokes, smiling, and, believe it or not, producing amazing things! There's, of course, a story about my son, who at 8 must be convinced that he doesn't have to work on a movie that he's making for six hours straight, not stopping to eat, just because he read that's when Steven Spielberg completed his first short film. I share this with you because we all have stories, and I'm sure you're thinking of your own unique family, with each family member having different balls to keep in the air. If not family, we've all had that college roommate whose "process" of getting work done is shocking in its absolute discordance with ours. So what do we do, as teachers, when we have a sea of faces, all who must learn to juggle the expectations of school with complex lives and personalities?

There's no easy answer, to be sure, but I've designed a new tool to give me some baseline information in order to begin triage. As you well know, there are a number of students who have the self-management piece down pretty well. What we need to do, of course, is to continue to support those who have this aspect mastered, but the first course of action in a new year needs to be to find where the gaps are and fill them. Many students don't have the metacognitive capacity to consider if they are a procrastinator, "calendarizer," or something else. I'm going to use a survey that I created in SurveyMonkey, called the "Student Learning Profile" (Figure 2.1). It will be given to the students, and I will disaggregate what I find and share with the students and parents (with student permission only).

Much of the survey itself is taken from work I did as a student in Dr. Peter Loehr's class as a part of my School Building Leader certification. His work, particularly "Intentionally Creating a Consistent School Culture Focused on Principles of High Achievement," has had a huge impact on how I perceive my role as the creator of classroom culture, and how I adapt to meet the specific elements that he's found to have the greatest impact on student achievement. Not surprisingly, his criteria address the social emotional needs of learners as actual predictors of academic success. His contention is that when the criteria are met, student engagement is increased and the intrinsic motivation is ignited, creating a burning desire in students to excel that we can't elicit externally. He explains:

> It is the increase in intrinsic motivators that produces an increase in engagement in learning and working activities. This is the type of motivation necessary to increase the engagement in the complexities of finding new solutions to new problems, opportunities, and challenges.
>
> (108)

SUPPORT MATERIAL

*from Dr. Peter Loehr's *Intentionally Creating A Consistent School Culture of High Achievement.*

1. *I know what is expected of me in my classes.
O Strongly DISAGREE
O DISAGREE
O AGREE
O Strongly AGREE

2. *In my classes, I have the materials and equipment I need to do my work right (correctly).
O Strongly DISAGREE
O DISAGREE
O AGREE
O Strongly AGREE

3. I am able to keep my binder or folder organized the way the teacher wants it.
O Strongly DISAGREE
O DISAGREE
O AGREE
O Strongly AGREE

4. My locker is organized so that I can quickly locate what I need and be on time.
O Strongly DISAGREE
O DISAGREE
O AGREE
O Strongly AGREE

Figure 2.1 Student Learning Profile (from Dr. Peter Loehr's "Intentionally Creating a Consistent School Culture of High Achievement")

5. *In one or more of my classes I have the opportunity to do what I do best on a regular basis.
O Strongly DISAGREE
O DISAGREE
O AGREE
O Strongly AGREE

6. *About every week (regularly) I receive recognition or praise for doing good work from at least one of my teachers.
O Strongly DISAGREE
O DISAGREE
O AGREE
O Strongly AGREE

7. I procrastinate (make up reasons to put off doing what I should be doing, avoid my work).
O Strongly DISAGREE
O DISAGREE
O AGREE
O Strongly AGREE

8. *My teachers regularly inform me how I am doing in my classes.
O Strongly DISAGREE
O DISAGREE
O AGREE
O Strongly AGREE

9. I like to use calendars that show me:
O one week at a time
O one month at a time
O an overview of the quarter
O I don't like calendars because...

_____

10. *There is at least one teacher at school who seems to care about me as a person.
O Strongly DISAGREE
O DISAGREE
O AGREE
O Strongly AGREE

That teacher, for me, is ...

_____

Figure 2.1 Continued

This is an important aspect of self-management because, as Daniel Pink contends in *Drive* and Carol Dweck in *Mindset*, so much of learning is based on intrinsic motivation and metacognitive understanding of how we think about our own learning (Figure 2.2). The survey provides important information that will help me ignite that spark, as well as a basis for adapting the culture of my room to the needs of my students. For example, if I have a room of self-admitted procrastinators, I might need to add in some checkpoint dates on bigger projects to support their learning. Additionally, if I have students who

Growth Mindset has taken on a life of its own—which isn't a bad thing. It just seems that we all know someone (or could be that someone!) who touts the amazing benefits of changing from a "fixed mindset" to one where improvement is not only entertained, but expected. Growth Mindset isn't something that we, as teachers, should "do," just like Differentiation isn't something we try to improve our evaluation scores. However, here are a few key ideas to remember in your own Flexible Classroom:

✓ Words matter. Be careful not to use limiting language.
✓ Make room for mistakes. If a student isn't challenged, the assignment will likely not engage either.
✓ Keep on keeping on. Perseverance is a key indicator of successful people, yet we don't always allow students to struggle.
✓ Don't just talk the talk. If you don't take risks, your students won't either.
✓ Help students find their passions and ignite their curiosity!

Figure 2.2 Just a Word about … Growth Mindset

feel disconnected, I might concentrate my energies into creating a safe environment and exploring what that means for all students. Will taking this survey take the place of good, old-fashioned teacher observation? No, but until a relationship exists, it is a way to assess the needs of students.

Google Calendar and Wearable Technology

Educators at this juncture in time are at a real crossroads, one that I believe can impact student learning exponentially. Technology. Devices. Smartphones. Tablets. iPads. Beats. Earbuds. Laptops. Whatever the technology is that our students love, we need to embrace it, and to learn from them how it can best serve all of our purposes. It might be tempting to compare our own experiences (or lack thereof) with technology, but as you recall the adults in your own life, did any of their "back in my day" stories ever do anything other than alienate you from them, as well-meaning as they might be?

Devorah Heitner, author of *Screenwise: Helping Kids Thrive (and Survive) in Their Digital World*, explains:

In my fieldwork, this overwhelmingly negative feeling that many parents and educators have about kids 'abusing' technology comes up over and over again, which is why I think of it as one of the most dangerous barriers to tech-positive parenting.

She notes, "A child who has used technology to support his goals and knows when to relate face to face and when to find other solutions will be prepared for the challenges of life." This ability to move through the world, both digital and actual, is at the heart of teaching in a Flexible Classroom, where the goal is to put the academic, social, and emotional needs of the student first.

Recently, I was teaching a particularly absentminded student how to set a reminder for himself using Google Calendar. He kept forgetting when he had a music lesson; like many schools, my students leave their core classes on a rotational basis, so as to not miss the same class all the time. This meant that he needed his instrument on different days, which he inevitably forgot.

He admitted that he was fully considering dropping out of band because he couldn't keep this straight. When I showed him how to set a reminder for himself on the morning of the lesson for two hours before (when he'd still be at home), he was amazed. As it turns out, he wasn't that impressed by the technology, but rather how I'd used it to set an alert *beforehand*, not when the actual lesson occurred. He had never considered using technology to remind himself of what was coming up.

This might seem unusual to some of you, but others are having an aha moment of their own! It is important, as educators, to realize that we all come to school with different paradigms and patterns, and the sooner we can help students with skills like self-management, the easier content will be to teach. Organizing time can be particularly difficult for students who are new to the country, live in chaotic households, or struggle conceptually because of learning disabilities. When you think of it this way, doesn't it sound inhumane to remark on a child's chronic disorganization in any way other than with compassion and empathy?

Carol A. Kinlan, in her article "Failure to Launch and the Disorganized Teenager," explores the difficulties that students without organizational skills encounter. Specifically, she mentions that boys have an even more difficult time developmentally, referring to one of her clients she sees as an educational consultant:

> Though his IQ was quite high, his B-s were largely a product of his disorganized approach to this schoolwork. Like many teenagers we see, especially young males, the cognitive tasks required to prioritize, balance and finish academic and other daily tasks develop slowly, sometimes well into one's mid-20s.

It is one of our many roles to help students adjust to the social expectations of new careers, as well as help ease the emotional burden of not being prepared by helping them to utilize every possible tool, especially technology.

Technology is enticing, and when we meet students where they are—especially if they like where they are—they are more likely to be successful. After working with my absentminded student, it occurred to me that I could send Google Calendar invites to get my students acclimated to the app. It had never occurred to me to use Google Calendar in this way, but I immediately got that "teacher-excitement-mind-racing feeling." I could share this with my students, Special Education co-teaching partner, and parents. In a Project Based Learning classroom, we can create a calendar for each individual project, even setting those "hour before" type alarms for tasks if necessary (Figure 2.3).

Another way I am going to start using Google Calendar is to add it to my website. This way, students who want to see the big picture can, and those who need to check it daily to see what is happening also have that access. It won't hurt to get them to flexibleclass.com to see the links to Quizlet, resources, and review sheets either! One of the main habits we should be attempting to instill is consistency. Some teachers do this by having students copy down the homework from the board on Monday morning; I believe that if we use the technology that they already use (like their phones), we will have greater success.

Though I've never used wearable technology with my students, I'm really impressed by how quickly the concept is becoming mainstream. The premise is simple: students wear technology (usually a watch) that uses biostatistics feedback to alert students to refocus or return to a particular task from which their mind might have wondered, or remind a student via a silent vibration to return to their seat. I have, however, set a timer on a student's phone, set to vibrate, for how long he should work on a task before taking a break, and

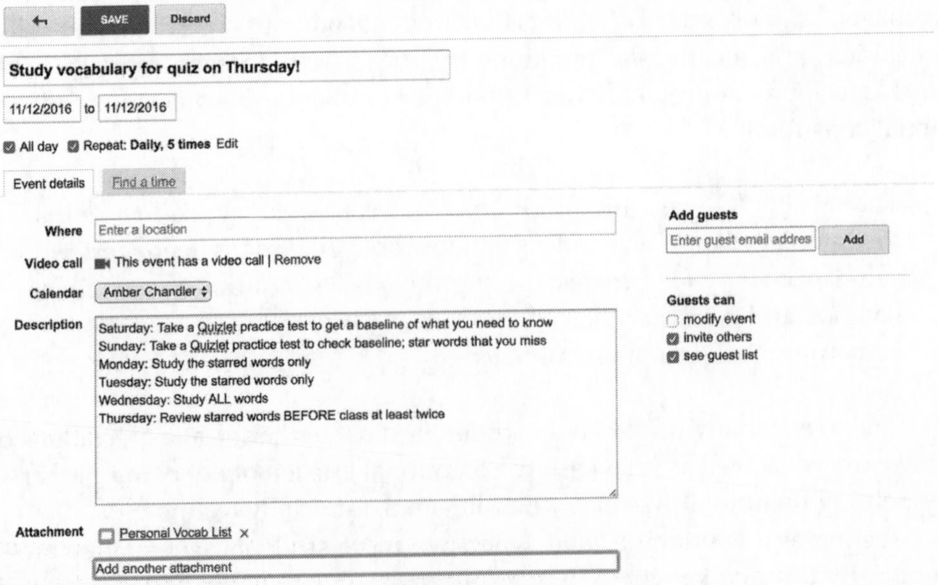

Figure 2.3 Google Calendar

the results are pretty amazing. Much like my anxiety and feelings of being overwhelmed, some students see an assignment looming in front them, no end in sight, and can't fathom how it will all get done—kind of like our to-do lists, right? When we can set mile markers and speed limits for our students who are flying along on their own rollercoaster road, we are able to assuage some of the anxiety, as well as set them up for future success where self-management is essential.

Provide a Due Date Range

In order to differentiate and also maintain high standards and expectations, I often use a due date range with my students. This idea grew from conversations I was having continually. "Mrs. Chandler, can I just hand this in? I don't want to lose it," or "Mrs. Chandler, can I give it to you on Monday? My computer is at my dad's house, and I won't see him until Saturday."

I'm embarrassed to say that for many years, I was more interested in the students doing what I asked by handing it in on a particular date than I was on the developmental scaffolding they may have needed. Through the years though, I realized that I was focusing on the wrong part of the situation.

Most of the time, the due dates were fairly arbitrary. Who amongst us hasn't collected an assignment on Friday, only to leave it piled on the corner of the desk for the following week?

Now, I accept most everything on a rolling basis, generally collecting things in a week range. This doesn't just support my students. I am also likely to give more feedback if I'm not sitting on 130 papers at a time. This approach also values my students' time. As I introduced Google Classroom, I showed my students how to use the comment feature, and I was struck by one of my student's answers when he wrote, "Mrs. Chandler understands the life of a middle schooler."

Aidan's perception is probably generous, but I try to recognize both their abilities and limitations, and let that knowledge of their academic, social, and emotional situations inform my teaching. However, teachers can't go it alone; rather, we need to tap into the potential sitting right in front of us each day: our students.

Anytime we can leverage our students' knowledge about themselves as learners, the more authentic the learning will be. Another way to help students learn about self-management is to provide opportunities for them to make decisions about due dates. Why not, instead of filling out a calendar for them, distributing the calendar, and allowing a Resource Group (my term for group of students chosen to work together at a specific table) to determine deadlines and reminders? Better yet, provide a blank calendar as a Google Doc, and have students collaborate on it as an actual aspect of their project, creating interdependence and an opportunity to build relationships while sharing about their lives. If students are discussing why a Thursday due date is better than a Wednesday one, sharing aspects of their personal lives in such a non-threatening scenario, the potential for developing relationships is created.

Create Interdependence

I jokingly say to my middle schoolers, "I know you're here to hang out with each other, but you still have to 'do school' while you are here." However, there's considerable truth to what I'm saying. As I was thinking about this topic, I googled "interdependence" and, surprisingly, the autofill finished with "interdependence in project management."

As I perused the results, one thing became clear: interdependence isn't just a skill to teach because it will help students manage their middle school projects, but it is something they will need in their adult lives. Article after article, the common thread was that employees need to be proficient with the following skills:

- ◆ leadership
- ◆ managing people
- ◆ negotiation
- ◆ time management
- ◆ effective communication
- ◆ planning
- ◆ controlling
- ◆ conflict resolution
- ◆ problem-solving

Not only am I able to share the real-world implications and applications to my students, but this thinking has prompted me to create a new "position" within my Project Based Learning classroom. I'm going to add "Project Manager" to the roles I have for students (Researcher, Lead Writer, Time Manager, Tech Coordinator, Lead Presenter, and Editor) when collaborating on projects (Figure 2.4). Additionally, students must pitch their projects to me with a detailed explanation of their team, individual roles, scheduling, and the process, product, and presentation that we will expect from the group (Figure 2.5).

Here are a list of project roles and the expectations for you during the project. Make sure that you are doing your very best, asking questions, and learning from one another. Study each role below and reflect on areas where you have strengths, and also on areas that will be a stretch for you. If it is a STRENGTH, highlight the role. If it is a STRETCH, put a star next to one of the areas you'd like to take a risk on (remember Growth Mindset people!)

Researcher: This person will dig for information via the library media center and online.
Ask yourself: do I have the time and desire to spend looking for information? Can I tell if a source is credible or not?

Lead Writer: This person will be in charge of preparing the text used in the project. You will need to feel comfortable typing the content, and working with the Researcher.
Ask yourself: am I comfortable writing independently? Do I love to write about all topics?

Time Manager: This person will make sure time in class during workdays is spent on task.
Ask yourself: am I willing to redirect my friends and acquaintances to get back to work (nicely!)?

Tech Coordinator: This person will need to be responsible for obtaining the technology needed for the group. This means checking it out from me and making sure to keep track of it. It means you decide what type of technology you use and how you might integrate it into your presentation. Prezi? Google Slides? Video recorded skit?
Ask yourself: am I responsible with my belongings and am I familiar with the best technology for this project?

Lead Presenter: This person will introduce the group, each person by name. This person will explain in a few sentences what the task was for the project. (For example: We were trying to create a visual dictionary of difficult words from the text.)
Ask yourself: am I comfortable speaking in front of a group? Can I remember names easily?

Editor: This person is responsible to edit all written material (presentations, essays, documents, etc.)
Ask yourself: is grammar my "thing?" Can I spot mistakes a mile away?

Project Manager: This person is the one who supervises all of the roles and makes sure everyone has what they need to do their part, as well as acting as a helper for any of the above.
Ask yourself: am I assertive enough to ask others how they are doing, and am I capable to jump into any role if the person is absent or falling behind?

Figure 2.4 Project Roles: Strengths and Stretches

A really great example of creating interdependence that I recently discovered is through Quizlet.com's "Live" option. I've used Quizlet for years, mainly to generate notecards and tests for my students. Occasionally, we do some of the group activities, but many features are best with small numbers, and my classes are closer to 30 than 20. However, as I was considering how I'd review the vocabulary for the final assessment of my short-story unit, I pulled up Quizlet to get a copy of the words, and I noticed Live. I watched the tutorial and was convinced to give it a try. I've never been happier with a vocabulary review.

Students may use their phones, iPads, or our class Chromebooks to login to Quizlet.live. The teacher who has generated the set will then hit "Create game." A six-digit code will appear on the screen. As students input the code, they will then be asked to enter their name. When all students' names are listed, Quizlet then generates teams based on the number of players. These teams are named after wild animals—the Penguins vs. the Camels vs. the Snow Tigers. My students are at tables, so I just shouted out which "animals" went to each table. Once the tables are assembled with teams, the teacher starts the game.

This is where the great interdependence occurs in a really fun way. Each team will have the questions on their screen, with each of the members of

SUPPORT MATERIAL

Names of proposed members (not to exceed 5):

_____ email: _____
_____ email: _____
_____ email: _____
_____ email: _____
_____ email: _____

Brief description of the process, product, and presentation you are planning:
Process: (What will the group be doing or exploring? What is your burning question?)
_____
_____
_____

Product: (What will you be making or creating to "show what you know"?)
_____
_____

Presentation: (How will you share what you have learned? Who is the authentic audience? What technology will you use?)
_____
_____
_____

Planning your time:
For each project we do, there is a presentation to prepare and a written component, so the work must be done by everyone involved. Please sign up for the role(s) that you will commit to. This means that you will create the slides and the written part of the document. Read the expectations carefully, as there are different amounts of work.

When, outside of class, do you have to work on this together? This could be studyhalls, Facetiming, in my room either before or after school, or via Google Classroom.
_____
_____
_____

You need to be aware that your grades will be calculated this way:
The products from your role + group essay grade = Avg of the two → essay grade (test)
Group slideshow grade + your job presenting = presentation grade (test)

Figure 2.5 Group Project Application

In the group, you need to decide on the following (some may have to do more than one position):

_____ Researcher
_____ Lead Writer
_____ Time Manager
_____ Tech Coordinator
_____ Lead Presenter
_____ Editor
_____ Project Manager

*By signing this agreement, you recognize that this is a huge project with three major test grades associated with it, as well as many classwork grades. You realize that when you submit slides or essays that you are ALL responsible for the spelling, mechanics, and grammar, as well as if it makes sense. You don't have to edit content, but the document and slides must be correct. There will be one slideshow submitted and one essay. All names must be clearly stated. If you become a burden to your group by not doing work on the planned timeline, you may be removed to complete the project yourself.

_____   _____
Student   date

_____   _____
Student   date

_____   _____
Student   date

_____   _____
Student   date

_____   _____
Student   date

Figure 2.5 Continued

the team showing different possible answers on their screen; thus, the teammates must talk to each other to see which person on the team has the correct answer. The goal is to get to 12 in a row, but if the team misses a question, that team goes back to zero. This was the cause of most of the commotion in the room, and soon they learned to really be sure before inputting an answer. When I say that my room was loud, crazy, and like a wild game of Family Feud, I wouldn't be exaggerating. We were studying vocabulary words. It was a beautiful thing, and as a nerdy teacher, I'm simply thrilled by the student engagement.

The best part of the game is that the students aren't competing against one another as individuals. Why would it be fun if Jane or Tom *always* wins (which is kind of how competition often works in middle school)? Instead,

they were on randomized teams. Better yet, after each round, they were randomized again, creating new combinations.

An additional benefit is that the collaborative competition and the use of
technology, coupled with the rotations, allows shy or standoffish students the
opportunity to interact in a low-pressure way. It was also really cool when
Khaled, a student from Yemen, was on a winning team. This was a chance
for him to be a part of our class in a meaningful way, even though he is still
very quiet. This activity brought out the best in all my students, and what
English teacher wouldn't be happy to hear a table debating the difference
between "tangible" and "palpable"? I also realized that the strategic grouping and regrouping of students into randomized groups goes a long way
toward helping students become acclimated with one another. There weren't
assigned leaders, and there weren't defined roles, as so often there are, but
instead a group of students working together, relying on each other to accom-
plish a goal.

As we are teaching and modeling self-management, I urge teachers to
be compassionate. We are not privy to the heavy loads some of our students
carry—either self-imposed through sports and activities, or circumstantial
due to familial obligations, trauma, or disability. The other day, as I said good-
bye to my daughter, who is in 6th grade, we both were shocked when she
said, "See you at 9:00." How is this possible? Am I a terrible mother? Believe
it or not, her schedule is very similar to other students'. School, play practice,
dinner/work on a project at a friend's house, and then youth group until 9:00
P.M. Obviously I wouldn't condone this breakneck schedule for her every day;
however, I do think all of those activities are crucial for her social, emotional,
and academic development.

That is, of course, the best case scenario. But, you know the truth. My
daughter's rollercoaster road is only partially controlled by her; caring adults
are there to take over anytime the route becomes too much. However, many
of you know that your students' roads are littered with accidents of all kinds
and look more like this: get sibling off the bus, help sibling with homework,
try to avoid conflicts with others living in the household, avoid abusers or
bullies, figure out what and how to eat, try to do homework without drawing
attention to oneself, drown out the fighting in the next room by blasting the
television, and struggle to fall asleep while feeling unsafe. The scope of this
book can't possibly touch the deeper interventions that are needed for these
students.

However, I refuse to sit idly by because I can't do enough. No one of us is
ever going to be enough, yet I know that in my own little room, in my own
little corner of the building, in my small space in the world, I do have influence, and so do you. We are the watched. Students wait for the intonations of

our voices, the touch on the shoulder, and the feeling that they are seen when they are in our presence. This book is going to help teachers do what we can, from where we are, with the tools that we have available to us as classroom teachers.

In my own way, and in a way I know you can use, I'm going to continue to share practical ways that we can help students with the social and emotional through the academic.

Helping our students become aware of their own self-management needs, allowing students to utilize technology, being flexible with a due date range, and creating opportunities for interdependence are ways I recommend for teachers to help students manage their workload while acknowledging and honoring their developmental capacity and their life outside of school.

Your Turn

How are you going to help your students keep all the balls in the air?

★ *Many students don't have the metacognitive capacity to consider if they are a procrastinator, "calendarizer," or something else.* How are you going to determine the needs of your students, particularly at the beginning of the year? Can you survey them? How can you use this information to guide instruction?

★ *Whatever the technology is that our students love, we need to embrace it, and to learn from them how it can best serve all of our purposes.* What technology do you have available? What about your students? What works best for you? What about your students?

★ *In order to differentiate and also maintain high standards and expectations, I often use a due date range with my students.* Are you able to have flexibility with due dates? Is there a way to stagger when you collect work in order to provide better feedback?

★ *Interdependence isn't just a skill to teach because it will help students manage their middle school projects, but it is something they will need in their adult lives.* What activities do you already do that encourage students to lean on each other to complete the task? Can you adjust what you are already doing to include a team component?

Post-Pandemic Principles

If pressed to choose the specific reason emergency pandemic learning structures wreaked such havoc on our lives—be it fully remote, hybrid, cohorted, or any other amalgamation of questionable practices—I'd hands down say that "keeping all the balls in the air" was impossible for students, families, and teachers alike. I've banned the "P word" (*pivot*) from my life, but the rotation from one method to another, multiple times in some months, was the reason most of us felt overwhelmed, stressed, and often unsuccessful.

My son began the year 2020/2021 in person, hybrid, on Mondays and Thursdays at school, asynchronous on Tuesdays and Fridays, with the expectation that he'd attend office hours as necessary on Wednesdays. Eventually, he became fully remote, attending Mondays and Thursdays online. Then, he was fully remote with online classes Mondays and Thursdays with every other Wednesday online. The grand finale: for the last three weeks of school he was online for all of his classes, every day. Seventh grade was a nightmare, and it had nothing to do with the content or his teachers. It had to do with the fact that the majority of schools across the country created Frankenstein schedules that had little chance of being effective and were more developmentally appropriate for a mature college student.

Families were pressed with unbearable choices, work schedules, and arrangements. We all wrestled with how to make it all work—to keep all the balls in the air—and if you were like our family, you probably failed more than once. Somehow, even though we were all juggling too many balls, we were also pretty critical of each other too. Families often felt that teachers weren't understanding of students' limitations or their unique needs. Teachers often felt that families were expecting too much from them and too little from their children. Students often felt that everyone was expecting too much. And, to a degree, I think we were all right. Keeping all the balls in the air is hard for many people, and adding a pandemic to the mix is like tossing a chainsaw into the juggling act.

My plan is going to be to go back to what I know best in terms of communication. I plan to post my students' scheduled work, with links, on my website flexibleclass.com. Each week, probably on Sunday night, I'll send out a reminder message that the next week is posted. I'll have a link in the reminder message which will take families to my site. This past year families were forced to learn a variety of platforms, some of which are amazing, but many that were confusing. I love Google Classroom from the teacher's perspective, but as a parent, it was exceptionally difficult to navigate for all the reasons I love it as a teacher. Each of my son's teachers used it a little differently, so finding what was due when was complicated. The sheer number of notifications was staggering. Yes, I'm sure we could have managed the notifications, but that was not a ball we were willing to pick up with so many others going. I believe that the simplicity of the reminder message will allow families and students to engage as they see fit without having to seek out the information themselves. I am going to be very careful to be very predictable and present the information the same way week to week.

What can we learn from this experience and apply to our lives post pandemic? As teachers, more than ever, we must make the routines, schedules, and expectations simple and clear. We must communicate with families in a predictable way, at regular intervals, with defined boundaries, but with the strong message that we are a team—the student, the families, and the teachers—and that we can work together for student success. *In short, the Post-Pandemic Principle we need to recognize is that the aforementioned chainsaw did some serious damage, and we need to do everything we can to make learning and school predictable and comfortable for students and families.*

3

Escaping the Echo Chamber

Teaching Self-Awareness

Developed by Collaborative for Academic, Social, and Emotional Learning and used with permission.

Humor me with an experiment. Grab your phone or log onto your computer. Go to the first social media site that you regularly use—Facebook, Instagram, Snapchat, or whatever the cool kids are using these days. Scroll through and start noting the variety of people you follow from different eras of your life and the wide variety of ages, from your 13-year-old niece to your best friend's mom who is in her 70s. Isn't it amazing how connected we are to so many different people? Now, scroll through again, but this time

DOI: 10.4324/9781003230311-3

look for the dissenting voice. Is there anyone who stands out, doesn't fit in, expresses opinions that make you uncomfortable? If you are like most people, you'll come to realize that though it *feels* like you have diversity, you only have different reverberations of the same ideas. Don't get me wrong. There are some people who have a balance, but think of how many times you've heard the term "unfriended" in the context of differing views about politics of all kinds—presidential, personal, religious, or sexual. I'm not advocating that we keep jerks around for comparison, but I'm concerned that this echo chamber finds its way into education and it is prohibiting our students and us from learning together.

I endured the long campaign leading up to the 2016 presidential election with gritted teeth, and surprisingly, from the chaos, I learned a new concept that has really impacted my thinking around Social Emotional Learning (SEL). I'm a bit of a media junky, so you can imagine how my head was spinning when I first heard the phrase "echo chamber." Good old Wikipedia explains it this way:

> In news media an **echo chamber** is a metaphorical description of a situation in which information, ideas, or beliefs are amplified or reinforced by transmission and repetition inside an "enclosed" system, where different or competing views are censored, disallowed, or otherwise underrepresented.

The more I learned, the more I realized that this concept plays itself out in schools on a microcosmic level each day.

Each day, my students come to school with their preconceived notions about teachers, education, English class, and authority. I, too, come with my preconceived notions about those same topics, but very rarely do we outright address the dissonance or gaps that might exist between us. Yet I somehow still want these students to listen and learn from me every day. Instead of approaching the difficulties inherent in these conversations, we retreat to the teachers' lounge where, more or less, our own ideas will be substantiated.

The *Washington Post* July 14, 2016, piece, "Confirmed: Echo Chambers Exist on Social Media. So What Do We Do about Them?" explains:

> The tendency to promote one's favored narrative is natural, but too much confirmation distances us from other perspectives and makes us unable to see the truth when it's finally presented—what the "Echo Chamber" researchers referred to as "a kind of cognitive inoculation." And in the end, a constant us-vs.-them mentality depersonalizes the holders of alternative views.

What strikes me most though is that we, as teachers, don't overtly acknowledge the spaces between, nor do we elicit enough feedback from our students or the dissenting voices to ever reach a version 2.0 of our own teaching. Until we are able to leave the echo chamber that keeps us all comfortable, we will never reach our students in the meaningful ways that can happen when we are communicating.

Sneak Peek

In this chapter, we will

★ learn how to empower students with "solution statements" instead of "problem statements"
★ investigate how slang, swearing, and register are critical considerations for our students as they learn to communicate effectively
★ embolden students to take charge of their own learning by thinking metacognitively

---

Problem Statements vs. Solution Statements

"I need a pencil," the slouching boy said quietly, as he looked right past me. He stood, seemingly agitated, shifting from foot to foot.

"I can let you borrow one. But, I want to tell you a better way to get one. Right now I feel like you are irritated at me because you don't have a pencil. When you don't look at me, I feel like you are mad. You seem like you want to run away because you keep moving around. Maybe you could ask a question instead of just stating your problem. Any ideas?" I said, slowly and carefully choosing my words. I wasn't trying to be condescending, and I didn't want teenage angst to mistake my tone.

"Can I have one?" he asked, glancing at me.

"Of course. Here you go," I said, opening my drawer. As I handed it to him, I asked, "Can I show you how this whole conversation could make both of us feel capable instead of awkward?"

"Whatever. Sure," he said, acquiescing, since he didn't really have any choice.

"Hi, Todd. I'm sorry to bother you. I seem to have misplaced my pencil. May I borrow one?" I said, modeling for him what a successful interaction would look like in this situation. I smiled and kept eye contact.

"So be nice. Is that what you're saying?" Todd asked, looking me in the eye for the first time.

"Yes. But it is more than that. It is the way you speak—with confidence, but politely, and how you listen—with your eyes and ears. When you are trying to communicate, you give off a vibe. You want to make that vibe the best you can."

Todd nodded and turned quickly away when the bell rang. Did this quick interaction make Todd a shoo-in for a Fortune 500 job? No, but it did pave the way for appropriate social interactions that involve speaking and listening.

At first glance this scenario may not seem to be so much academic as a question of manners; however, a closer look reveals that the Common Core Standards require students to: *"Adapt speech to a variety of contexts and tasks, demonstrating command of formal English when indicated or appropriate."* The best part of addressing the speaking and listening standards is that it is a literacy issue that can be advanced in any classroom situation.

I'll be the first to tell you that the overt conversation I am suggesting here is a bit uncomfortable at the onset. However, where else in the curriculum can you have this kind of immediate and useful impact? As we project what our students are going to need in the future, we can be sure that communication is crucial. This is a power standard that will pay great dividends as we shape students' speaking and listening skills to meet the challenges of the 21st century.

One of the things I love at this moment in education is the reevaluation of what expertise is necessary and which skills we've been teaching out of habit. I vividly remember teaching my students how to use MLA style, explaining how to remember the specific parts of a works cited list. That was fewer than 10 years ago, yet it seems like a horrible waste of time to today's students because of advances in technology and websites like NoodleTools that will generate your works cited for you, as long as you plug in the information. As technology continues to evolve, the need for memorized and rote tasks will be replaced by a surge in the 21st-century Four Cs described by the Partnership for 21st-Century Skills (a collaborative of both business and education interests): critical thinking, communicating, collaborating, and creating.

Being able to adapt your speech to a variety of scenarios is not only useful, but expected. Though these types of overt conversations seem forced at first, you'll be surprised how quickly students will pick up on the correct social cues and adapt their speaking and listening skills. Push through your initial doubts about this tactic, and you will do your students a favor that just might get them a job interview, an internship, or simply help them ask for help finding what they need in the library.

The simple switch from what I call "problem statements" to "solution statements" is truly a gigantic step in moving our students to self-advocacy from learned helplessness. However, there is another underlying dynamic that I hadn't thought of until I learned about the echo chamber concept. What if this student has been taught that this submissive and helpless tone is the appropriate one to use with adults or authority figures? What if this is the tone and comportment that this student sees in other areas of his life? On the other hand, what if the school and its teachers have simply accepted this type of communication? Are students mimicking one another in their attempts to communicate their needs because it has become the norm for the classroom? Or, also likely, what if these conversations are just awkward, so we let them slide? What if we didn't teach fractions because the lesson wasn't our favorite? We can't accept the mediocre when it comes to the social emotional aspects when we wouldn't tolerate it from an academic viewpoint. We must have the difficult conversations and model the behaviors that will most benefit students.

The Social Currency of Register

My son Oliver, a 3rd grader, loves to yell "Burn!" when someone says something that might be considered insulting. It is, to say the least, annoying. But I must remind myself, and some of you I'm sure, of how we said annoying things as well. Here are a few of my faves (see what I did there?): *all that and a bag of chips, as if, eat my shorts, gettin' jiggy with it, hella*, and the all-time most annoying: *not!* I actually cringed as I typed these phrases that I once thought were "cool." Yet, slang is a sign that you fit in or, unfortunately, that you don't.

Because slang, and swearing for that matter, have social significance in arenas outside of school—including in sports, homes, and the streets—we must not diminish the way our students speak in circumstances where this type of communication is crucial for their success, or even survival. Most of us have our "teacher voices" and when we use them on our spouses, they aren't too pleased with it. Try saying, "Please clean up your area. We share common space, so let's be considerate!" In my case, it is sad, but true, that I have some pretty embarrassing slang that I use amongst friends and at home. As a teenager of a grunge, *Wayne's World*, and *Clerks* infused world, I use the word *dude*, mostly when I am addressing someone when I am excited, as in "Dude! Did you know there's a *Simpsons* marathon on Thanksgiving weekend?" On the other hand, we all know how cringeworthy it is to hear an adult try to appropriate the latest teen phrases. By all means, don't announce to your homeroom that you are "low key addicted to that filter." (Which, my daughter informs me, means that you are *very* addicted to a certain filter that you use for pictures, mostly on Instagram.)

Seeing the social and emotional weight all types of language can carry, we must not be dismissive, but we don't want our classrooms to sound like a playground—at least most of the time. How can we teach students to appropriately switch registers, or styles of speaking, without devaluing any of the communication our students rely on to fit into their environments? First, we must explain and demonstrate the power of words. My favorite activity I've ever done with this is what became known as the "Blueberry Pancakes Experiment." I was explaining to students that we need to be careful when we use language because we have an influence on both how people perceive us, as well as what those people then project to the world about us (Figure 3.1).

The premise is simple. If a powerful group of people begin using a word or phrase, they can create a trend toward using it, even if the users themselves don't understand the origins or the real meaning. As 8th graders, my students are at the top of the pecking order, so they assume a certain attitude. One day in class, as I was explaining this, I suggested that we create a phrase ourselves. Immediately noting the enthusiasm, we agreed that we'd pick a phrase and start using it very regularly. We had to agree on a definition, and it had to be something original, and for the experiment to work we promised to never

"Register" is just another name for style. The 21st Century communication paradigm is difficult to decipher in that it is still evolving. It is, and will continue to be, important for students to be able to switch registers—often in the same conversation. This is not easy to teach or model, but whenever possible we should be empowering our students with both opportunities and examples of register switching. Here are the five registers and ideas about how to include them in your own Flexible Classroom:

✓ Static Register. This is frozen language and doesn't change. The Pledge of Allegiance and taking attendance are examples. *There is nothing wrong with having specific call and response in class.*

✓ Formal: One-way participation; no interruption; exact definitions are important. *Students can assume this register when they are presenters.*

✓ Consultative: Two-way participation; background information is provided. Interruptions are allowed. *Teaching students to ask clarifying questions works well with this concept.*

✓ Casual: In-group friends and acquaintances; no background information provided; slang is common; interruptions common. *When students work in Resource Groups, this is the register they may converse in.*

✓ Intimate: Non-public; tone of voice more important than wording, may have a private vocabulary. Can include swearing. Also includes non-verbal messages. *Students should know that this register is valued, but not for the school setting.*

Figure 3.1 Just a Word about… Registers

reveal the meaning. If someone asked, we'd just shrug it off. After many suggestions, we decided that we'd use the phrase "blueberry pancakes" to mean "amazing" or "unbelievable." What happened next was one of those teaching moments where you just sit back and smile (until your principal calls, which mine did).

Students began dropping the phrase into all types of situations. When one of their friends makes a three-pointer, my students chimed in with "That's so blueberry pancakes." In math, when a student received a 100 on a quiz, "Blueberry pancakes!" My students so enthusiastically spread the phrase that by the end of the second day, 6th graders were using the phrase, though with less accuracy in meaning. I had about 100 students at the time and within 48 hours, the phrase infiltrated our school of 1200 students. I was thrilled beyond belief. And then, the phone rang.

"What are you teaching those kids, Chandler?" my principal, Mr. Courtney, asked without saying hello. He was kind of blunt like that, and as teachers, we found it refreshing.

"English," I said back. I wasn't being sarcastic, exactly, but I just didn't know what he was talking about, and with him, blunt was also preferred.

"I just got a call from a 6th grade teacher who isn't sure if she is being insulted or not because her students are calling her 'blueberry pancakes.' They told her they heard it from an 8th grader, so I asked the first one I could find. He said he couldn't tell me, and that you were the one who started it." He continued, "What are you doing?"

Impressed by my student's dedication to our plan, I explained to him just how well my lesson was working, and he suggested I inform the staff the next time I create a new word for the lexicon, but I could tell he thought it was pretty "blueberry pancakes" himself. When I debriefed with my students and told them how much influence they had wielded, they were impressed, but some were offended. "Stupid 6th graders didn't even use it right," someone complained, pointing out that no one would call their teacher "blueberry pancakes." That would be weird. But, we then had an excellent conversation about how people don't always know what they are saying exactly, but are influenced by those around them.

The Blueberry Pancakes Experiment helped my students see how they had power over language, and once you establish that with your students, you'll be able to help them navigate between registers without offending anyone. These guided notes are helpful as you explain registers to students (Figure 3.2). This isn't something I'd formally assess, but I would keep returning to it. Another way to extend this activity is to have students create more complex scenarios on the back of the handout and then pose them to each other. Those conversations will be even more authentic and meaningful than

"Register" means what style of talking you use

Static Register	Formal Register	Consultative Register	Casual Register	Intimate Register
This is frozen language and doesn't change. "The Pledge of Allegiance" and "The Lord's Prayer" are examples.	One-way participation; no interruption; exact definitions are important. Presentations are a good example.	Two-way participation; background information is provided. Interruptions are allowed. Students in their Resource Groups	In-group friends and acquaintances; no background information provided; slang is common; interruptions common.	Non-public; tone of voice more important than wording, may have a private vocabulary. Can include swearing. Also includes nonverbal messages.

Which register for which scenario?

1) Discussing the latest ELA quiz as you leave class _____

2) Dinner with your family _____

3) Studying with your Resource Group _____

4) Singing the National Anthem _____

5) Hanging out at the school dance _____

6) Trying to get your oil changed _____

7) Ordering at a restaurant _____

Figure 3.2 Say What?

teacher-generated examples that will be just a step behind, no matter how good we are at register recon.

Slang and swearing are problematic, to be sure, but if the conversation about language is neutralized by framing it as an academic issue, not a socioeconomic or cultural one, the tension fades. When a student uses language that isn't school appropriate, I don't make a big deal of it, but I will say, "Switch registers," and it has a neutral, nonjudgmental impact.

I've likened it to coming to class with a notebook for another class. I don't disapprove of your other notebook, but I do want you to have the right one for our class. However, and I'm sure many people won't necessarily agree with this, if students are talking amongst themselves quietly or having a private conversation, I don't interrupt and correct swearing or slang when I catch snippets of it.

Allowing students to have access to different registers for different circumstances actually acknowledges the complexities of communication. Obviously, if I heard derogatory, racist, or sexist language, I'd make it known that it wasn't acceptable in any circumstance. AMLE's "This We Believe" frames it this way: "An effective middle grades curriculum is distinguished by learning experiences that address societal expectations while appealing to young adolescents and offering them opportunities to pose and answer questions that are important to them" (17). The conversation about registers is one of the most important I have all year because we are learning together, not a teacher passing judgment.

Metacognition

If you've ever consoled a child who failed a test or didn't make the team, one of the things you might have noticed is that students are not very self-aware. Recently, at a post-conference, I asked a young lady what grade she thought she earned, based on the criteria we had set forth.

"B," she said without a second of hesitation.

"Tell me more about that," I said, hoping to elicit some clue to her thought process.

"I got a 'B' on my math test this week, and I scored 4 points in the game, so I think I'm having a 'B' kinda week," she replied, as if I were just too dense to understand that this is how the world works.

Truth be told, my student didn't have any idea how she had done on the assignment because she had not thought about her own thinking—in other words, she was not spending any time in what I call the "metacognitive minute." The phrase was born several years ago when my frustration level was through the roof. Over and over, I couldn't get past the fact that my students could take a reading comprehension quiz on the chapters from the night before, then hound me about their grades constantly. Not only was I not too thrilled about their grade obsessions, I was in disbelief that a person could be this clueless about his/her own learning. How could you not know what you didn't know?

Finally, one day I instituted a "Metacognitive Minute." It is going to sound extremely simple, but I can promise it makes a huge difference. Each day I write the Daily Learning Goal on the board (essentially my objectives) and introduce it immediately. Students copy it on the "Metacognitive Minute Recording Sheet" (Figure 3.3). For example, maybe the goal is "I will understand metaphors." I then ask some questions about the Daily Learning Goal. For example, "So, what will it look like if you understand metaphors?" Students will shout out, "I'll recognize them," or "I'll be able to use them," or "I'll know what they mean." This takes two minutes, tops, and as they become used to it, I drop the questioning.

With about two minutes left in class, I return to the Metacognitive Minute, and ask students to stand up and "shake it out," or something physical to change their state. I then tell them to sit back down and take out their "Metacognitive Minute Record Sheet." I tell them to go back to their DLG (Daily Learning Goal) and determine which level they thought they'd reached and to create an action step if needed. If students are lost, they know it is time to get help immediately, and they'd record this information in the "SOS" column. If students have questions, but feel confident that they can figure it out, they record their information in the "Follow Up" column, meaning they will have to take some action before the next day, generally checking notes with some other student. If students feel confident, they write in the "Awesome" column, and they are free to help other students.

- Metacognitive means to "think about your own thinking." This is a way for us to realize if we understand what we are supposed to be learning or if we need to take some action steps.
- When you enter the classroom, copy down the Daily Learning Goal (DLG). During class, keep this goal in your mind as I teach, you participate, and students contribute. You'll be checking yourself before you leave.
- At the end of class, you'll need to figure out how well you understand the DLG. Here's a way to determine what you should do next:

SOS	FOLLOW UP	AWESOME
▣	▣	▣
I don't get this. I won't figure this out alone. Go see the teacher **NOW**. Take action. This is on you!	I'm not sure. I need to do something: talk to a friend, look at the notes, or research online **BEFORE tomorrow**.	I get this! I am SO ready to help others who might not get it just yet. **READY!**

Sample chart:

Today's date:	Today's Daily Learning Goal:	Self-assessment:	Actions I need to take:
10/2/16	I will recognize metaphors and understand how they are used in "The Most Dangerous Game."	I can recognize metaphors, but I am foggy on how the author is using them.	I'm in the "FOLLOW UP" area. I'm going to talk to Brianna at lunch to see if she can tell me what the author is doing. If she doesn't know, I'll Google it tonight.
10/3/16	I will write my own metaphors.	I can't do this.	This is an SOS. I'm going to get a pass to see Mrs. Chandler during studyhall.
10/4/16	I will be able to recognize metaphors, write my own, and summarize the author's purpose for using metaphors in "The Most Dangerous Game."	Wow. I actually can do all three.	I rock. I'm going to see if anyone needs help.

Metacognitive Minute Record Sheet for

_____

(your name)

Figure 3.3 Metacognitive Minute Recording Sheet

Today's date:	Today's Daily Learning Goal:	Self-Assessment:	Actions I need to take:

Metacognitive Minute Record Sheet for

_____

(your name)

Figure 3.3 Continued

It is really cool to have students scramble over at the end of the period to get a pass for study hall because in the Metacognitive Minute they realized that they may know what a metaphor is, but don't know how to use it and need help. Sometimes students will ask me to share them on the Google Slides I used for class, so they can check something out. Finally, after years of trying to formatively assess students, I have the tool to know how they are doing in the process of learning. AMLE emphasizes that "because of young adolescents' drive toward independence, they should be provided with opportunities to contribute to and take ownership of their own educations," but reminds middle level educators that "students must be nurtured in making choices about curricular goals, content, and activities, as well as the means of assessment" (19). The Metacognitive Minute allows me to successfully juxtapose independence with nurturing.

This may not sound like a revolutionary tactic, but I came up with it while working on my National Board Certification, and it has dramatically changed my own thinking. It bothered me that I relied on so many quizzes to check understanding, and I felt both bewildered and frustrated when they didn't seem to learn from taking them. I had been plagued with uncertainty, yet to be an accomplished teacher I needed to know what my students learned (and didn't!) and adapt from there. How would I know what they learned if they didn't? Metacognition is a skill that I can teach them so that everyone is on a successful path, knowing what next steps we need to take together.

CASEL (Center for Academic, Social, and Emotional Learning) defines **self-awareness** this way: *"The ability to accurately recognize one's emotions and thoughts and their influence on behavior. This includes accurately assessing one's strengths and limitations and possessing a well-grounded sense of confidence and optimism."* For students who "get it," I am instilling confidence for them as we move through difficult material. For those who don't "get it," I'm helping them to recognize their own thoughts, but more importantly influence their behavior when met with a limitation, modeling for them a necessary feedback loop: when you need help, you must advocate for yourself.

Sometimes our students are stuck in their own private echo chamber where they continually confirm their own poor conceptions of self and school. They may have heard negative things from others, but as we all know, it is easy to let a narrative play out, over and over again, because we don't challenge it. Again, echo chambers aren't limited to our students though. For years, I told myself that I couldn't run a 5K. I wasn't in great shape (I wasn't), I had weak ankles (I do), I didn't have time to train (I didn't), but when I started thinking about all of this narrative stuff, it occurred to me that I needed to push the limits of my own abilities. I needed to push past my own poor conception of myself—even though it was all true—and make it happen. I did it. It wasn't pretty. I didn't run, that's for sure. But I didn't walk either. I jogged. And I even heaved. But I did make it, and I may never run another one, but it taught me some important things about myself along the way.

One of the most difficult things when talking about education is to acknowledge that our experiences as teachers are so wildly different, that it can seem that we don't have the same job at all. The "problems" I have in my suburban district may seem absurd to my friends who work in high-need schools. On any given day, I receive at least a few emails from parents. My open houses are packed. We talk about "helicopter parents" and "tiger moms." Other teachers dream of such problems. However, we can stand behind one commonality: all students come to school with their own sort of baggage—which comes in all shapes, sizes, and even name brands. Teachers can positively impact how we help kiddos become better students and citizens when we push their experiences a little wider, challenge their preconceived notions, and make ourselves vulnerable as well. We can empower our students to get out of their own way and step out of their echo chambers, and while we are at it, we can make sure we aren't stuck in one ourselves.

Your Turn

How can we help students escape their echo chamber while checking ourselves too?

★ *Until we are able to leave the echo chamber that keeps us all comfortable, we will never reach our students in the meaningful ways that can happen when we are communicating.* In what topics do you think you might be experiencing this echo chamber effect? Personally? Professionally? Socially? What can you do to change that?

★ *Being able to adapt your speech to a variety of scenarios is not only useful but expected.* What are some ways that you can provide students with opportunities to try out different social situations? How might you start this conversation?

★ *I had been plagued with uncertainty, yet to be an accomplished teacher I needed to know what my students learned (and didn't!) and adapt from there.* In what ways do you use formative assessment? Is there a way to allow students the opportunity to self-check that fits into your subject area well?

★ *Sometimes our students are stuck in their own private echo chamber where they continually confirm their own poor conceptions of self and school.* How can you assess students' beliefs about themselves and school? What will you do with the information?

Post-Pandemic Principle

If you've never been the victim of a social media attack, consider yourself lucky. It seems that localized pages for communities, schools, and groups pop up on Facebook as a place to vent, test-trial balloons of conspiracy theories, and, unfortunately, at times, attack someone in the hopes of creating a mob. In the fall of 2020, I decided to teach *The Pigman*. My reasons were pretty straightforward: students like it, it was different enough from their own lives to give them an escape, and the psychology aspect of it is a fun way to connect with kiddos. I'm very transparent with everyone about what I'm doing in my classroom, with my doors truly open to families, grad students, other teachers, admin, politicians—anyone. So, in my typical fashion, I shared the assignments with my students and families. Within a few hours, my name was mud in a rogue Facebook group. (These too, have been popping up. When members are asked to follow the rules of one group, they will quit, form a rogue group, and all sense of propriety or norms take over.)

My wild, radical act, worthy of a weekend of bashing? I had created a page in my digital notebook where students were to compare our current time period to the 1960s era in order to establish an understanding of the setting of the novel. My example was a picture of a protest in 1960 and a picture of a protest in 2020. Suddenly, I was indoctrinating students about Black Lives Matter (which was nowhere in my example or the digital notebook) and trying to psychoanalyze my students. Or, in other words, I was trying to show my students that the age they were living in was similar to the time period in the book while trying to get to know them through fun quizzes. Luckily, I am confident in my justification for my book choice and its alignment to the curriculum and standards. More luckily, former students and parents jumped in and called off the attacks, but not before I had to send a letter home to my current students and their families explaining myself *and* offering a different option if a student's family did not want them to read the book. It was, in short, exhausting.

This experience really shook me. Why? The parents who were vehemently attacking me were doing so out of *their* strong beliefs. I was teaching from *my* strong beliefs. How can I have the kind of "Caring Classroom" community if this was the climate? What could I do to assuage parents' fears that I didn't have the best interest of their students in mind? How could I take the necessary risks to reach their children if I was going to be constantly scrutinized? I was feeling burnt out in September. I remember sighing and saying to my co-teacher, wait until we do the social justice unit with the movie *Zootopia*.

You might be wondering how this negative experience could possibly create a Post-Pandemic Principle. Flash forward to spring, when I almost always do *The Outsiders*. I knew that if some people were objecting to *The Pigman*, I'd surely have those who didn't want me to teach *The Outsiders*, a book about gangs, smoking, drinking, and violence. (Or, what the book is actually about: looking for acceptance, socioeconomic differences, mob mentality, and what makes a hero.) I decided I'd communicate with my students and families, overtly telling them my reasons for teaching the novel, clearly voice my disapproval of the unsavory parts, and offer to have a phone conversation or a video call with families who might still have questions. By this time, all families understood that I was aggressively working to help their children, advocating for them on every front, and patiently and flexibly helping through the year. No one asked for more clarification or requested a phone or video call.

*Post-pandemic, there is a lot of distrust that has crept into our everyday lives. We must reasonably and respectfully approach families with our intentions for their children, especially if the content we are teaching hits a nerve. The echo chamber is dangerous, and the only way to move forward and create the momentum we need to reinvigorate schools is to work with those who may not understand us, or us them. As educators, as experts, we should not have to explain our intentions or choices, but it is in our best interest, and the best interest of our students, to explain more than we ever have before and consider our choices **carefully.***

4

Whatever Happened to Afterschool Specials?

Preparing Students for Responsible Decision-Making

Developed by Collaborative for Academic, Social, and Emotional Learning and used with permission.

For a long time, I thought it was just me whose moral compass was tuned in at 3:30 P.M. to learn how to handle the complex world around me. For those of you too young to know what an ABC "Afterschool Special" was, it was a television show that ran for 25 years and was meant to help students deal with

DOI: 10.4324/9781003230311-4

both social and personal issues. Social Emotional Learning (SEL), for many of us, was doled out in two-hour increments.

I'm never sure what age the intended audience was, but my mom always let me watch them. I was usually accompanied by my sister, who was two years younger, and my backyard neighbor, who was a year older. Back when television was organized around time, not the other way around, we were always sitting on our plaid couch, ready for the opening music. These weren't the reality shows my own daughter loves; rather, these were movies written with the explicit intent of teaching school-age children about the social and emotional issues we'd face, and how we were supposed to handle them. Via the amazingness that is Wikipedia, here are a few of the titles that I recognized: "Just Tipsy, Honey," "First, the Egg," and "Just a Regular Kid: An AIDS Story."

What fascinates me now, as an adult, is just how many people I know who learned about social issues, and how we were meant to handle them, via these specials. I remember, nearly 30 years later, episodes about anorexia, suicide, and alcoholism, and I can now recognize just how influential these shows were. Why? As impressionable kiddos, we were looking for ways to handle the world around us, especially the topics no one wanted to talk about.

Clearly, the world is a different place, but can't you just imagine the types of afterschool specials that we need right now? The world may have changed, but the social and emotional needs of kiddos to make sense of the world around them, and the necessity to learn what to do in complex situations, have not. In fact, I think that the topics that no one wants to talk about are still widely ignored. With so many different perspectives, a global community can be a wonderful thing, but there has stopped being a clear set of guidelines for young students. I'm not going to suggest that we make the moral decisions for our students, but this chapter is going to delve into the role of schools, particularly teachers, in helping our students become responsible decision-makers in a world where many adults have stopped providing moral guidance.

Sneak Peek

In this chapter, we will

★ inventory our own thoughts regarding responsible decision-making
★ learn how to help students develop personal ethics
★ learn to incorporate responsible decision-making into our classroom culture

Tell Me How You Really Feel: Inventory Your Thoughts

Through the years I've discovered—as many of you have too, I'm sure—that when you have relationships, not just class lists, students begin to look to you for guidance. It has never been in my nature to tell anyone how (or who) to be. Yet, I believe it has become increasingly important to reach hearts and heads. It may sound trite, but I can promise you that no one will ever remember the phenomenal worksheet you gave them. What they might remember is how you helped them navigate the world. If I'm honest, most of what I teach in content could be learned by a well-developed tutorial, but helping a student who is drowning in decisions can be life altering. Some people, mostly those who don't teach, might think I'm overstating the impact teachers can have. I know, for a fact, that my guidance has changed lives, and if you are holding this book you have stories to tell too. Don't let the noise from the outside world ever make you doubt the important work that occurs in your classroom, work that is so great in magnitude that it is simply not measurable on an assessment.

AMLE's description of the tremendous privilege and responsibility of shaping students' lives through a "hidden curriculum" (one that is not explicitly taught, but deeply intuited) gives me chills:

> In fact, this aspect of learning is sometimes so profound and long lasting that it overrides learning that is more traditional. Lives are often shaped more by small individual actions, probing questions, subtle reminders, earned commendations, and personalized challenges than by direct instruction.
>
> (18)

What I love about this statement is that it implies relationship and emotion—both of which create retrievable memories.

Additionally, research shows that learning that is not in the context of a relationship is not as retrievable as memory that is encoded with emotional attachment. *Brain World Magazine*'s article "Learning & Memory: How Do We Remember and Why Do We Often Forget?" explains:

> Emotions can be a catalyst or an impediment to learning. It has been estimated that 95% of our reactions are unconsciously driven by the amygdala and only modestly impacted by the executive centers of the cerebral cortex. Although ours is generally considered a rational brain, it is an emotional brain, where feelings receive first priority. A student who is upset is one who cannot learn and will not remember content information well during assessment.

Students whose emotional needs are being met in my classroom have a better chance of remembering what I am teaching, both for an assessment, but also as a larger schema of information that guides their decision-making. One opportunity we have in education right now is to guide our students in making responsible decisions. It is time to step forward, even if it is out of character, and claim the hearts of our students.

As you approach your students' social and emotional needs, you're going to need to take stock of your own non-negotiables and determine what criteria you use to make responsible decisions. This is soul searching. What will you stand for? As I approached these questions, I thought of what I wanted for my students. Not a list of rules, but a list of what mattered to me. On the first day of school, I use a handmade poster I made to introduce myself. Here's what's on it:

> Be kind!
> Take risks.
> Listen actively.
> Do your very best.
> Everything counts!
> Share.
> Be your own hero.

It doesn't say *all* that I mean, of course. What it really means is be kind to all people no matter their race, religion, sexual orientation, social status, level of education, or kinds of clothes they wear. However, those are lessons they will learn in an authentic context throughout the year. Take some time to figure out what you want to value in your classroom as you help students make responsible decisions. Use the "Claiming Your Non-negotiables" worksheet (Figure 4.1) to help you sort through your thoughts and draft some life rules that inform your own decision-making.

Helping Students Create Their Own Personal Ethics

If you are thinking, "Wait, I have biology to teach, not ethics," or "Do you know the curriculum for my 5th grade? I'll never have time for this," you wouldn't be the first to question the wisdom of taking time away from the curriculum to teach values of any kind. In fact, I think that the higher the stakes of the testing, the less likely teachers are to want to explore ethics and values or focus on our students' decision-making. Yet, I'd like to suggest that deeper learning will happen when we are able to expose our students to authentic scenarios as a part of a Flexible Classroom that values students as individuals.

How can ethics play a part in a biology class? To me, the better question is how could it not? Infusing decision-making into a biology class can serve dual purposes. Students will be highly engaged in the content in order to authentically apply the learning, thus moving the information from their short-term memory to their long-term memory. Additionally, students are able to rehearse their decision-making based on personal ethics, a skill that will greatly benefit students socially and emotionally in their futures. This

(a guided exercise to discover your rules for life)

Look at this word list. Read through it a few times. *Highlight no more than 10 words* that strike you as extremely important. Cross out words that don't matter to you. You'll have some words left over, and that's ok.

abundance	acceptance	accomplishment	adventure	balance
beauty	boldness	challenge	charity	commitment
dependability	determination	devoutness	empathy	enlightenment
expressiveness	faith	flow	freedom	generosity
genuineness	grace	gratitude	heart	holiness
honor	hospitality	independence	inspiration	intelligence
joy	justice	leadership	liberty	love
loyalty	meekness	moderation	neatness	obedience
optimism	order	passion	peacefulness	pleasure
popularity	recognition	recreation	respect	restraint
teamwork	thrift	transcendence	truth	unity
uniqueness	usefulness	valor	victory	vision
wealth	winning	youth	zeal	zest

Answer the following questions honestly. Take your time. If you are stuck, ask someone who knows you very well and who will "tell it like it is." Don't think too much. Let your answers evolve; that means cross things out and change the wording. This is a living document, so it should reflect the latest experiences.

What are your three greatest accomplishments?

1) _____

_____

_____

2) _____

_____

_____

Figure 4.1 Claiming Your Non-Negotiables

3) _____
_____
_____

When you look at the above three accomplishments, is there a theme that emerges? Is there a certain word or idea that is linked to a highlighted word from your list above?
_____
_____

What are your three greatest failures or disappointments?

1) _____
_____
_____

2) _____
_____
_____

3) _____
_____
_____

When you look at the above three failures or disappointments, is there a theme that emerges? Is there a certain word or idea that is linked to a highlighted word from your list above?
_____
_____

Now, take these insights and create five "non-negotiables" that you want or don't want in your life. These should be short and to the point. They will not include an explanation:

1) _____
2) _____
3) _____
4) _____
5) _____

Reflect: How do these non-negotiables fit into the culture of your classroom?

Figure 4.1 Continued

activity (Figure 4.2) is a great place to start. The teacher can have students group themselves according to the topic, position on the topic, or which quote they agree with more. The teacher could also allow students time with each grouping, and then allow students to present individually or with peers.

How about our 5th grade classroom teacher, the one bogged down with curriculum? Colonization is a social studies curriculum topic for most 5th

Task: Choose one of the ethical dilemmas mentioned below by Dr Koehler and research the potential pros and cons of using genetic knowledge to make decisions. Create a digital representation of your findings (PowerPoint, Prezi, Infographic, or other digital representation) to share with the class. Keep the following two quotes in mind and be prepared to side with either Einstein or Hawking:

I shall never believe that God plays dice with the world. —Albert Einstein
God not only plays dice, but also sometimes throws them where they can't be seen. —Stephen Hawkin.

"Bioethics and Human Diagnostics" by Gus A. Koehler, PhD

Testing for genetic defects is generally considered to be helpful and to increase possible treatment options. The issue becomes much more complex when genetic information has implications for reproductive choice or portends an unhealthy future for a currently healthy person (for example, having a mastectomy to prevent the potential future occurrence of a genetically-based cancer). Related issues include: disclosure of a genetic defect; availability and affordability of genetic counseling and health insurance; and employee screening.

Figure 4.2 Ethical Decision-Making in Biology

graders. As a good hook before starting the colonization unit, students can work together on the "Colonizing Quandary: Space Exploration" activity (Figure 4.3). This activity also has cross-curricular implications, as it is easy to expand into science standards, while the research and writing involved meet English language arts (ELA) standards. It is a hands-on activity that lends itself to ethical decision-making and leads into some complicated colonization questions that come with the founding of the United States.

In my ELA class, I plan to teach the graphic novel *Maus* this year. It isn't an easy book, as it addresses the Holocaust in a graphic novel. The major players are depicted symbolically. Jews are mice, Nazis are cats, and Americans are dogs. There is an abundance of history that I'll need to cover, since I'll be getting to it before the social studies curriculum. Though I'm certainly teaching a graphic novel, as well as some history, symbolism, and theme, I'm using this opportunity to discuss responsible decision-making with my students. It is a daunting task to approach 8th graders with arguably one of the most complicated and controversial ethical dilemmas the world has ever faced. To be honest, I've taught this unit before without the responsible decision-making aspect, and I felt that it was too one dimensional, and my students were too far removed from the complexities.

As I planned this unit (again), I knew that I had to do something differently. This time, I'm planning to do more frontloading. Before we begin the novel, we're going to spend a few weeks accessing the students' personal priorities, rehearsing ethical decision-making, and eventually writing their own credo to explain their beliefs. As an ELA teacher, I have the luxury of creating expansive units, but it is also an investment in their future understanding of the novel. Additionally, I'm convinced that writing a credo will help them find their footing a bit as they move through middle school. One thing that

Did you know that there's a pretty decent chance that in YOUR lifetime, people will go to space to live there? Crazy, right? Let's explore this idea! Here are the roles for your research and conversation:

Who:	Does what?	Questions to consider	Product to hand in
Scientist	Examine the probability (chance) that colonization could occur in space.	How would people arrive there? How would people breathe? What supplies would we need to keep a person healthy?	Write a three sentence summary of your findings.
Colony Planner	Plan how a community in space would need to be arranged.	Would all the living spaces be connected or would there be separate groups? How are those groups arranged?	Draw a map of the colony as you imagine it to work.
Sociologist	Consider how a space colony could function.	Who is in charge? Is there a president? School? Government? Churches?	Write a short paragraph describing the colony's way of life.
Historian	Record the information from the Scientist, Community Planner, and Sociologist, in your own words.	What will people in the future want to know about this colony? Why did people want to colonize in the first place? Is the colony different than earth in significant ways?	Write a list of 10 bullet points that would be helpful to students who need to learn about the colony.

You will have two class periods to research these questions and prepare the product that is listed. You'll share your findings with the class. Do your best work to make your colony amazing. Make sure to:

* Give your colony a name.
* Create a motto for your colony that relates to why you left Earth to create a new world.
* Be detailed, using lots of adjectives and sensory details. Remember, this is a new world!

Figure 4.3 Colonizing Quandary: Space Exploration

is noteworthy about this assignment is that it is mostly independent. I run a Project Based Learning classroom that is largely collaborative, even in their writing, but I want to impress upon them that their ethics are deeply personal, and we all have to find our ways to live, which they will express in their credo.

However, I don't want my students to begin in isolation. They are so social, and thinking about ethics is going to draw them in. They are so used to bouncing ideas off of each other in their Resource Groups that I don't want to take that routine from them. The first activity I'm going to do is the "Personal Priorities Thermometer" (Figure 4.4). It is a kid-friendly conversation starter that allows students to begin the conversation about what matters to them in a non-threatening, conversational way. To build upon these foundational conversations, we will discuss (and likely debate) the scenarios presented on the "Ethical Dilemmas" (Figure 4.5) handout.

I intend to give students plenty of time to talk in small groups, but I think that it is crucial for them to rehearse some of their ethics in front of the group. Learning from each other is an important part of my Flexible Classroom

Directions: On each "thermometer" place a star nearest the description of your feelings about the topic. After you've filled out your opinions, chat with your Resource Group to see what you share in common, and areas you differ. Mark their opinions with O's.

COOL→ No strong opinions, don't really care, not interested in the topic, haven't heard of it
LUKEWARM→ Not a big deal either way, take it or leave it, not worth arguing about
HOT→ Very important, this is a dealbreaker for me, I can't believe people don't see how important this is

COLD   LUKEWARM   HOT
----*
Friendships and close relationships

COLD   LUKEWARM   HOT
----*
Family and family events

COLD   LUKEWARM   HOT
----*
School, grades, academic recognition

COLD   LUKEWARM   HOT
----*
Sports, teammates, victory, competition

COLD   LUKEWARM   HOT
----*
Performing, creating, communicating

COLD   LUKEWARM   HOT
----*
Spirituality, religion, charity, afterlife, sense of purpose

COLD   LUKEWARM   HOT
----*
Recreation, hanging out, playing video games, relaxing

Figure 4.4 Personal Priorities Thermometer

approach, and though they'll ultimately write their credo (Figure 4.6) alone, I want them to approach the concept itself as a group. Formulating statements of their beliefs is laying the groundwork for future conversations about the topics of the novel: What do you do in the face of evil? Is silence the voice of complicity? How should we respond to deep loss? I'm confident that this approach, which coaches students through the process of responsible decision-making, will be beneficial for their understanding of the novel, as well as for their futures.

Incorporate Responsible Decision-Making into Your Classroom Culture

Some states have implemented standards to ensure social and emotional learning becomes a part of that state's educational landscape. According to CASEL's "Policy Recommendations":

An ethical dilemma is a complex situation where the solutions will cause equally important beliefs to conflict with each other, and it can seem there isn't an "easy way out."

With your Resource Group, take turns reading the dilemmas. Discuss each until you feel that you'll be ready to defend your choice to the class. Use the lines to take notes.

To hack or not to hack?

A hack is a code that will allow a player in a game to give themselves an advantage that other players don't have. For example, a level up or an extra weapon would be a hack. Hacks are not particularly hard to find out, but people new to the game might not know. These hacks are not the same as a "trick" that allows you to learn more about the game. A hack is a "cheat." Servers try to prevent hacks and gamers can be banned, sometimes even if they just "think" you are hacking. **Should people hack or not?**

_____

_____

_____

Speak now or spend more?

In the lunch line, you say your ID number to pay, and notice that it was charged to someone else's account. Do you correct the person at the register, do nothing, or grab an extra snack? **Speak now or spend more?**

_____

_____

_____

"Show and tell" or "hide and sneak"?

Your best friend is sleeping over. Around midnight she gets a text from a number that she doesn't know. She asks, "Who is this?" and the other person sends her an inappropropriate picture. You want to wake up your mom, but your friend is freaking out that she will get in so much trouble because her mom already thinks she shouldn't have a phone. She's convinced that her mom will take away her phone and begs you not to. **"Show and tell" or "hide and sneak"?**

_____

_____

_____

Figure 4.5 Ethical Dilemmas

There have been three different approaches to developing K-12 learning standards for social and emotional learning. Some states have developed free-standing, comprehensive standards or goals for social and emotional learning. Other states have developed clearly articulated standards that are focused on a particular aspect of social and emotional learning. The majority of states integrate learning goals that are relevant to social and emotional learning into other academic content areas.

On the federal level, both sides of the aisle supported legislation in 2015 that would further SEL. Though a positive step, implementing standards is a tricky proposition (Figure 4.7).

However, as teachers, we do have the opportunity to help students reach their greatest potential, both personally and professionally. Responsible decision-making is an area that we can immediately thread through our existing curriculum and connect to proven best practices. For example, teachers can allow students to create a class constitution that will help regulate behaviors and attitudes within the class. Though at times this can seem time-consuming, we are doing two things. First, we are allowing students the opportunity to make decisions. For some students, it is shocking how little control they

Ralph Waldo Emerson, a great activist and writer, once wrote, "To be yourself in a world that is constantly trying to make you something else is the greatest accomplishment." That is why, for this assignment, you are **on your own**. I don't even want you to share your ideas (gasp, right?!). That is, I don't want you to share until your great reveal--the presentation of your ideas.

You are creating a written statement that expresses what you stand for and who you are. You may use straightforward language or you may choose to be poetic. Your credo should be written in a way that screams your name!

I understand how challenging this will be. I'm going to do it too, and frankly, it makes me nervous! *This requires such truth that no one else can do it for you*. To guide you through this process, see the suggestions below:

Choose between 5 and 10 beliefs that you have that make you, YOU! You might want sections and headings, or it might be told in one longer narrative. **BOLD** the individual words or phrases of your belief. There is not a specific length, but if you don't have at least 4 or 5 sentences for it, it is probably NOT a belief. For example, mine are going to be:

family and friends first
be exceptional
take risks
jump in with your clothes on
never miss a chance to cuddle
eat dessert first
stay up late
travel (literally and figuratively)
write it down
compliment often

Be positive and respectful. Please avoid telling your audience what we should do; instead, tell us what you do believe and what works for you. Understand that there will be people who do not agree with your ideas. That's ok because your ideas are **ONLY FOR YOU**!

Be personal. Write in words and phrases that sound like you. Read your essay aloud to yourself several times, and each time edit it and simplify it. Your diction should be comfortable for you. You won't be reading this to the class, but if you did, we should be able to "hear" you in it.

After you have completed your essay, you will create a Prezi, Haiku Deck, Piktochart, Google Slideshow, PowerPoint, video, photo collage, piece of artwork (painting, sculpture, etc), musical recording, or some other product that will be your presentation medium. You will each have 5 minutes to present. This means that you will need to choose to either briefly talk about all of your beliefs OR share one of them in a deeper way.

You will submit your essay via Google Classroom. A copy of this assignment and the Essay Grading Guide are in the stream.

Figure 4.6 Personal Credo: This I Believe…

Essay Grading Guide:

"A" essays → These essays are personal, developed, and grammatically sound. They are easy to read and sentences flow, making it easy to move from one idea to the next. It is easy to identify the core values and beliefs of the author.

"B" essays → These essays are personal, but may lack some development or have grammatical mistakes. They might include fewer transitions and could seem choppy. It is easy to identify the core values and beliefs of the author.

"C" essays → These essays are formulaic, may need more development, or have serious grammatical mistakes that impact reading. They are choppy, and it is could be difficult to identify the core values and beliefs of the author.

Papers that are below a "C" will be returned. I'll help you after school to rework your writing and guide you through the areas that are causing you to be less than your best.

Presentation Grading Guide:

"A" presentations: These presentations are unique to the author. The medium chosen is appropriately designed. All writing is easy to read and spelling is correct. The speaker is loud, clear, and enthusiastic.

"B" presentations: These presentations are unique to the author. The medium chosen might have some flaw in design or is not easy to understand. Writing may be harder to read or there could be spelling errors. The speaker may need prompting to be louder or clearer. The speaker might not be enthusiastic.

"C" presentations: These presentations are more generic. The voice and uniqueness of the author is unclear and the medium might confuse the audience. Writing might be hard to decipher or contain many errors. The speaker might need several promptings to be louder or clearer. The speaker might be dismissive or uninterested.

*If your presentation does not meet the "C" level, I will rehearse with you after school and give you the opportunity to present again the following week.

Figure 4.6 Continued

have over any part of their lives. By creating opportunities for students to decide and reflect, we are helping them develop real-life skills and rehearse for bigger decisions.

The second thing a class constitution can do is help create a culture of collaborative learning to replace the adversarial situations that students had gotten themselves into. Many years ago, when I was teaching junior English in summer school, I started the first day with the plan to create a class constitution. Obviously, this was a tough crowd, but I wanted to teach them that teachers and students can work together; my goal for the summer was that they pass English, but it was going to be in a classroom where students and teachers learn together. Within the first five minutes, the activity was failing because they weren't making bylaws that they wanted; they were simply regurgitating all of the school rules that they'd failed to follow in the first place.

As excited as I am that schools are starting to take the social and emotional needs of our students more seriously, I'm not fully comfortable with SEL Standards because the types of learning we are talking about are so amorphous and individualized. However, I'm all too aware that if it isn't measured, it might not be taught. I don't have the answers, but I will say that as soon as there's a standard with benchmarking, we lose some of our autonomy and are tied to timelines and comparisons. "Best practices" will emerge that may be fabulous for your inner city classroom but would fail miserably in my suburban school. For example, at an SEL conference, I was sitting next to a group from Atlanta who were talking about the power of home visits. Trust me when I say that in my corner of the world I'd probably get in trouble for dropping into someone's house. There are three factors that I think must be considered when rolling out SEL Standards:

✓ Socio-economic considerations: The cost to implement new standards correctly is expensive. *The last thing we need is another mandate that enlarges the gap between students' access to a quality education.*

✓ Ample time to implement: For example, Illinois has a standard for late high school that requires a project that will impact the needs of a community. *It takes years to develop the skills and community collaboration that would be necessary for this type of project to be successful.*

✓ Quality professional development: It is crucial that this SEL is not reduced to two hours on a staff day. *Implementing without true understanding has a best case scenario of surface improvements, and a worst case scenario of actually damaging fragile social and emotional needs of students.*

Figure 4.7 Just a Word about … SEL Standards

As I walked around, I heard one student say, "She should just give us naptime," followed by howls of laughter. Deep breath. Here we go, I thought.

"OK. I can give you naptime. Tell me about that," I said, suddenly gaining the attention of 25 disgruntled teenagers.

"It's too early. We need sleep. I got class after this too," the boy said, clearly not expecting much.

"How long is a good naptime?" I asked.

"I dunno. Ten minutes, I guess," he said.

"OK, done. Can you write that on the board for me?" I said, as I handed him the chalk (like I said, it was a long time ago). Each class was 1 hour and 40 minutes long. I easily could concede 10 minutes if I got the other 90 minutes.

"So, I'll do even better. How about a five-minute break halfway? Then, all your work is due at 9:30. If you finish it, you get the last ten minutes to nap. I'll even turn the lights off. Bring a pillow, whatever you need," I said, gaining confidence that this might work after all.

It did work. Amazingly, that room of teenagers gave me their attention— at least as much of it as I could expect early in the morning on the hottest days of summer. We had made other bylaws that gave them some say in the way class was run. They were allowed to have drinks because, believe it or not, they weren't allowed to in any other class. On Fridays, they could bring breakfast. They all chipped in a dollar on Thursdays and a kid who worked at the grocery store would stop and bring us a breakfast pizza. But they also agreed to be on time, not swear at each other or me, and to do all of the assignments, with the exception of one. They wanted to be able to just say, "Nope.

I didn't do that one. I was busy," and I'd say OK, mark it down as the free assignment, and no one would be mad.

Those students were the first that I'd ever given that much leeway to. I had no idea that it would be such a turning point for me. That summer we read a novel, wrote a personal narrative, and did a how-to essay. This was in only five weeks. I had assigned the how-to essay to help them see that they had knowledge that we would all find valuable. I was amazed that one of the girls could take apart a computer and put it back together again. Another girl made us a class flag by quilting. A boy who wore a bike chain as a belt showed us all how to do tai chi. I learned as much as they did, and I made sure they knew it. They were rowdy, sometimes off task, but all in all, they worked well together and the class ran smoothly. This was summer school, and I was exhilarated. How could that possibly be? When the summer ended, and the students filed out, I remember thinking, "Why can't all classes be like that?" The answer: me. I've since developed the "Class Constitution" (Figure 4.8) that is ready to use at the beginning of each year. It's a little more formal than my fly-by-the-seat summer experiment!

As a teacher, we have so much more control over our individual circumstances than we believe. Find what you want to do and make it educationally sound. Yes, they had a drink. Have you read this article about hydration? As a matter of fact, they do have a break. Have you seen this amazing research about the attention span of teenagers? You get the idea. Research and be ready to stand behind your ideas. That, by the way, is at the center of real responsible decision-making. Would I do something that would get me fired? No. I had turned down their idea to walk across the street for a smoke break. After class on the first day, I went down to the assistant principal's office and filled him in on what I was doing. To this day, I credit that class with teaching *me* about responsible decision-making, and the power that comes with it.

SUPPORT MATERIAL

The students of Room ___ have created this living document to govern the community. Just as the framers of our Constitution set out define their goals, here is our aim and purpose for our community:

_____
_____
_____

We agree that the members of our class should have the freedom TO:

1) _____
2) _____
3) _____
4) _____
5) _____

Figure 4.8 Class Constitution

We agree that the members of our class should have the freedom
FROM:

1)_____

2)_____

3)_____

4)_____

5)_____

We are a class free from fear. This means that we are kind to one another, and we take risks because that's how to grow. We acknowledge that we are a work in progress and sometimes we'll mess up. That's ok. We are a class that accepts mistakes and grows from them. We are a class that will support one another in and out of the classroom. Our community is physically and emotionally safe. We accept each other as we are: skin color, sexual orientation, gender identification, religion, and personalities of all types are respected. We hereby decree that this Constitution is our guide. We will reconvene with a Constitution Convention at the end of each quarter to assess our success.

Signed: _____

Date: _____

Figure 4.8 Continued

Your Turn

How can we promote responsible decision-making in our classrooms?

★ *The world may have changed, but the social and emotional needs of kiddos to make sense of the world around them, and the necessity to learn what to do in complex situations, have not.* What did you personally struggle with while in school? What struggles might students have that you don't fully understand?

★ *Through the years I've discovered—as many of you have too, I'm sure—that when you have relationships, not just class lists, students begin to look to you for guidance.* What are some ways that you can provide students with guidance? How might you start this conversation?

★ *It is a daunting task to approach 8th graders with arguably one of the most complicated and controversial ethical dilemmas the world has ever faced.* What complex topics lend themselves to your content area? How can you help students talk about these topics and rehearse responsible decision-making?

★ *Some states have implemented standards to ensure social and emotional learning become a part of that state's educational landscape.* What are your thoughts on standards for SEL? If you were to create them, what would be your focus?

★ *Responsible decision-making is an area that we can immediately thread through our existing curriculum and connect to proven best practices.* What lessons or activities do you have that include opportunities for students to rehearse decision-making?

Post-Pandemic Principle

Ungrading: Why Rating Students Undermines Learning (and What to Do Instead) is a collection of essays from some of my favorites, like Joy Kirr, Alfie Kohn, and Starr Sackstein, and I highly recommend it if you've found yourself wondering about going gradeless or moving toward more standards-based assessment. I've known for quite a while my position on grading, retakes, rubrics, and the like, but I haven't, until recently, been able to articulate exactly what I want students to know about my philosophy of grading, and this book pushed my thinking. Sure, my students are happy with feedback, glad for opportunities for retakes, and know that I truly understand that we all learn at different rates, at different paces, and in different ways. However, during the pandemic, I had the opportunity to think about what exactly I wanted students to learn about learning. Since I knew that the year was a wild experiment anyway, I chose to have conversations about learning with my students far more than I ever have before.

With direct contact time way down, I needed a way for my students to keep learning when I wasn't there. In a non-pandemic year, I don't give homework, but since I only saw students for two days in person for much of the year, they had to, by necessity, do work at home. I hated the prospect of "at-home learning," because I knew that they were already inundated from all of their other classes with "asynchronous" work, which in reality, was just homework. I needed an easy, measurable, and engaging way for my students to continue their education at home. I landed on Edpuzzle, an amazing platform that allows you to search lessons created by other educators, or to upload videos yourself, and then create self-scoring multiple-choice questions or extended responses. The key for me to Edpuzzle is that I can see how long students spent on a question, whether they went back to watch the video segment again to find an answer, and I can make my own videos.

At first, there was some resistance to Edpuzzle for a really interesting reason: accountability. Unlike so many other really great tools, I don't have to take my students' word for it. Students would send me frantic emails that all sounded basically the same: "I'm sorry. I rushed through the Edpuzzle. Can you reset it and let me take it again?" I'd always respond the same: "Sure! I'll just put your grade in the gradebook for now, but after we chat in person, I'll reset it for you." This may sound like an evil plan, but I had my reasons. I wanted to have a face-to-face conversation about not making this a habit. I wanted them to look at me and explain the situation. I would always reset it and let them take it again. However, I'd always record the original grade in the "notes" of my gradebook. It would read "Good effort! Original grade

55%" in the notes, but reflect the new grade in the grade column and their average.

By noting the students' original grade I was doing three things. First, I was letting their caregivers know what was happening. I wanted their families to know that their child was rushing and not giving the assignment the time it needed. I also wanted them to understand that their child was responsibly seeking to do better, and I wanted families to know that this was an option. I'm not going to lie. It was, and is, and will be, a huge pain to go through this process, but it will only last for a little while for most students. Most students will, after a few retakes, begin to slow down and "do it right the first time." However, there will be students who are immature or whose caregiver is on their case to get a higher grade, who will need for me to reset and allow another chance to learn the lesson.

The platform is free, compatible with Google Classroom, and collects data that is easy to share with students. However, the main reason I've continued to use Edpuzzle is that it holds students accountable in measurable ways. This data is priceless when meeting with families because we can stop talking about how Suzy isn't good at reading comprehension and instead talk about how Suzy doesn't spend enough time actually doing the reading, or how Joe may struggle with vocabulary, but he isn't taking advantage of the opportunities to retake Edpuzzle quizzes. Too often, since school for most of us was a "one shot deal," caregivers assume their child simply struggles when instead the student *isn't* actually struggling through and putting in the time. By allowing retakes, the work was always without risk, and families and caregivers were able to help students.

In my attempt to have open dialogue with my students, we frequently discussed how they felt we were doing. They did not love our poetry unit, as you can see in Figure 4.9, and they hated the digital notebooks we attempted. In all fairness, we hated them too. It was definitely a technology tool that we tried and failed with; however, we only used them for about five weeks until we asked how it was going. When they hated it, we were happy to try something different. I was always particularly concerned by testing because students were given so much less time face to face with us, so we utilized a variety of review tools.

At the end of the year, I was curious about what they would say we should keep from our pandemic learning year, and what we should get rid of (Figure 4.9).

The Post-Pandemic Principle here is simple. Students need accountability and flexibility simultaneously. It isn't enough for us to tell them to "study" without providing real guidance through that process. Students quickly learned what a hassle it

Please choose activities that we should KEEP for next year.

109 responses

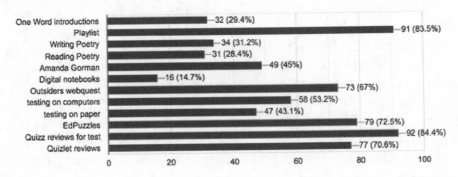

Figure 4.9 Student Survey

became when they were lazy or uncommitted the first time through. When they put in the time and rewatched the video segments they didn't understand, they were able to be successful. In essence, Edpuzzle forces students into a metacognitive feedback loop, which is exactly what students need to learn to be independent. The different study tools helped students to help themselves, and they were able to practice multiple times for tests and quizzes, all in a risk-free environment. When we help students truly prepare for a test or quiz, it should be anticlimactic, as they should already understand what they know and don't know.

5

Relationship Skills

Don't Let Them Get Your Goat

Developed by Collaborative for Academic, Social, and Emotional Learning and used with permission.

I have a special place in my heart for the frequent flyers to the school nurse. What better way to escape a classroom or situation that isn't working for you than to go to the one place in the school where the adult's job is to actually ask you how you are feeling? If they were giving away miles for my frequent flying back when I was in 5th grade, I could have taken my whole family cross-country. Some teachers don't seem to remember that the experiences of

DOI: 10.4324/9781003230311-5

emotional pain, fear, and anxiety are downright visceral. If you haven't felt the strong kick in the stomach of failure, you should consider yourself lucky. But most of us have, and for children, the nurse's office can provide a safe haven, or in my case, a mini therapy session.

"What's the matter?" Mrs. Louis asked me, shaking her head, but taking me by the hand. We walked back to the tiny closet space that was a makeshift office.

"My stomach hurts," I said, weakly. I knew the next questions by heart.

"Like butterflies? Like spinning in circles? Like you need to go to the bathroom? Like elephants stampeding?" Mrs. Louis asked without a hint of mockery, even though she asked me these questions at least three times a week.

"Elephants," I said, feeling silly that this was how we talked about my problems.

"What now?" she asked roughly. Elephants was our code for the huge kick-to-the-gut feelings I had when I was made fun of.

"Michael told everyone to call me Amber Brain instead of Amber Rain. Now that's all anyone will call me," I explained.

"Honey, you can't let them get your goat. Some of the kids who say that are mean. But some are just kidding. And some are jealous. If you cry when they say it, the mean ones will say it more," Mrs. Louis said matter-of-factly.

I'd love to say that her advice worked, but it didn't. What did work though was my relationship with her. She knew how to get me pieced back together and back to class. When I think back to this time, I'm always struck by her phrase, "Don't let them get your goat." I'm positive I didn't know what she meant, but it didn't matter. Mrs. Louis was my person.

To begin every school year, I tell this story. And then I tell my new students that they don't know me yet, but I'm offering to be *their person*. I tell them to come to me if their lockers won't open, they rip their pants, they are crying, they need lunch or a pen or a Band-Aid, or if they want to use my phone to call home. As you might expect, many 8th graders look away skeptically, but some need this reassurance immediately, and over the course of the year, many more come to me simply because *we all need a person*.

Sneak Peek

In this chapter, we will

★ examine practical ways to connect with our students
★ learn to implement relationship building into our curricula and culture
★ empower our students to be Upstanders

I See You: Connecting with Students

I am horrible at learning names. You'd think I'd get better, and maybe I have, but I still hate the first weeks of school when I am getting to know my students. Over the years, I've come up with ways to help me learn names. As soon as I can connect a story to a kiddo, I usually remember the name. One of the ways that I stumbled upon this was an amazing life-altering activity that my co-teacher, Laura Klein, introduced me to. (How is that for a build up? Life altering is hardly what you'd expect from a get-to-know-you activity, right?)

We created a "One Word Challenge" for our students (Figure 5.1). The idea wasn't our own, but it was created to be shared and even co-opted. The authors of *One Word That Will Change Your Life* are Dan Britton, Jimmy Page, and Jon Gordon, and they wrote the book expecting teachers, leaders, pastors, and coaches to use their idea to motivate those of us who don't quite hit the mark when it comes to New Year's resolutions.

Like many fabulous ideas, the premise is pretty simple: instead of creating a list of self-defeating resolutions that usually are limiting in some way (quit smoking, stop procrastinating, no more dessert), the authors ask us to choose one word, only one, and to invest our energy into that word.

Because I have entered a school building every fall for 37 consecutive years, my real New Year's Day is September 7. From the moment I entered as a kindergartener in the fall of 1979 with my first-day dress, crooked bangs, uncomfortable new shoes, and Snoopy lunch box, I knew I belonged in a classroom, and I never looked back, even when I needed frequent trips to the nurse. I make it my goal that all students feel safe and supported in my classroom. This activity allows an emotional connection before the educational one.

The One Word Challenge is a baby step into my Project Based and collaborative classroom. More important, though, I realized this year that it allows me to *see* my students for the first time. I highly recommend doing this activity early on because it places teenagers in the position of raw vulnerability (where growth happens) within the context of a safe classroom. Each student creates one slide with his/her particular word, shares it with me, and I create a slideshow set to their music, further validating the important journey that they are on. It offers a great touchstone to return to as the year progresses.

For those of you who might feel like this "touchy feely" activity is a waste of time, I promise you, the energy you use on the frontside will pay massive dividends that can't be underestimated. If it feels like "fluff," take a few minutes to come up with your own one word, examine how a small

There are many smart people who believe that we are what we think about, or what we **consciously** turn our attention towards.

This is similar to an athlete getting "PUMPED" for a game, narrowing her attention to the smallest detail of the game and blocking everything else out. Or, a musician who **FEELS** the music in his bones.

We are going to begin our year with each of us choosing one word that we will consciously turn our attention towards throughout the year.

Your word is something to keep you **MOTIVATED**!

One Word Challenge directions

CHOOSE ONE WORD (adjective) TO FOCUS ON THIS YEAR.

1. DEFINE IT TO FIT YOUR INTENT.
2. WRITE AN "I WILL…" STATEMENT TO PROVIDE AN EXAMPLE OF HOW YOU WILL FOCUS ON THIS WORD.
3. INCLUDE POSITIVE VISUALS AND CAPTIONS.
4. INCLUDE YOUR NAME.
5. CREATE A GOOGLE SLIDE AND SHARE ME ON IT.

*I'll be putting all the words together to share with you **WHO WE ARE** and **WHAT WE ARE ABOUT**! Send me a link to any song that you think would motivate us.*

Figure 5.1 One Word Challenge

shift in your thinking could impact students over time, and then think of that small shift exponentially. Dare to try something when you aren't sure of the outcome, and you are modeling the Growth Mindset from day one. Not only is this good karma, if you will, but sound educational practice, backed by research. AMLE's "This We Believe" calls for an adult advocate for every student who will assist in their academic, social, and emotional development.

As the year progresses, it is important to continually find ways to learn about your students. I've been guilty in the past, so I don't fault teachers who do their mandatory three days of class culture building, and then retreat into the curriculum. Before I really fell in love with the idea of Social Emotional Learning (SEL), I missed opportunities to connect with and help my students because I was thinking more about what most other people were always talking about: benchmarks, data points, and growth. There's nothing wrong with these things, and I pay attention to all three. However, I've found that when I pay attention to the art of teaching rather than just the science of it, I can find ways to demonstrate to my students that I genuinely care about them while also helping them grow intellectually and emotionally.

Other Ways to See and Connect with Students

This year, one of the things weighing on my mind was what to do when students don't learn what they need to. Two new practices for me have dramatically changed the way students feel about my class and, crucially, how they see my earnest interest in their actual growth as people, not just pupils. I decided that I was going to *see* my students' needs, and I was going to meet those needs—no matter what it takes.

The first idea I had was to allow students open-note quizzes and tests. I had made a passing comment to one of my classes that I didn't see the point of memorization with the world at our fingertips via our smartphones. One of my students raised his hand and asked, "Then why do you have tests then?" He wasn't challenging me in a negative way, but it flustered me. I was perplexed because I didn't have an exact answer at the ready, but I was so excited that our classroom community allowed him to ask this question and know that I'd take it seriously. I thought about it, and I couldn't come up with a reason students couldn't use resources on their tests. Isn't that what I preach all the time: look it up, use the dictionary, ask your Resource Group, talk to an expert, google it, etc.? I gave students a crash course in what types of notes they should take (Figure 5.2). On the day of the test, students showed up with all kinds of notes.

Not only did the notes help the students, it was also a great way for me to collect data. As I graded, when a student didn't do as well as I'd expected, I was able to crosscheck whether the students' notes were incomplete or inaccurate, or if the student was having problems even transferring what they had on their notes to answer the questions. Without fail, the data provided to me by the notes was as important as the grade itself.

For example, one of my students had meticulous notes, but had really bombed a section. When I looked more closely at what she turned in, it

I'm always telling you to use your resources, Google it, ask an adult, look it up, and ask a Resource Group member. So, when it comes time for the next quiz or test, I'm going to allow you to prepare ahead of time by creating notes. Here are some of the types of information that you might want to record:

Non-fiction

→ names of important people or places
→ author identifying information
→ lists of any kind
→ sequences that you notice (first, second, initially, next)
→ title headings and subheadings
→ bolded words and their definitions
→ a summary statement
→ questions that the author raises (and answers, if supplied)
→ the claim the author is making

Fiction

→ PETS (place, environment, time, situation)
→ exposition
→ the complications that make up the rising action
→ the climax
→ the falling action
→ the resolution
→ the protagonist and antagonist, as well as secondary characters
→ themes that emerge
→ symbols and possible meanings
→ a claim that you can make about the piece
→ quotes to support that claim

You may organize your notes any way you'd like. This means that you can color code, handwrite, type, pre-write, draft an outline, or any other method to organize your thoughts. Make sure your notes have your name signed on each page. This signature tells me that these are your notes and that you have not photocopied them or copied directly from someone else. You may, however, share information and have great conversations about the notes you are taking. In fact, I hope you do! This is a form of studying in itself, so I'm looking forward to seeing what you produce. You will hand these notes in when you take the test. Happy notetaking!

Figure 5.2 Open-Note Guidelines

was clear that she was missing that entire section of notes. I looked at her attendance, and sure enough, she had left early that day. I was then able to have a conversation with her about a real-life skill: when you miss school (or work, later in life) you need to make sure that you find out what happened. It doesn't seem like an aha moment to an adult necessarily, but when I was able to show her, to really pinpoint it for her, I was confident that the lesson she learned would impact the way she handles absences in the future.

I collected another data point that applied more generally across all of my students. It told me something about my teaching. The section that most students struggled with was the literary vocabulary. We'd practiced identifying similes, metaphors, hyperbole, imagery, dialogue, personification, foreshadowing, flashbacks, and symbols. I noticed that many students missed personification. When I glanced at the students' notes, I found that most of them had only written down one example, even though I'd given several. I'm still not sure why—and I'll have to go to the source (my students) to figure it out, but I do know that when my attention is turned to these gaps, my teaching will improve.

However, even if I'm not sure what caused the gap, it was too big to ignore. If the goal is for students to learn, and if I could pack my ego away for a while, I could demonstrate to my students that the goal is learning and growth, not grades. I decided I'd offer a "Points Buyback" for the section of the test that had caused problems across the board (Figure 5.3).

I wanted my students to know that I did *see* them, that I did notice when a huge group of students didn't understand, and that I cared enough to help them learn. When I was talking to a colleague and mentioned this, I was surprised by his response: "Aren't you just inviting trouble?" He went on to say that students would think it was my fault they didn't learn something. I thought about it for a while, and I think he's right. If a big percentage of students don't get something, that *is* on me. And what's wrong with that? If we want our students to own their own learning, why not use my own vulnerability to show them how to be both humbled and willing to learn?

Allowing open notes and "Points Buyback" is definitely not common practice in my building, and I irritated quite a few people who heard about it. There were several complaints, but that's what happens when you shift the paradigm from grading to learning. I don't blame those who question me on this because most teachers, my former self included, are rule followers for the sake of following the rules. That's how schools have always been run. It was not until I started questioning "what's the point of this?" that I moved from a compliant teacher to an innovative one. Schools are built on a rigid system when, in my experience, a Flexible Classroom is a better learning environment for students.

My "rules to live by" (as opposed to classroom rules) include the directives "Do your very best" and "Everything counts." I mean what I say. If that effort wasn't a student's very best, I believe I should allow that student the opportunity to pursue excellence. And, if "everything counts," as I think it does, doesn't it speak volumes about a child who is willing to do an hour assignment to improve their already good grade? It tells me that they are valuing the work that I am asking them to do, and they are willing to put the time into being the very best they can be. So what if other teachers won't allow the same options as me? I don't even mind if the other teachers tell students they disagree with me. Why? Because the world is full of conflicting bosses who all want things done their way, and students themselves need to be flexible too. Though these are academic activities, and they originated from assessments, the truth is open notes and retakes are relationship building when our students recognize that we want their success badly enough to *do whatever it takes.*

*Some of you did really well on the test, but the literary terms tripped you up. What can you do to help yourself (and your grade!)? You can complete this challenge within the week, and for every word you successfully master, I'll give you a point back. YOU MUST COMPLETE THE ENTIRE ASSIGNMENT, EVEN FOR THE WORDS YOU DID NOT MISS.

Section One: Write the definitions of each of the literary vocab words. All of the words are on my Quizlet under "Literary Terms." You can find the link on flexibleclass.com on the ELA8 landing page.

1) **Simile:** _____
   _____
   _____

2) **Metaphor:** _____
   _____
   _____

3) **Symbol:** _____
   _____
   _____

4) **Personification:** _____
   _____
   _____

5) **Hyperbole:** _____
   _____
   _____

6) **Flashback:** _____
   _____
   _____

7) **Foreshadowing:** _____
   _____
   _____

8) **Dialog:** _____
   _____
   _____

9) **Imagery:** _____
   _____
   _____

Section Two: This is the part that gave you trouble. You need to review these terms carefully, and gather examples. There are links on flexibleclass.com under ELA8 on the handouts page. Use those links to write down 2 examples for each literary term. Then, you will need to create 1 original example of your own. I know this is tough, but you need to OWN these words for the rest of your life!

Simile:

example #1 _____
_____

Figure 5.3 Literary Terms "Points Buyback"

example #2 _____

_____

original example (you make it up!)

_____

_____

Metaphor:

example #1 _____

_____

example #2 _____

_____

original example (you make it up!)

_____

_____

Symbol:

example #1 _____

_____

example #2 _____

_____

original example (you make it up!)

_____

_____

Personification:

example #1 _____

_____

example #2 _____

_____

original example (you make it up!)

_____

_____

Hyperbole:

example #1 _____

_____

example #2 _____

_____

Figure 5.3 Continued

original example (you make it up!)

_____

_____

Flashback:

example #1 _____

example #2 _____

original example (you make it up!)

_____

_____

Foreshadowing:

example #1 _____

example #2 _____

original example (you make it up!)

_____

_____

Dialog:

example #1 _____

example #2 _____

original example (you make it up!)

_____

_____

Imagery:

example #1 _____

example #2 _____

original example (you make it up!)

_____

_____

Figure 5.3 Continued

Helping Students Develop Relationship Skills

Ray Mathis, health educator for 33 years, turned speaker and author, is someone who caught my eye with his quick, to-the-point LinkedIn posts. Day after day, I'd scroll by, stopping to read when I got the chance. One of the reasons his posts jumped out at me is that he draws upon his wealth of experience and writes extensively about bullies, bullying, and ways to dial down the emotions when managing classrooms of at-risk students. As a former teacher, he can speak candidly about the pitfalls teachers face in the classroom, while also offering practical advice. As I think about my role in the social and emotional lives of my students, I love what Mathis says about the reasons students cause problems at school (emphasis mine):

> At the risk of sounding like Father Flanagan, I have always believed that inside each troublesome kid is someone who has always just wanted the kind of life he/she has seen so many others have. However, he or she has just never been able to figure out how to get that for him/herself. Many start to lose hope, and often resent others for having it. That's often the motive behind bullying. **Our best hope is always to seek out that child and give them hope, and the tools to have the kind of life they'd like.** This won't happen by simply demanding they behave, and punishing them every time they don't.

What then is the best way to give students hope and tools? I'd like to suggest that we are overt in our approach because students can smell a disingenuous person with a secret agenda a mile away. There's nothing wrong with purposeful classroom culture building with the premise that we can all learn from one another. I have no problem explaining that we need to be open to the potential relationships that life provides us with. I make a huge point of promoting budding relationships by allowing students to work together on projects, sit together often, and meet in my room during my free periods. The more I can model what good friends do, the better chance my students have of moving past their individual reservations.

Teachers, myself included, feel the pressure to keep up with content. I'd argue though that five well-spent minutes can so positively impact relationships that the time "lost" to culture building is actually an investment. One of the areas I feel very strongly about is providing students the opportunity to build up each other in a safe way. Some students never receive compliments, so I love a quick activity introduced to me by Kayla Marsh, called "Fishing for Compliments!" (Figure 5.4).

The activity gives students the opportunity to discover positive impressions that others have of them. Kayla facilitated this activity with my graduate students, and we found it remarkable how much it improved our well-being to simply be appreciated for who we are. Students put their name on the worksheet. Students then stand in a circle, crushing the paper into a snowball. We then did a snowball fight, throwing the papers playfully at each other. We each

Your name: _____

Directions: When you choose a snowball, write a compliment about that person inside the fish. We will repeat three times. When we are done, everyone will have 3 fish full of compliments!

Figure 5.4 Fishing for Compliments!

grabbed a snowball. Then, we opened it up and wrote a compliment about the person whose name was on the worksheet. After about a minute, we repeated the process, picking a different snowball. We repeated again. After the third snowball fight, we returned the slip to the student. Each student was given a couple of minutes to read their compliments. We then debriefed how we felt, and which compliments meant the most, and which were perhaps surprising.

As I studied the research about the power of positive self-image, I ran across an amazing study in *Medical Daily* by Stephanie Castillo. She explains:

> If someone's fishing for a compliment, it means they really want you to acknowledge something about them or their work. It's a transparent move, sure, but it may be a successful one, too, according to a working paper from researchers at the Harvard Business School, London Business School, University of Michigan, and University of North Carolina-Chapel Hill.

Castillo points out that "researchers find that it can 'lead to behaviors and interaction patterns that make you more engaged with people, more creative, and better able to perform under pressure.'" We certainly felt our moods improve! Imagine, now, the impact this might have on a tough Monday morning. So, though students are being directed to "fish for compliments," the results are great for their self-esteem and how they engage with others. Plus, it is an opportunity to talk with students about how to take a compliment, a problem many adults have too (Figure 5.5).

Learning to give a compliment is an art; however, I'd argue that learning to take one is too. So many of us, for myriad reasons, are unable to simply say, "Thanks" when someone says something nice about us. Pay attention the next time someone compliments you and how you respond. You might be surprised to find that you actually deflect it or downplay your accomplishments. We somehow believe it is more virtuous to decline a compliment, but this is a serious mistake in thinking! According to "Mastering the Delicate Art of Responding to Compliments" in *Psychology Today*, Susan Krauss Whitbourne, PhD. offers this advice:

- ✓ Don't disagree, but DO accept a compliment at face value: If you disagree, you are actually creating an argument with their judgement. *You can say thank you and move on to another topic.*
- ✓ If you feel like you are hogging the spotlight, redirect: If someone else deserves credit, or at least a share, there is nothing wrong with redirecting. *Saying, "Well, I can't take all the credit. Susan was really an amazing leader" then you are agreeing with the complimenter and coming across as humble.*
- ✓ Use humor: If you really hate the praise, joking it off is ok, but don't deny it. *If a compliment makes you feel like the complimenter is trying to have power over you, it is ok to defuse with humor. For example, if someone says, "That is really an improvement over your last race," the complimenter might be taking a slight dig. If you answer joking, "Well, that didn't take much, but wait until next time," then you have retained the power.*

Figure 5.5 Just a Word about … Taking a Compliment

Another useful tool is the Mood Meter. It is a part of the RULER program created by the Yale Center for Emotional Intelligence. I first heard about this tool at the NOVO Foundation Social Emotional Learning in Action national conference, where I presented a short documentary about my students and our journey together to create a Flexible Classroom. I mention this because I was in *way* over my head at the conference. Some schools who were there had entire programs, led by administrators and teams of trained people. Other schools had mounds of data about the positive impact of programs they had implemented. A few schools had outside companies coming in to assist.

There I sat with my co-teacher, Laura, thinking of our friendly little classroom, on a long hall, in a far-off wing of my building, mostly ignored by anyone not in my 8th grade class. I'd never felt more discouraged. It entered my mind that we'd been selected to participate by mistake somehow. But, the more I listened, the more I realized that I could implement all kinds of activities and culture-building projects, and we had the power to normalize positive relationships in our own room. The takeaway for me, and for you if you feel alone in your journey to empower students with social emotional skills, is that you can create a space where the rules are different. The rules are rules to live by, not rules to make students compliant. You can, from your own little space in the world, change lives. This may sound like a cliché or a silly truism, but I think it crucial that we honor the work we do as educators and not minimize its impact.

The ladies at our table explained that they used the Mood Meter daily. At the beginning of the year, there is a huge assembly where a speaker comes in to talk about how their moods can impact learning. Each student has a laminated Velcroed card that they carried from class to class and place on Velcro strips on the corner of their desks. They use dry-erase markers to put a check next to the color that represented their current mood and feelings:

RED feelings: high energy, irritated, scared, anxious, mad, fidgety
BLUE feelings: low energy, sad, lonely, depressed, tired
GREEN feelings: low energy, relaxed, peaceful, comfortable
YELLOW feelings: high energy, happy, excited, curious

I immediately thought of the multitude of reasons this wouldn't work in my building. Resistant teachers, an untenured principal, cost of supplies, training. Fortunately, I have a partner for all of the ideas others don't want to do. Next year, Laura and I will create Mood Meters. We'll probably sit on her back deck with piles of craft supplies. We'll probably feel awkward talking to new 8th graders about this when they haven't been exposed to this type of "touchy feely" thinking. We're going to show the movie Inside Out, and look at brain research to support the importance of monitoring mood. This may seem like a topic for self-awareness or self-management; I agree with that, but I think that the type of vulnerability and honesty required to pull off something like this will teach students how to maintain and nurture relationships, no matter their own mood or that of others. Would I like to have a schoolwide initiative? You bet. Would I like professional development? Of course. But, if I take my own advice, I must take risks like this to grow as a teacher.

Empowering the Upstanders

No matter where you teach, there will be bullying behaviors that surface. I'm not an expert on bullying, but Rosalind Wiseman, author of Queen Bees and Wannabes, is, and her insights about Upstanders are guiding my approach in the classroom. First and foremost, we need a clear definition: an Upstander is a person who stands up for him- or herself, as well as stepping in when trouble arises for anyone else. Wiseman contends that an Upstander doesn't judge the people in the situation, but rather the Upstander looks at the situation that occurs and intervenes. What that means is that even if the Upstander thinks the kiddo being picked on is annoying, the Upstander won't allow it because no one should be singled out and picked on.

I'm going to put this right out front: this is hard stuff.

Last summer we were at Darien Lake, an amusement and waterpark. My son and I were at the top of the waterslide, right under a huge bucket that kept dumping water on us. There was a hold up in the line and everyone was tired of being drenched. A big guy yelled up to the front of the line, "What's taking so long?"

"This girl won't go down the slide," the teenage attendant said, literally pointing at the girl.

"Get out of the way!" another man yelled.

"Just go!" a little boy behind her said, imitating the adults.

"I'm trying to make her go, but she won't," the attendant said.

"Walk back down then," the big guy yelled.

My son looked at me, and I knew we'd reached the moment where I had to intervene. I grabbed his hand, and scooted my way through the line.

"I'll take care of it," I said, and the crowd parted. This, by the way, is the best part of teacher-as-superhero complex. If I see an injustice that involves kiddos, I feel compelled to get involved, and I somehow feel I have the authority to do that.

"What's wrong, honey?" I asked, touching the little girl's arm. She was about 9 or 10 years old. She jerked back quickly. Her eyes were darting everywhere. She was rocking back and forth. I knew she was in some sort of sensory overload. I stepped away from her and down the steps.

"OK. Let's walk back down," I said, imploring her to come with me. By this point, it had been a good five minutes. She came down the steps to me.

Someone in the crowd yelled, "Get out of the way. The girl wimped out. She's coming down."

The little girl turned back around and ran to the top of the stairs, clearly in full-on distress.

At that moment, I was so overwhelmed that I didn't know how to help the little girl. What kind of jerks would treat a small child this way? I had to get her down.

My poor son, all of 7 years old, asked the most important question thus far: "Where is her mom?"

I asked the attendant to radio down to the bottom and ask the lifeguards to see if they could locate the parent.

Right then, a distraught woman came bursting through the crowd. She hugged her daughter, who didn't recoil this time, but instead broke into horrible sobs, and I almost did too. My blood pressure was through the roof. I was shaking from the confrontation, and I realized I'd been squeezing my son's hand too tight. Suddenly, I was exhausted.

And there you have it. We tell our students to "stop others from bullying" and "don't be a bystander" as if we are saying dot your i's and cross your t's, no big thing. I'm a well-educated grown woman with two kids, with zero vested interest in whether strangers would ostracize me, not an insecure pubescent who could face all kinds of social consequences, yet we act as if our roles are the same. They. Are. Kids.

To me, this is the elephant in the room when you talk to kiddos about bullying and bystanders, Upstanders and "trusted adults." I told my students the story about the little girl at Darien Lake, and I shared with them how awkward the entire experience really was, and I explained to them that it really stressed me out. I told them that they needed to know the truth. Being the Upstander isn't easy, instantly rewarding, or fun. Instead, I explain, the reason we need to rise to the occasion is because the bullies will stop. Not all the time, for sure. But there is power in numbers.

One of my major concerns for my students is that they scoff at the idea of "trusted adults." When I tell my students on the first day of school that I want to be their person, I am always surprised by how quickly they do need me. It is for small things, often: stuck lockers, forgotten phone cords, or a late pass because they were in the bathroom too long. Girls and boys come to me about these small things, and then, when something does happen that needs a *trusted adult*, I'm it. Here's something that I've learned this year that is breathtaking to me because of the potential it has to improve schools from the most grassroots level. When a group of students share the same *trusted adults*, the same "their persons," the entire group can be transformed because real relationships and Upstanders are normalized. I'm certainly not at this spot in my teaching career, but I can tell you that the vibe I have in my class that I teach with Laura, a person who is everyone's person (mine too), is vastly different than when it is just me. There is power in numbers.

In an effort to be more overt, next year I'm going to use this "Upstander Go-To Guide" (Figure 5.6) to lead discussions early in the year to help students

"Silence is the voice of complicity"

What does the quote above mean? Look up the word "**complicity**" and rewrite the quote in your own words here: _____
_____

Would you consider it "speaking up" for someone if you don't say anything to your peers, but act on their behalf?
_____
_____

An Upstander is someone who stops a bad situation from getting worse. Sometimes being an Upstander just means making others feel comfortable when the situation is awkward. You don't have to pick a side. In fact, you will be more successful if you don't. **Address the situation**. Other times, you'll need to take a stand to stop the situation. If a situation needs an Upstander, be ready. Here are some good and horrible ways to get involved.

Figure 5.6 Upstander Go-To Guide

SITUATION:	HORRIBLE WAYS TO GET INVOLVED:	GOOD WAYS TO GET INVOLVED:
A student sits down at a table at lunch, or the classroom, and everyone stops talking. The student looks really nervous. No one says a thing. The student starts to stand up to leave.	*"Where do you usually sit?"* (if the person isn't sitting there, there's probably a reason) *"Why are you sitting here?"* (don't put people on the spot) *"We don't have enough room."* (if you don't, ask a teacher to allow you to pull up a chair) YOUR EXAMPLE: _____ _____ _____ _____ _____	If you don't know each other, introduce yourself and others (you are making the situation easier for all students) If you know each other, recap what was just being said, *"Hey, sit down. We were just talking about…"* Or, ask a question everyone can relate too like *"Can you believe how much homework we have tonight?"* YOUR EXAMPLE: _____ _____ _____ _____
In phys ed, a girl comes out of the locker room alone. She is wearing shoes that aren't considered "cool." You are sitting along the wall, and some of the kids in your group yell "Where'd you get THOSE shoes?"	*"Don't make fun of her. She might be poor."* (she can hear you, and if she can't afford the "cool" shoes, pointing it out doesn't help) *"Stop. She can hear you."* (if you say this, you are as guilty as those who were saying it) YOUR EXAMPLE: _____ _____ _____ _____ _____	Stand up, walk away. Say loudly, so the girl can hear you, *"I'm not talking about people."* (making it not-ok to talk about people is the first step) Stand up, walk away. Say loudly, so your friends can hear you, *"Not cool."* YOUR EXAMPLE: _____ _____ _____ _____
In homeroom, you hear that there's a picture of a student that is making the rounds on social media. Apparently, it is very unflattering and could be inappropriate and kids are sharing it.	Ask someone to share it with you so that you can see what they are all talking about. (you never want anything sent to you that is negative in any way) Go up to the student and say, "Do you know about the picture? That is awful." (talking about this to the person might make it worse) YOUR EXAMPLE: _____ _____ _____ _____ _____	This one is too big for you alone. Report this to a trusted adult. To figure out who that is, think of a person in your school who stands up for kids, won't tolerate any negativity, and you know will take action. Guidance counselors are trained to handle situations like this. Your name doesn't have to be brought up. YOUR EXAMPLE: _____ _____ _____ _____ _____

Figure 5.6 Continued

become more familiar with the concept of being an Upstander. I've come to believe that we must do overt "training" sessions with our students because the situations they are in are so complex that they need prior experiences to draw from. We should teach these moments, and the moral dilemmas as well, as exercises in critical thinking. This need to expose students to solutions before the situations happen brings me full circle back to those Afterschool Specials. It also brings me to a final point about those schools with whole programs in place for SEL.

If I compare my efforts to those schools', I'll never be able to help those in my school, in my own little corner of the world. There are some of you who are holding this book who have classrooms full of students whose problems are absolutely life altering, and my ideas could seem idealistic and naive. You are probably right. My hope though is that this book will make everyone come to see the dire need for educators—in any situation—to step up and be *that teacher, that trusted adult* that so many kiddos don't believe exist. Be that *trusted adult. Be their person.*

Your Turn

How can we build relationships with students, help them build relationships, and encourage them to be Upstanders?

★ *Some teachers don't seem to remember that the experiences of emotional pain, fear, and anxiety are downright visceral. If you haven't felt the strong kick in the stomach of failure, you should consider yourself lucky.* What can you do to help students who are experiencing emotional pain, fear, and anxiety? Are there any practices or procedures that need adjusting to better your relationships with these students?

★ *There's nothing wrong with purposeful classroom culture building with the premise that we can all learn from one another.* What are some ways that you can provide students with opportunities to build up each other? How might you encourage budding friendships?

★ *Being the Upstander isn't easy, instantly rewarding, or fun. Instead, I explain, the reason we need to rise to the occasion is because the bullies will stop. Not all the time, for sure. But there is power in numbers.* In what ways can you build consensus with students and create power in numbers? Are there any curricula that would support this idea?

Post-Pandemic Principles

In a recent webinar, I asked the participants what they missed during their time as pandemic teachers (that time when they had to abandon all of their normal ways and teach in crazy configurations, as well as cram more content into less time). Of course no one said spelling tests or lectures. They said they missed the connections with students, the small group time, and especially the opportunity to really know their students. At the end of the school year, my co-teacher, Laura, and I were feeling really sad about this last part—not knowing our students the way that we always do. We had a final exam to prepare for, but we decided we'd take some time to connect with our students one last time before we sent them to high school. We only had about five days that we could give over to a project and presentation, which is our typical way of getting to know our students. We've found that students take pride in work that they will be sharing with an authentic audience, and we benefit from how each presentation forms the foundation of our learning community.

We decided to give students an opportunity to reflect on the pandemic or reflect on their whole lives. The task was to create a five-item "playlist" that would help us, as a class, to understand who they are as people. I explained that they could narrow this to the last year and a half, if they wanted to think about what they were watching, listening to, or engaging with while quarantined and hybrid. Or, if they'd rather not spend their time reflecting on the current time period, they could look back on happier times. This was an important decision because I wanted students to have an authentic and meaningful experience doing this, but I wanted to be sensitive to the fact that some students may have lost relatives or may have experienced some pandemic-related trauma—lost jobs, lost security, illness, etc. While I wanted those who could process trauma through this project to have the opportunity to do so, the last thing I wanted to do was to make them relive trauma that they were not ready to address. Most kiddos chose to focus on their whole lives, rather than the pandemic, with a few notable exceptions. Two students who lost someone to Covid paid tribute with their playlist, and we were able to offer support as a community.

Having my own 13-year-old is helpful in so many ways when I'm trying to be in the know about pop culture. When I ran the idea by my son, Oliver, he thought it was good, but added that I should also let kiddos know that they could include TikTokers and influencers to their playlists. He also added that allowing students to include gaming could possibly help students identify others who were into the same games and help make connections. His suggestions were definitely helpful, as several students noted that they didn't know how much they had in common.

One of the takeaways we had as a group was that they shared more than they ever knew. For example, there were at least four or five people per class, over the course of all five of our classes, who listed "Life Is a Highway" as one of the songs on their playlist. Each playlist entry required a link to the video and a six- to eight-sentence paragraph explaining the significance of the media chosen. Over and over again, kiddos explained that they had watched *Cars* more times than they could count, and that "Life Is a Highway" is one of the first songs they had learned all the lyrics to. I loved to watch students bond over how much they loved a movie when they were in elementary school. Eighth graders can be standoffish, to say the least, as they are constantly fighting to project their emerging identity; yet, here we were, having a singalong. (The template and example playlists are free on the resources page on flexibleclass.com.)

The post-pandemic takeaway is this: give students an opportunity to share their "media" in a safe and nonjudgmental space and it will help students connect with one another. We are going to do this playlist activity first thing in the fall, as it will help students find some common ground, and it will be our sneaky way of getting an authentic writing sample. By creating five slides, we will have a really good baseline to set goals for their writing for the year. It will allow us to set routines about how to use technology, work independently, and act as an audience. Students want to share who they are, and we need to give them a safe space to do so. My co-teacher suggested that we create a bulletin board that shows all the ways that their choices intersect, helping students who have been isolated for so long find common ground and hopefully new friendships.

6

Social Awareness

"We All Have to Try"

Developed by Collaborative for Academic, Social, and Emotional Learning and used with permission.

When I was in college, I had a baby blue Chevy Cavalier Rally Sport, affectionately known just as "The Cav." The Cav's bumpers were covered with my newfound political beliefs (Clinton/Gore 1996), musical tastes (Indigo Girls and some Dancing Bears), and a few notable quotes, my favorite being "Silence is the voice of complicity." When I was a new parent, I had a purple PT Cruiser, the closest I could come to a mom van. It had bumper stickers too, but they definitely told a different story, a story of places we'd been,

DOI: 10.4324/9781003230311-6

like Chimney Rock, North Carolina, or who we'd become: "Proud Parent of a Blasdell Student of the Month."

Then a few years ago, my amazing husband surprised me with the car of my dreams, a red VW Beetle. The first thing I thought about was what stickers I'd put on this dream car. I thought quite a bit about it; after all, the bumper space on my most impractical small car is valuable real estate. Two years have passed, and I have yet to mark my car with my belief statements. Don't get me wrong, I have definitely been close. I just can't seem to find anything that puts the whole "me" out there the way I used to. I'm not growing up, don't worry. Instead, I think I've reached a moment in my own development where I honestly just think "It depends" about almost everything! Music tastes? It depends on which decade of my life you want to talk about. Social causes? As a mother, woman, wife, daughter, or teacher? Quotes? Well, it could be profound one day and "mom logic" the next.

This situation has served as a little existential crisis for me, so imagine my surprise when the answer came to me at a matinee movie of *Zootopia*. Judy Hopps, the spunky protagonist, gives her rousing final speech, and says, "Turns out, real life is a little bit more complicated than a slogan on a bumper sticker. Real life is messy." Not only does this get to the heart of my dilemma, it is a reminder to all of us about the nature of belief itself. We are always changing, and real life is messy. Though we may be tempted to, bumper sticker versions of our complex lives are dangerously oversimplified, which is exactly why I've put off writing this chapter as long as I could. Social awareness is such a nuanced conversation that I fear missing something. I can't help but think that many teachers feel just like me, and instead of addressing social awareness, we gloss the surface and have a few well-placed posters to make everything feel copasetic. The truth is, talking about social awareness brings important issues to the forefront, and these are issues that most people, myself included, have sometimes tiptoed around. However, it is time for teachers to take a stronger role in creating critical thinkers who are able to identify bias and stereotyping in order to become informed, productive members of our communities.

Sneak Peek

In this chapter, we will

★ investigate how to discuss bias and stereotyping through film
★ learn how to intentionally model the message of empathy
★ embolden students to take control of their narrative

Film Basics: Lessons in Movies and Messaging

I could spend several pages spewing my Film Theory 101 knowledge at you, pointing out the phallic symbols that are seemingly everywhere in Disney movies, discussing the rise of product placement, and analyzing the stereotyping of nearly everyone (white males included) that is perpetuated by the movie industry. Though I could choose to swear off movies, or write enough that you might want to, I promise that is not what I'll do, for one very specific reason: I love movies. All kinds of them. My husband and I have gone to the movies, on average, once a week for 20 years, totaling about 1000 movies together, and though he'd claim I ruined some of them with all my analyzing, he still takes me, so maybe he secretly enjoys my rants.

In all seriousness, it is crucial that we accept movies as one of the vehicles by which our students arrive at their perceptions of the world. We can help them learn about stereotyping and bias through a film study. All types of films would do, but I'm choosing *Zootopia* because it is the middle ground between some of the more hard-hitting (and R-rated) movies I might have chosen. In some other life, with different students, I'd love to teach *American History X*, *Precious*, *Schindler's List*, or *The Color Purple*, but I think a non-threatening genre is the best way to meet students where they are, and focus more on message than how to interpret a movie. Don't be fooled by the fact that *Zootopia* is an animated movie, as it is intensely political.

With that said, I do start with a lesson called "Film Basics" (Figure 6.1). After we've talked about movie elements, I distribute the "Film Review Assignment Sheet" (Figure 6.2) and the "Film Review Grading Guide" (Figure 6.3) because I always like students to know the purpose of what we are doing. As we watch *Zootopia* together, there's lots of stop and starting, so this isn't some "put in a movie" lesson plan, but rather a series of teachable moments orchestrated by my strategic discussion points of the movie.

Students should follow along on their "*Zootopia* Viewing Notesheet" (Figure 6.4), and eventually use the "Film Viewing Notesheet" (Figure 6.5) for their independent review. Students don't usually have this experience of movie watching, so there might be a little pushback at first, but I've found that students like to learn how to have these types of conversations. I also include an "Easter Egg Hunt" (Figure 6.6) that helps students see that filmmakers know exactly what they are doing with every element of the movie. Too often, they miss the ways that they are manipulated, and this is a great precursor to the conversation about media bias.

I recommend that you use the "*Zootopia* Teacher's Guide" (Figure 6.7) to prepare when to stop and start, and come to your own conclusion about

When making a film, there are many decisions that a director makes in order to create a specific effect on the audience. Here are some film basics, along with how an audience might react:

Aerial shot: a shot taken from an airborne device, generally while moving
Sets the mood, could be nostalgic, or could be emphasizing the setting

Allusion: an expression designed to call something to mind without mentioning it
If you are familiar with the allusion, it is like an inside joke

Backlighting: the main source of light is behind the subject, silhouetting it
Emphasizes the character as a type, creates drama or suspense

Bridging shot: a shot used to cover a jump in time or place
Directors use calendar pages, newspaper headlines, or seasons to show time

Camera angle: marks the location from which the shot was taken
bird's eye view: taken directly above the scene to establish the landscape
worm's eye view: shot looking up from the ground, such as from a pet or child

CGI (computer generated animation): allows artists to add LOTS of detail
One giraffe in Zootopia has 9 million CGI hairs on his body

Character: the people who are in the movie (even if not seen on screen)
flat character: not developed, someone who just plays a role, "mechanic"
round character: developed, someone who seems real, not just a role
static character: does not change over the course of the story
dynamic character: changes over the course of the story
main characters: the protagonist, antagonist, and the prominent members
secondary characters: add to the scene or story, but are not prominent

Easter Egg: an unexpected feature in a movie , included as a joke or bonus
Pixar incorporates MANY Easter Eggs, making some people believe all
Pixar movies happen in the same world

Flashback: a scene or sequence of the past inserted into a scene set in the present
Shows the backstory, develops characters and motivation, sets up conflict

Pacing: the speed by which the story unfolds
Fast pacing can overlook character, but slow pacing can be too boring for some

POV shot: a shot which shows an image from the specific point of view of a character
Provides an alternate version of events, puts audience in a different mindset

Scene: the uninterrupted record of time and space depicted between edits
Each scene can be a sequence of the plot or build understanding of character

Stereotype: a widely held but oversimplified image of a person or thing
Directors sometimes use a stereotype so that audiences can immediately
recognize a person or situation ("dumb jock," "lazy cop," or "soccer mom")

Voice actor: an actor who is the voice of an animated character in a film
Directors can choose well-known actors to subconsciously invoke the actor, or
a lesser known or unknown voice actor to create an original

These are just the basics. If you are really into this sort of thing, check out nyfa.edu, which is the New York Film Academy Student Resources page.

Figure 6.1 Film Basics

what you'd like to focus on. I'll say this: I looked everywhere, and a scene-by-scene guide didn't exist on the internet, so I spent a Saturday night with my son creating this guide because these conversations are too complex to just fly by the seat of your pants—at least for me. I'll be doing this unit for the first time as our final unit for the school year. I imagine that year to year this conversation will change, based on both the students and life

We are going to study two films together. The first, I will be walking you through very carefully, teaching you to how to "see" through different lenses to analyze both the movie and the message. For the second film, you'll be doing this alone. You may use any G or PG movie you'd like, as long as your family agrees to it.

We'll be looking at *Zootopia*, the 2016 Disney movie about a city of anthropomorphic (talking) animals who tackle questions of bias, stereotypes, drug addiction, overcoming obstacles, feminism, and the nature of hierarchical relationships. We will be looking at this film as both a "movie" and a "message."

There are four graded assignments associated with this unit:
The first is to take notes on the **Zootopia Viewing Notesheet.** It will be very important to have specific details later when you are collaborating with your resource group to answer questions about the movie.

The second is to watch a movie of your choice, either alone or with a partner or two, and fill out a **Film Viewing Notesheet**, just as you did for *Zootopia*. This one will actually be even more important, as it will help you write your review. You should be viewing the movie through the lens of bias and stereotyping. This means that you will focus on whether or not the movie uses bias and stereotyping.

The third assignment is to write a **Film Review.** You will write, either alone or with your partners from the Film Viewing Notesheet assignment, a review of the movie you watched. You will critique the movie, focusing on the movie making itself, as well as the message. It will be up to you if you cover these equally. The review **MUST** address this question:

Does (insert movie title here) use bias and stereotyping? If so, for what purpose? If not, how does the director avoid it?

The final assignment will be to **create a presentation** about your movie. It could be that you create an alternate trailer, make an "At the Movies" kind of talk show where you review the movie on screen or in a live skit, or some other way to share your opinions about the movie with the class. Whatever you come up with will need to be uploaded to your website, and you will present it from there.

Figure 6.2 Film Review Assignment Sheet

situations that I have in my room. I do recommend that you use this lesson with students with whom you already have a relationship, as it will need to be an open and honest conversation if there are going to be aha moments. As I was discussing this plan with my husband, he jokingly said, "Are you sure you want to stir that pot?" He knows the answer, but his point is well taken. This is not a "get-to-know-you" activity, but rather, for me, a culminating activity of a year building up students and tearing down preconceived notions.

Full disclosure: I wasn't sure that I wanted to "get into" this conversation either. The movie made me ask, "Wait, did she just say that?" uncomfortably while glancing at my children to see which conversation we'd need to expound upon later. But that is exactly why I need to teach this, and I think it is why you should too. When I'm not sure about something, I vet my idea through the sources I trust. What does *Teaching Tolerance* have to say about this movie? The Fall 2016 edition's "Staff Picks: What We're Watching" section describes it this way:

Disney's *Zootopia* is a timely lesson in inclusivity. This animated movie takes place in a spectacular, multi-habitat city where predator

	Above standard	At standard	Approaching standard
Review addresses bias and stereotyping	There is carefully crafted analysis of bias and stereotyping that provides specific evidence from the movie, as well as commentary regarding the director's intent.	There is analysis of bias and stereotyping, with evidence from the movie, as well as some ideas about the director's intent.	There is some analysis of bias and stereotyping, but it is mostly identification of these elements. There is very little, if any, discussion of the director's intent.
Review uses film basics vocabulary to discuss the cinematography	There is nuanced references to the film basics vocabulary, and the insights are well-developed about the cinematography. It is entertaining to the reader.	There is references to the film basics vocabulary, and the writer attempts to discuss the cinematography. The insights remain unexplored.	There are some film basics vocabulary, but it may be misused or incorrectly interpreted. Cinematography is not discussed, or is incomplete.
Review meets the following requirements: typed, double-spaced, around 350-500 words, and includes all relevant specifics about the film (actors, director, release date, rating, etc).	All requirements are met, with specific details and accuracy.	All requirements are met, though specific information may be lacking.	Missing one or more of the requirements. Student should make an appointment with me to complete the assignment.
Review is written in an entertaining, yet thoughtful way. The sentences are sharp, correctly punctuated, and vary in length.	The review is entertaining and thoughtful. The writer uses a variety of well-constructed sentences. Accurate grammar and spelling throughout.	The review is entertaining and thoughtful, but may need elaboration. The writer uses a few different sentence types. Mostly accurate grammar and spelling throughout.	The review is incomplete or inaccurate. The writer does not use a variety of sentences. Grammar and spelling are often inaccurate.

Grading Guide for Film Review Assignment

Figure 6.3 Film Review Grading Guide

and prey live in peace. … Packed with fun and messages of inclusion, Zootopia is a great resource for the elementary classroom!

Hayley Glatter's article, "A Cartoon Gateway to Real World Issues," in the December 29, 2016, issue of *The Atlantic*, online edition, explains exactly why it is important to broker these conversations:

In addition to the broader ways *Zootopia* prompts young viewers to condemn racism and stereotyping, subtle, don't-blink-or-you'll-miss-them moments also prove bitingly relevant in 2016. Judy calls Nick

As we watch Zootopia, we'll be stopping to talk about issues of Social Justice. Social Justice is the distribution of wealth, opportunities, and privileges within a society. Pay attention to the messages that are directly introduced, but also pay attention to what isn't being stated, but instead inferred from the way characters and situations are portrayed. *MOST INCIDENTS COULD BE LISTED IN MULTIPLE COLUMNS--JUST CHOOSE ONE.*

Bias: prejudice in favor of or against one thing, person, or group compared with another, usually in a way considered to be unfair to one group	**Stereotyping:** a widely held, but fixed and oversimplified image or idea of a particular type of person or thing, perpetuated by classifying all of the group the same way	**Sexism:** discrimination or devaluation based on a person's sex or gender, as in restricted job opportunities, or other opportunities, usually creating dominance of male over female	**Racism:** a belief that inherent differences about various racial groups determine individual achievement or abilities, creating dominance and inferiority
Example: The Mayor asks, "Do you think I'm going to believe a fox?" (56:26)	*Example:* The Yak at the Mystic Oasis Spring Naturalist Club is dirty with flies buzzing around him and seems out of it. Negative "hippie" image. (37:17)	*Example:* Gideon Gray says that a bunny cop is the most stupidest thing he'd ever heard of. (2:45)	*Example:* Judy says, "I'm not just some token bunny." (16:13)
Example:	*Example:*	*Example:*	*Example:*
Example:	*Example:*	*Example:*	*Example:*
Example:	*Example:*	*Example:*	*Example:*

Figure 6.4 *Zootopia* Film Viewing Notesheet

"articulate"; a character is scolded because "you can't just touch a sheep's wool"; and Judy feels demeaned when someone calls her "cute" just because she's a rabbit. In this way, the movie progresses from a common refrain children may have heard before about not judging a book by its cover and reminds adults of more tangible, memorable nuggets of truth.

Either alone, or with a partner or two, watch a movie using a "Social Justice lens." Social Justice is the distribution of wealth, opportunities, and privileges within a society. Pay attention to the messages that are directly introduced, but also pay attention to what isn't being stated, but instead inferred from the way characters and situations are portrayed.

Title of Film: _____

Director: _____

Release date: _____

Top Stars: _____

To whom is the movie marketed? _____

As you watch, determine what type of messaging there is related to the following topics. Jot down notes and specific examples in the chart on the back of this sheet.. You might want to write down the time in the movie that the incident occurred (for example 3:23 would mean 3 minutes and 23 seconds into the movie)

Remember, you'll be using these notes to write your review, so be detailed. Use additional sheets as necessary.

ageism	anti-immigration	bias
bullying	careers	class
censorship	"cool"	gay rights
gender discrimination	gender identity	hate
"handicaps"	intolerance	intelligence
"jocks"	language diversity	nationality
"nerds" or "geeks"	poverty	race
racial profiling	religion	stereotyping

Figure 6.5 Film Viewing Notesheet

As all teachers know, those "memorable nuggets of truth" provide perfect teachable moments. There are many movies that are thought-provoking, and each teacher can choose what works best for the curriculum (Figure 6.8).

Am I nervous about this unit? Absolutely. Many students in my suburban, homogenized school have never thought about any of the ideas that this unit addresses, and that is unacceptable. Will we stumble a bit as we work our way through this together? I'm sure. But I'm not going to sit around waiting for someone else to do this work because some of these students are going to be voting in the next election, and it is unconscionable to me that they might not be prepared in any way to elect our president because they've never been given the tools to be socially aware. I have to admit that the I feel an urgency in helping students as I see some of the problems they face both at home and the scenarios being played out around the world. Middle school kiddos need us to clear a path for them sometimes. AMLE's observation that "young adolescents also witness and experience the negative results of homelessness, racism, drug and alcohol abuse, crime, international terrorism, wars, domestic

An "Easter Egg" is a small hidden reference in a movie or video game

Can you find these 20 references in the movie? What have I missed?

1. Dumbo's real name is Jerry Jumbo Jr. (hint: also a reference to Ben and Jerry's Ice Cream)
2. *Bambi*
3. *The Godfather*
4. *Breaking Bad* (Woolter and Jesse)
5. Han's Pastry Shop (Hans from *Frozen*)
6. Nick Wilde looks A LOT like 1973 *Robinhood*
7. Lucky Cat Cafe from *Big Hero 6*
8. Many hidden Mickey Mouse pictures
9. "Life isn't some cartoon musical . . . *Let It Go!*"
10. The movie *48 Hours*
11. Emmet Otterton = *Emmet Otter's Jug Band Christmas*
12. Jerry Vole= Jerry Vale
13. Zuber= Uber
14. Just Zoo It= Just Do It
15. Targoat= Target
16. Elephants dressed as Anna and Elsa in Tundratown (which looks like *Frozen*)
17. Duke Weasleton in *Zootopia* is voiced by Alan Tudyk who is the Duke of **Weselton** in *Frozen*. In *Zootopia*, Duke Weaselton corrects Judy for pronouncing his name Weselton, and in *Frozen*, the Duke of **Weselton** is mad that his name is pronounced Weasleton.
18. Baloo's scratching scene in the 1967 *Junglebook*, singing "Bare Necessities" is very similar to the "Naturalist" Community scene--where all the animals are bare.
19. Bootlegged movies: *Wreck It Rhino*, *Wrangled*, *Pig Hero 6*, *Meowana*, *Giraffic*, and *Floatzen 2* (the last three weren't released when *Zootopia* opened)
20. When Judy whacks the train car, it is similar to the *Star Wars' Millenium Falcon* coming back to life in *The Empire Strikes Back*.

Figure 6.6 *Zootopia* Easter Egg Hunt

This guide is designed as a tool to teach students about bias and stereotyping, as well as issues of social justice through the movie *Zootopia*. I've listed the times when the film should be stopped, as well as what is being said, and my comments on it. Your comments may be different, and that's ok! The important thing is the conversation. This is just a sampling, so I'm sure you'll find others that you might want to use.

2:45 **"Bunny cop . . . most stupidist thing I ever heard."**
Gideon Gray is stereotyped as a "hick" while also being sexist about Judy's plan to be a police officer when she grows up.

7:20 **"As Mayor of Zootopia, I'm proud to announce my 'mammal inclusion initiative' has produced its first . . ."**
Self-congratulatory speech made about Judy's becoming a police officer. This is an allusion to affirmative action.

Figure 6.7 *Zootopia* Teacher's Guide

13:53 **"A bunny can call another bunny 'cute,' when when other animals do it, it's a a little . . ."**
Clear reference to the "N-word," as well as other terms reappropriated.

14:00 **"Flabby, donut loving cop, stereotyping you . . ."**
Clawhauser is the stereotypical police officer who catches himself stereotyping Judy for being a little bunny.

16:13 **"I'm not just some token bunny"**
Judy uses the work "token" here to allude to the practice of hiring a minority as a gesture driven by mandates, not inclusion.

19:30 **"You probably can't read Fox, but we reserve the right to refuse service to anyone."**
The elephant in the ice cream parlor tells this to the fox. In recent history, this could be referring to a bakery turning down the request to make a wedding cake for a same-sex couple's wedding. Historically though, this has been a racial issue.

20:15 **"You know, it just burns me up to see people with such a backwards attitude towards foxes. You're a good dad, and a real articulate fellow."**
Judy, in her attempt to sympathize with Nick Wilde, the fox, is quite patronizing, which he then points out, and it goes right over her head. Joe Biden, referring to Barack Obama, says: "I mean, you got the first mainstream African-American who is articulate and bright and clean and a nice-looking guy."

23:56 **The sign in Nick Wilde's neighborhood reads "Savage" instead of "Salvage"**
This foreshadows the use of the phrase "go savage" to describe the violence caused by the Night Howlers.

49:19 ***Godfather* parody of Italian mafia**
This scene is replete with the ironic Mr. Big, who is a tiny mouse, with his big polar bear thugs, and the Italian princess who gets what she wants, and the idolized grandmother.

51:00 **"From one predator to another"**
An attempt to parallel the conversations that those of the same race might have.

56:18 **"Or maybe any aggressive predator looks savage to you Rabbit. . ."**
Suggestion that animals that are Prey see all Predators as a threat; essentially, this is a way to talk about racial profiling.

56:26 **"Do you think I'm going to believe a fox?"**
Law enforcement pointing out that they won't believe someone based on their bias against a particular group.

59:57 **"If the world is only going to see a fox as shifty and untrustworthy, there's no point in trying to be anything else."**
Nick says this to Judy, illustrating a classic argument about the role bias and stereotyping plays in the perpetuation of generational poverty and violence. Ultimately, how one is viewed becomes the self-fullfilling prophecy.

1:01 **"You can't just touch a sheep's wool."**
Judy says this to Nick when he is touching Assistant Mayor Bellwether's wool. Clearly a reference to fascination with "otherness."

1:07 **"It may be time to consider their biology. The only animals going savage are predators."**
This is an accurate statement in that the only animals going savage are predators, but it fails to consider any other information that might be relevant, instead relying on a broad sweeping generalization.

Figure 6.7 Continued

1:11   "They seem to be reverting back to their primitive, savage ways.""So, we must be vigilant."
       This is when Judy's bias reveals itself at the press conference.

1:13   "It's not like a bunny could go savage." (Judy)
       "You're not like them." (Judy)
       "There's a 'them' now?" (Nick Wilde)
       "You know what I mean. You're not that kind of predator." (Judy)
       "Are you afraid of me?" (Nick)
       This conversation shows that Judy is really afraid of Nick, as she reaches for her fox repellent,
       which Nick points out as making an impression on him when he saw it at their first meeting.

1:14   "Did that predator just threaten you?" (reporter)
       "No, he's my friend." (Judy)
       "Are you saying we can't even trust our own friends?" (reporter)

       "Have you considered a mandatory quarantine on predators?" (reporter)
       It becomes clear that the media wants to bait Judy into responding in an inflammatory way.

       "We don't know why these attacks keep happening, but it is irresponsible to label
       all predators as savages."
       Gazelle, the pop star, makes this announcement at a rally for peace.

1:19   "I thought she was talking in tongues or something."
       Gideon Gray makes this comment about Judy, who seems to be talking nonsensically. He is
       referencing, and disparaging, Pentecostal Christians, whose religious practice includes "speaking
       in tongues."

1:20   "I think someone is targeting predators on purpose and making them go savage."
       Judy says this, invoking Malcom X's contention that the White Man is behind the problems in
       the black community. For example, he said, "They send drugs in Harlem down here to pacify us.
       They send alcohol down here to pacify us! Why, you can't even get drugs in Harlem without the
       White Man's permission!"

1:21   "You bunnies are so emotional."
       Nick says this to Judy, further normalizing the sexism.

1:29   "We're on the same team Judy. Underestimated. Underappreciated.
       Aren't you sick of it?"
       This is Assistant Mayor Bellwether's plea to Judy that the they must stick together. It can equate
       to race, but it also can clearly be seen as a Feminist mantra.

       "Hero cop killed by savage fox."
       Assistant Mayor Bellwether paints the picture of how the media will love this headline.

       "Prey fears predator, so you stay in power?"
       Judy asks Assistant Mayor Bellwether if this is her plan.

       "Fear always works."
       Assistant Mayor Bellwether replies to Judy's question. The ploy to keep races afraid of each
       other has long been a theoretical position.

1:33   "We all have limitations. We all make mistakes. Which means—glass half full—
       we have a lot in common. The more we try to understand each other, the more
       exceptional we'll be. We have to try. So no matter what type of animal you are, try.
       Try to make the world a better place. Look inside yourself and realize that change
       starts with you. It starts with me. It starts with all of us."
       This is Judy's big speech to end the movie at the ceremony for new officers, one of whom is Nick
       Wilde. The movie's solution to the bias and stereotyping are offered here.

Figure 6.7 Continued

violence, and child abuse" (9) is disturbing, but accurate. And, like "This We
Believe" implores educators, I feel I have a "responsibility to assist students
in dealing with such major societal issues" and to help "foster responsible,
moral decision makers, and discriminating, enlightened consumers" (9).
Though it might not be a lesson I set out to teach as I look at a curriculum

Movie:	Social Justice Domain(s):	Best for:
The Lorax	Justice and Action	This is a Dr Seuss story with an environmentalist slant. It is a great first look at how individual actions can make a difference.
Finding Dory	Identity, Diversity	This is an animated film that also takes on pollution, but it also focuses on Dory whose short term memory loss mimics the experience of some students with ADHD. She finds help and structure to be successful.
A Place at the Table	Justice, Action	This is a documentary that explores "food scarcity." It examines places where this is common, and speaks with some who are living meal to meal.
Dolphin Tale	Justice, Action	This is another environmentalist flick. It spurs action and reiterates the need to take charge.
Big Hero 6	Identity, Diversity, Justice, Action	This is an animated movie that touches on a wide variety of issues. The boys are grieving, as their parents have died. There's also sinister uses of scientific discoveries, but also a very strong commentary on the notion that we choose our own families sometimes.
He Named Me Malala	Identity, Diversity, Justice, Action	This is a documentary about Malala. Most students will be familiar with her, but the perspective is inspiring.
12 Angry Men	Justice, Action	This classic takes on the justice system and classism. Most appropriate for 8th grade and up.
Erin Brokovich	Justice, Action	This is a Hollywood version of a "regular person" taking on the system. It deals with pollution and the resulting health issues in a community. It is best for late high school students.
John Q	Justice, Action	This is also a Hollywood version of a "regular person" taking on the system. It deals with a distraught dad who can not afford the heart transplant his son needs. Disturbing and thought provoking. It is best for late high school students.

Figure 6.8 Thought-Provoking Movies to Teach Social Justice

map, sometimes we are convicted to help students in an area that might go uncharted unless you forge ahead.

Modeling the Message: Empathy in Action

Dr. Brene Brown is a research professor at the University of Houston Graduate College of Social Work, and author of *Daring Greatly* (2012). She spent a decade studying vulnerability, courage, authenticity, and shame. Her work is breathtakingly raw at times, and I've personally loved her ideas for years; however, it wasn't until I began looking at the social and emotional needs of my students that I truly grasped the significance of what she asserts. In her Ted Talk, "Listening to Shame," Brown explains: "If you put shame in a petri dish, it needs three ingredients to grow exponentially: secrecy, silence, and judgment. If you put the same amount of shame in the petri dish and douse it with empathy, it can't survive."

The reason this particular quote struck me is that the thing I remember most about middle school was shame—body shaming, clothing brand shaming, grade shaming, family shaming—you name it, it was there in some form or another. Worse yet, middle school is a breeding ground for all three ingredients to make shame grow: secrecy, silence, and judgment. I can't tell you the number of times I've asked a distraught student, "Why didn't you tell someone?" and am met with a look of resignation, a belief that I just don't get how the system works. What occurs to me is that we haven't taught our students any other way to deal with the barrage of embarrassments and setbacks that adolescence brings, so no wonder they suffer in silence.

"Modeling" has always been an important issue with me. There are many teachers who believe that by modeling the work we expect students to produce, we are "spoon-feeding" them to conform to our expectations. I feel very strongly that models are not only good practice, but a necessity. How can I expect a student to know what a persuasive essay sounds like unless I provide models? How can I think a student should use semicolons unless exposed to them regularly? So what if they "copy" or imitate what I provide? Some would argue that they aren't producing authentically, but I'd counter that it is out of confidence in form and structure that true creativity can grow. The same is true for modeling the message of empathy. How can we expect students to practice empathy if we don't give them good models to follow?

We teachers encounter students every day who we *feel* for—whatever that means for us. The key is whether we feel sympathy or empathy. This is where Brene Brown makes a huge distinction that is important to our practice. Her video, "Brene Brown on Empathy," is a cartoon short that demonstrates that fixing a person's problem is not often what is needed or even possible, but sharing a listening, caring ear is something that we can all do. We learn that "when we feel heard, cared about, and understood, we also feel loved, accepted, and as if we belong." Sympathy, on the other hand, robs us from connecting with each other, with the powerful party standing in superiority over the object of pity. Teachers must learn that we cannot solve all of our students' problems, but we can stand with them as supportive empathizers who don't seek to solve, but instead model grace and acceptance so that they too can respond to others with empathy.

Ultimately, when we teach students to be empathetic instead of sympathetic, we are teaching them a different way to view the world. When people express political and religious views that differ from ours, we must not allow these differences to become barriers. If we are able to use the lexicon of empathy, we will be able to step outside of ourselves and create a more tolerant environment. For example, look how a lexicon of empathy (Figure 6.9) works in the following scenarios.

Admittedly, it can sometimes seem so much easier to let things slide, but it can be very powerful to address situations as they arise, modeling the empathetic response. Just recently, the day before break, Tom, a boy on my hallway, bumped Jason accidentally, knocking his books and papers everywhere. Jason, whose stuff went flying, immediately tried to deflect attention, saying, "Don't worry about it." This let Tom off the hook, so he turned to walk away. I wanted to walk away myself. This was socially awkward. But it was also a moment that needed addressing. I called over to Tom, "Hey, let's go help Jason. I know you didn't do it on purpose, but it stinks to be him right now," looking over at Jason scrambling to pick everything up. When we came back to help him, Jason looked really relieved. When Tom gave Jason a hand to pull him up from the ground, he said, "Sorry, dude. I really didn't mean to bump you." Jason, of course, mumbled a "No big deal," but it was a big deal, and embarrassing. When we went back to help, we participated in the situation, shouldering some of the moment's awkwardness.

Now, this doesn't seem like a big deal. And I could be reading more into it than I should, but I really felt it was important to put Tom into Jason's shoes, to show him how much it would stink if the roles were reversed, even if it was an accident. There are countless opportunities throughout the day where we can model the message of empathy. When students started asking each other "What did you get?" on a test, I stopped and had a conversation about why that question puts every single person in an awkward position. We talked about all the possibilities: what would it feel like if you got a grade that you were embarrassed about, what about if you got a 100, or what if you were just a private person, or did much better than your best friend who you knew studied a ton?

Again, this might not seem like the most pressing problem in school, but when we find ways to address these social emotional needs, students and teachers are better for it. When we can embed these lessons within curriculum, we create deeper learning experiences that are more student centered

Situation:	Sympathetic Response:	Empathetic Response:
A young girl with a hijab sits down on the school bus. She is the only one with a head covering and is being stared at, her face turning red.	*Poor girl. Too bad she has to wear that thing. I'll be nice to her.* [the girl is to be pitied]	*I imagine that it must be difficult to be stared at like that. I hate when I'm embarrassed.* [the girls share common experience]

Figure 6.9 Lexicon of Empathy

| Spelling is very difficult for Tom. Students in the class notice that he fails many tests, but no one says anything or offers to help. Sometimes people whisper about it. | *Tom can't help it. He's not very smart. My parents say we should just ignore it when he fails. It's not his fault.*

[invisibility develops] | *Tom seems really good at learning music. Maybe we can make some songs together to learn spelling, and he can teach me guitar.*

[everyone has talents and something to offer] |
| Donald's sister has Down Syndrome and frequently has problems transitioning from school to the bus at the end of the day. A teacher sees Donald trying to help her. | *I'll take it from here, Donald. A boy your age shouldn't have to deal with this.*

[taking over and judging] | *Donald, what usually works? It must be tricky taking care of your sister, but she sure loves you. Can I walk with you?*

[deferring, standing with someone, positivity] |

Figure 6.9 Continued

and memorable. As teachers, we can all teach empathetic listening skills that will foster student learning and a better classroom climate (Figure 6.10). If we help students "do school" better, they will "do life" better later, and by teaching students overtly how to be empathetic listeners, we are preparing them for a future that values this type of soft skill.

When a friend is having a problem, a sibling is struggling with something you have been through, or a parent is stressed out, are you an empathetic listener? Sometimes, in our excitement to talk ourselves, we aren't really listening. Look at the empathetic listening tip on the left, and make up an example in the box to the right.

Be creative in the example you create. In a few minutes, be ready to share your example or even act it out! Pretend you are teaching this to a younger student, so really spell it out. I've done the first one for you (I'm thinking you might be nervous if you are doing the task correctly or not—so giving you an example is a gesture of empathy!)

Maintain eye contact	John is talking to Suzy about how depressed he is that he didn't make the basketball team. She really does feel badly for him, but she keeps checking her phone. *It would be much more empathetic to maintain eye contact.*
Ask clarifying questions about the situation	
Share an example of a time when you were feeling the same way	
Ask how the person is feeling	

Figure 6.10 Empathetic Listening

Ask if there is anything you can do	
Don't interrupt	
Offer resources	

Figure 6.10 Continued

Teaching Students to Control Their Narrative

When I was in middle school, I wanted to try out for the volleyball team. I told my dad about it, and he went to the library, checked out a book about volleyball, and told me he'd make sure I was ready in the fall, if I would just do what he told me. All summer, we did drills, he made me run "suicides" in the backyard, and I would lie in bed at night, setting the volleyball until my arms burned. Though he taught me much about volleyball, he was definitely more of a what we now call a "life coach." I attribute much of my success in life to my dad because that summer he taught me the power of visualization and positive self-talk. These may be catchy phrases to some, but to my dad, and then to me, they were lifeboats.

My dad grew up very poor, with an alcoholic father, and was the first to graduate high school in his family. My parents were married as teenagers, but my dad was driven by the desire for stability—which his childhood had lacked. He worked in a printing factory, first running a collating machine, then managing, and eventually he worked his way up to a salesman position, which is when he discovered books on tape to pass the hours in the car. It was during those hours that he earned his real education—Zig Ziglar, Stephen Covey, Norman Vincent Peale, Dale Carnegie, Napoleon Hill, and eventually Tony Robbins. Their words became his, and his became mine. A nice story, right? Yes, but why is this at the end of a chapter about social awareness?

Social awareness isn't simply understanding the world around you, but rather also knowing that the people around you are going to make assumptions about you. Those assumptions might be right, or they might be wrong, and very little can be done to change their minds. However, it is crucial that we control our own narrative, tell our own stories, and don't let anyone define our path except for us. So many times I see that the social influence on my students—from parents, siblings, friends, music, television, the internet, etc.—are so influential that they don't seem to have a chance. This is why, as a teacher, I take every opportunity to help students find their voice, and it is why I require public presentations of almost everything we do (see Figure 6.11).

When students are confronted with a social reality that doesn't meet their personal vision of themselves, they are often swayed by the social reality because they don't know how to stay the course. That is why they need lifeboats. They need mantras. They need belief statements. They need quotes to live by. They need ammunition. This is where they need visualization and positive self-talk—to pull them back to shore, out of danger. For example, if we help our students visualize their lives in technicolor, to really flesh out every detail of what it will be like to go to college, they are then able to summon that visualization when they are tempted to do something that doesn't fit that plan, like drink and drive or have unprotected sex. DWIs and babies are not in that vision of their world.

Just as my dad poured positive talk into my life, giving me the right inner voice, we can provide for our students. They need to have hours upon hours of positive self-talk "downloaded" and at the ready because there will always be naysayers or "dream snatchers" who wish to measure our students by some social constructs that should not define them. If we can fill their heads with our voice, let them echo our belief in them, they will, like I did, merge those voices and find their own. They will be able to talk themselves through stressful situations, moments when they are being judged or labeled, or written off because of the color of their skin, the brand of their shoes, or who they pray to.

As we teach our students to be empathetic, and compassionate, and socially aware, we also have the obligation to prepare them for those they

---

With the world at their fingertips, the "like" button at the ready, and literally thousands of texts per day to audiences of hundreds, students today are completely comfortable with authentic audiences—at least virtual ones. How disappointing would it be then, to work for hours on a project only to have one person (the teacher) view it? We must prime our students for a world where constant connectivity has created an exponential audience. Here are some tips for showcasing student work with authentic audiences:

✓ Have students publish Vlogs (video blogs) or videos of their presentations on YouTube. *Getting 2000 views on YouTube is validation that their work matters.*

✓ Skype with other classrooms, or set up virtual field trips for your students about their projects. *Twitter is a great place to find like minded teachers who want to share their classrooms digitally.*

✓ Presenting to the school board, Mayor's office, or Village board are excellent ways to engage students with the community. *Introducing students to these venues is a great way to encourage civic responsibility as well. They have legitimate concerns about their community, and if they have suggestions, they have a right to be heard.*

Figure 6.11 Just a Word about ... Authentic Audiences

will meet who are not "enlightened" because all too often we are defined not by our successes, but by someone else's version of our story. This is why we must embolden our students to control their own narrative, to write the story they want to be in, and to create for themselves the roles they wish to have.

Learning for Justice (A project of the Southern Poverty Law Center) is an organization committed to overtly teaching students the skills they need to be empathetic, productive, and informed citizens, empowered to successfully navigate the complexities of our society. It has created the "Social Justice Standards: The Anti-bias Framework," which provides Anchor Standards and Domains (Figure 6.12). The domains are Identity, Diversity, Justice, and

IDENTITY

1. Students will develop positive social identities based on their membership in multiple groups in society.
2. Students will develop language and historical and cultural knowledge that affirm and accurately describe their membership in multiple identity groups.
3. Students will recognize that people's multiple identities interact and create unique and complex individuals.
4. Students will express pride, confidence and healthy self-esteem without denying the value and dignity of other people.
5. Students will recognize traits of the dominant culture, their home culture and other cultures and understand how they negotiate their own identity in multiple spaces.

DIVERSITY

6. Students will express comfort with people who are both similar to and different from them and engage respectfully with all people.
7. Students will develop language and knowledge to accurately and respectfully describe how people (including themselves) are both similar to and different from each other and others in their identity groups.
8. Students will respectfully express curiosity about the history and lived experiences of others and will exchange ideas and beliefs in an open-minded way.
9. Students will respond to diversity by building empathy, respect, understanding and connection.
10. Students will examine diversity in social, cultural, political and historical contexts rather than in ways that are superficial or oversimplified.

JUSTICE

11. Students will recognize stereotypes and relate to people as individuals rather than representatives of groups.
12. Students will recognize unfairness on the individual level (e.g., biased speech) and injustice at the institutional or systemic level (e.g., discrimination).
13. Students will analyze the harmful impact of bias and injustice on the world, historically and today.
14. Students will recognize that power and privilege influence relationships on interpersonal, intergroup and institutional levels and consider how they have been affected by those dynamics.
15. Students will identify figures, groups, events and a variety of strategies and philosophies relevant to the history of social justice around the world.

ACTION

16. Students will express empathy when people are excluded or mistreated because of their identities and concern when they themselves experience bias.
17. Students will recognize their own responsibility to stand up to exclusion, prejudice and injustice.
18. Students will speak up with courage and respect when they or someone else has been hurt or wronged by bias.
19. Students will make principled decisions about when and how to take a stand against bias and injustice in their everyday lives and will do so despite negative peer or group pressure.
20. Students will plan and carry out collective action against bias and injustice in the world and will evaluate what strategies are most effective.

Figure 6.12 Anchor Standards and Domains; Source: *Teaching Tolerance*

Action, and the 20 anchor standards follow CASEL's Competencies—beginning with oneself and radiating outward to finally becoming socially aware and actively taking part in creating a better world.

When we meet the social and emotional needs of students, the rest will follow. When we are able to ignite passions, teach empathy, and embrace differences, we will heal our little corner of the world, which is a start. Teachers have the amazing privilege to have exponential influence, and it is time we harness it. It is too easy to think that one person can't make a difference, and it is tempting to believe that people have already made up their minds. To that end, at the close of *Zootopia*, Judy gives a rousing final speech that encapsulates the role I think teachers must assume in this complex society:

> We all have limitations. We all make mistakes, which means—half-glass full—we have a lot in common. The more we try to understand each other, the more exceptional we'll be. We have to try. So, no matter what type of animal you are, try. Try to make the world a better place. Look inside yourself and realize that change starts with you. It starts with me. It starts with all of us.

I know, I know. Sappy Disney ending, right? I'm deciding right now, though, and I'm asking you to stand in agreement on this, that we're going to be OK with that. We don't have to sugarcoat reality, but as far as I'm concerned there's nothing better than peddling hope and optimism that starts with personal responsibility.

Your Turn

How can we help students to become empathetic and socially aware?

★ *The truth is, talking about social awareness brings important issues to the forefront, and these are issues that most people, myself included, have sometimes tiptoed around.* Have you been hesitant to talk about issues of social awareness? What is holding you back?

★ *In all seriousness, it is crucial that we accept movies as one of the vehicles by which our students arrive at their perceptions of the world. We can help them learn about stereotyping and bias through a film study.* What films would be appropriate for your subject area and grade level? How can you incorporate them?

★ *What occurs to me is that we haven't taught our students any other way to deal with the barrage of embarrassments and setbacks that adolescence brings, so no wonder they suffer in silence.* What can you do in your own classroom to help students to handle the daily stresses of life? How can you create a culture where students are able to share their embarrassments and setbacks?

★ *However, it is crucial that we control our own narrative, tell our own stories, and don't let anyone define our path except for us.* In what ways can your class, and even your school, help students define their own path? How can we show students the many options available to them?

Post-Pandemic Principles

The *Zootopia* social justice lesson from this chapter won #2 blog of 2017 and #2 blog of the decade on ShareMyLesson.com, a free sharing site created by the American Federation of Teachers. I still remember watching the movie with my family at the theater and knowing that I had to use the movie to address racism, sexism, and bias. Similarly, as I watched *Cruella*, the dark Disney prequel to *101 Dalmatians*, I knew that this film must make it into my classroom. Though far less hit-you-over-the-head with the message, I saw the potential immediately. Cruella is a villain, to be sure, but she provides the viewer with a character arc worth exploring and applying to those in the world around us with whom we seem to have nothing in common. Due to the political climate, it is crucial that we teach students to see more than a political message, and humanize the people who might not have the same view of the world.

If we are ever to come together as a society, it is going to be because we intentionally, deliberately, and systematically seek to understand one another. This isn't a popular notion, for good reason. Why would we want to know more about people with whom we are at odds? Why would we want to seek to understand "them," when no matter which "them" you mean translates to an enemy based on ideology. The fundamental nature of our country is at stake, and it couldn't be a sloppier, more complicated time to try to help students critically think about issues and their place in the world, but it also couldn't be a more important time either.

Once again, just like with *Zootopia*, there are other movie options to help students, but also like *Zootopia*, *Cruella* just "hits different," as my own children would say. As Common Sense media puts it, "Sinisterly superb, this is a well-crafted, phenomenally acted, artistically drenched triumph that's a whole lot more responsible than most other villain-as-main-character films. And yet it does make a hero out of a criminal. So, there's that." I intend to teach this movie as a character study, a look at identity, and a way to question the stories we tell ourselves. Cruella experiences bullying, is a bully, and also has an aha moment when she realizes that the bravest, most rebellious and radical thing she could do is to be true to herself instead of playing a part. This is the "stuff" of very good discussions with teenagers! My own teens were riveted and as we spilled out of the theater, they were both talking a mile a minute about how amazing the movie was. My son, Oliver, and my daughter, Zoey, are very different types of kiddos, so the fact that they both were entertained and intrigued, across gender as well, was enough of an endorsement for me to begin my plans.

The most important thing we can do is to help our students with social awareness by helping them to understand that there is "more to the story" than meets the eye in nearly every situation. We must convince them to do the work to get to know one another instead of making snap judgments based on class, clothing, musical taste, or political affiliation. The Post-Pandemic Principle to help students become socially aware is to humanize the "other" and help students make sense of the complex landscape we've found ourselves in.

Restoration

Circles and Bubbles for Healing

Developed by Collaborative for Academic, Social, and Emotional Learning and used with permission.

I spent a year piloting a program for at-risk high school freshmen whose goal was to "restore what was lost" while emotionally supporting them, academically challenging them, providing community, and holding them to high standards. We began with the idea of "restoring" their belief in themselves, their education, and their possibility. In that year, we were fortunate to have an entire period a day devoted to Restorative Circles, and the transformations were amazing. These students' problems weren't solved, but rather they

DOI: 10.4324/9781003230311-7

learned strategies and gained community, which was then able to bolster them for the rest of their experiences. I am incredibly thankful for the chance I had to work in that setting, and I'm excited to translate those lessons into a plan for all types of classrooms.

I believe 100% that post-pandemic teaching—whenever that may finally occur—is going to be about restoration. For the foreseeable future, we are going to need to understand that our role as educators is not only to teach content, but to bring consistency, caring, and compassion to our classrooms. Students have lost so much, but with the loss of their "normal" education, they have lost stability, friendships, rites of passage, and the belief that everything will be OK. In addition to the pandemic experiences, students witnessed and experienced some of the most racist, sexist, and homophobic news cycles that I've seen in my entire 47 years. It is no wonder that the kiddos are not OK. However, as educators, we've always been that source of stability and hope for students; now, we are going to need to *intentionally* embark on years of healing. I believe that learning to use Restorative Circles and bubbles will provide a path forward that we can help our students navigate, while also growing ourselves.

This chapter is going to provide an overview of how Restorative Circles can help educators reclaim the hearts (and, simultaneously, the minds) of our students. My experience with Restorative Circles is small but powerful. I'll be sharing resources and advice from Jesse Brodka, a former board member of the Erie County Restorative Justice Center, Restorative Practices facilitator, and the person who gave me the confidence to try "circles" with my students. Jesse is a senior at Canisius College and a former student of mine. He's on fire for the power of this practice, but more about him and what I learned a bit later in the chapter.

The other part of this chapter is going to include resources on what I'm going to call "bubbles." I've checked pretty extensively, and I think this nickname is all mine! Restorative Circles take time, organization, and can lose their potency if the group is too large (though I've participated in large groups that were facilitated beautifully). I'm going to introduce my solution to the "this all sounds great, but I don't have the time/space/energy/ room in my curriculum" issue that could rightfully stop some of you from attempting restorative work. The pressure is real for educators to do it all, and with the introduction of bubbles in your classroom, you can utilize every minute of class time without sacrificing the things you *must* do. With that being said, I'm hoping to convince you that you absolutely, positively *must* do some sort of restorative work in your classrooms, whether it be full Restorative Circles or bubbles. *Students need us to help them restore what has been lost.*

Sneak Peek

In this chapter we will

★ learn how to get started with Restorative Circles
★ learn how to get started with restorative bubbles
★ learn the dos and don'ts of facilitating conversations

The Student Becomes the Teacher

I've written extensively about Project Based Learning, and one of the most exciting units that I do is on passion projects. No matter which iteration, students have full choice over their topic (their passion), their products, and even their methodology for presenting what they've learned. Depending on the age, experience, and abilities, I provide levels of support along the way. I teach a class at Canisius College for education majors called "Adolescent Literacy in a New Literacy World" where we explore the many types of "literacies" that teachers can incorporate in their classrooms, depending on their subject area. Topics include financial literacy, health literacy, and media literacy. Their final project was a different sort of passion project: students should choose a literacy that they believed was essential for students in our classrooms. It could be a literacy that we studied or one that we had not discussed.

Jesse Brodka is a clever mix between a wise philosopher, a squirmy 12-year-old boy, and an ambitious college kid. He has a winning smile and a twinkle in his eye, a nervous laugh, a goofy confidence, and is not shy about all the quirky things that make him *him*. When he asked me if he could facilitate a Restorative Circle for his final passion project, I was intrigued. When he warned me that it would take a little over double the time allotted, I knew that he was truly going to present a *passion*, not just a final project. I agreed, and it was one of the best decisions of my life. Jesse believes, as do I, that Restorative Circles can help students have emotional literacy.

I went on to use what I learned from Jesse to begin using Restorative Circles in the at-risk program I was piloting. I invited Jesse to guest facilitate on Fridays, and my students' skepticism, apathy, and occasional disdain were no match for Jesse's enthusiasm, commitment, and clear belief that "this stuff works." I include this anecdote about Jesse because it is important for all of us as educators to learn from our students and also be willing to get out of our comfort zone. I'm still not as expert as Jesse at facilitating—I still worry about curriculum—but I have experienced the power of restorative work, and I implore you to give it a chance.

Why do I believe so strongly that this is what students need? One Friday, about six months into my year in the at-risk program, I was absent and Jesse couldn't make it either. I'd left notes for the sub to give the students a study hall since we wouldn't be there to facilitate our "circle time." When I came back to school after the weekend, I was met by my students who were excited to tell me that they had done circle time *without us*. As it turns out, when the sub had told them they had a study hall, one of my students—I'll call her Leigh—had volunteered to facilitate our circle because, as she told the sub, "We need it before the weekend." My sub note said, "Students didn't want a study hall. Leigh volunteered to facilitate, and all the students participated. It was really amazing to hear them talk like they did. I'll sub anytime!" This is important for so many reasons, but most significantly is that these students recognized that they *needed* to take charge of their mental health and emotions, and *they* could do it without our help.

Restorative Circles

I'm going to tell you right away that I am not a certified trainer, but I have facilitated Restorative Circles with great success in my classroom space, as well as been a part of several. There's an ephemeral magic to circle time, and it always seems oversimplified to try to explain the synergy that happens, but I will try my best to make the idea clear. I met up with Jesse for coffee and asked his advice about explaining the complexities of Restorative Circles, especially when many readers may not have ever experienced one. Here's the guidelines we developed together.

Set the Space

Of all the "scary" moments of starting something outside of my comfort zone, this might have been the trickiest. Depending on your grade level, it might feel awkward or forced. For me, I felt like an impostor. I knew this was good stuff, for sure, but I didn't know exactly how to sell this to a bunch of jaded freshmen. Fight through it. It is worth it! I fumbled my way through, and when students know that you are being authentic and are coming from a place of caring, they are more respectful and helpful than you'd ever imagine. Jesse explained to me that in order for Restorative Circles to work, the experience must be differentiated from "school," that we must "intentionally set the space. Make it clear that this is different. This is special."

Arrange students into a big circle where everyone can be seen. Then, talk about that choice. Why a circle? Jesse suggests that we encourage a discussion about the symbolism of a circle, and make sure it is clear that the purpose is to make sure *every* voice is heard. There will be those students who are in their glory, who live for this sort of thing, but there are many, many others who would be missed unless a specific order is established.

Establish Norms and Values

Because this is new to most students, it is important to establish norms and values *with* the group, not *for* the group. Norms refer to behaviors that are "normal" behaviors associated with a situation. For example, a norm in most classrooms is that students raise their hands and are called upon by their teacher before speaking. Values are those things that are important to a person or group. It is the combination of these two elements that will make the group run smoothly. Norms are fairly easy to establish because most of the school world drills these behaviors into students. However, it is important to point out that this space is different. What, particularly, would make a circle work best? How should people act? Here's a partial list from our group, remembering that these kiddos struggled deeply with school:

1. Always listen fully. No phones.
2. Don't laugh at anyone.
3. No slurs or swearing.
4. Don't tell other people what to do.

Establishing the values was a much tougher proposition, and one that is much more raw. Jesse recommends some version of "Be present. Be real. Be open." Many times, students are going to value a particular thing because they've experienced its violation. When you look at some of the items on my students' list, you'll see what I mean:

1. Don't lie.
2. This is a closed circle. *Keep your mouth shut.* (Confidentiality)
3. If you hurt someone's feelings, apologize, even if it wasn't on purpose.

Confidentiality was the most important part of our norms and values setting session. Students needed to understand our parameters as teachers and court-mandated reporters. We were crystal clear that if they ever threatened to hurt themselves or anyone else, or that they were being abused in any way, that we'd have to help them by reporting the information to proper authorities. We emphasized that it was our job, but it is also how people operate in a caring community: when you are in need of help, you get it.

Students should write their ideas on notecards and place them on a table or even the floor in the middle of the circle. Gathering around all of their ideas is powerful as each of them puts themselves "into" the circle. Point out that this is intentional, and that the norms and values are created by this group, and each group might be different. Before the second meeting of the circle, record the norms and values on a poster or chart paper, as you'll use it at the beginning of each circle time to recalibrate. It is also helpful for times when a new member is present or if someone has violated the "code." I chose to talk about norms and values in terms of codes, since students are experts at code switching, depending on their circumstances. Codes for circle time are likely very different from those they'd normally use, but that is the point. Circles are special, and this experience is different.

Choose a Talking Piece

A talking piece is a physical object that can be transferred from person to person. The only person who can speak is the person who holds the object. In these complicated times, it is OK if you choose to have a digital version of this. If students are distanced, you could have their list of names up and move a pointer from person to person. It is always more compelling to use a physical piece, but teachers will find a way.

There are many ways to choose a talking piece, but as the facilitator there is an opportunity to make yourself vulnerable with your students. You may choose an item that is meaningful to you (but that you'll also let people touch often), and explain why it is important to you. I chose to use a Minion stuffed animal that I had been gifted. I explained that Minions were important to me because they remind me of my family vacation to Universal Studios, and the actual stuffed animal was important because the student who had given it to me had also really struggled in my class but had ended up doing well because of *lots* of conversations with me.

You can also have students bring in an object that means something to them that they'd be willing to let the class use. Have each student put their item into the middle. Take turns going around the circle once, letting every student who wishes to speak (see later) explain why the item is significant. Then, go around again, asking students to choose an item that isn't theirs, just one that resonates with them for some reason. Ask students to share a sentence about how that item makes them feel. Note if any item is a favorite. If so, ask to use that item as the talking piece. If there are several, a show-of-hands vote could narrow it down. I don't personally use this method because kiddos can get their feelings easily hurt, and if they really want their item chosen, it can become a distraction. However, I've seen this method done a few times with variations, and they were successful.

Honor Abstention

At this point, you are probably thinking about a student who would absolutely not want to participate. Perhaps, you would have been that person. That's OK. Honor every person's decision to abstain or "skip" if they aren't ready or interested. Almost every group I've been involved with as a participant and a facilitator has had at least one chronic abstainer. However, as time passes, students will gain comfort and grow bored of not participating. In my conversations with non-participants, most claim that the circles are still calming and allow them to reflect on things, even if they aren't ready to share. Very important: keep asking for participants, give those who have misgivings space, and before you know it, you might be surprised when a usually apprehensive student suddenly participates. It wasn't suddenly—it was because you continuously created an inclusive environment!

Recalibrate

Whenever a circle is convened, make sure to recalibrate by going over the norms and values. Jesse demonstrated this for me, and I stole his style. He never read from the list, and he asked students by name to share from the list. No one was really put on the spot—the "answers" were in front of them, but it did require students to speak and be a part of the recalibrating. Then, once the norms and values are reviewed, do what I call a "whip around."

A whip around is a question that should not elicit deep thought or emotional baggage. Either/or questions are great for this. Burgers or tacos? Summer or winter? Dogs or cats? Any question with a limited number of answers works well too. What's your favorite month? What's your favorite holiday? What's your favorite color? What's your favorite song? Best fast food? Once you've gone around the circle one or two times with a re-entry type question, you should do a check-in.

A check-in can be something that people do all at once, like a "fist to five" (0 fingers held up is awful, 5 is amazing) or you can go around the circle and ask students a simple, "In two sentences, tell us how you are doing." It is crucial to take the temperature of the group before you facilitate a true conversation within a circle. Case in point: one Friday Jesse and I were going to facilitate a conversation about obstacles facing our students in terms of completing assignments. Definitely a touchy subject, but we wanted to get information to help them. However, during the check-in portion, not a single member of our circle held up more than three fingers, while the majority held up one. Several had zeros. Jesse and I shared a look, and with a quick shake of his head, Jesse switched the question, asking, "What's your number one feeling right now?" Our conversation was heartbreaking, but it was helpful and productive, and it allowed our students to know that we cared about them deeply. As a closure, Jesse told them our original plan, and students were visibly touched that we had been willing to accommodate their needs—which is the point!

Facilitating Conversations in a Circle

Now that you know how to facilitate a conversation in a circle, you might be wondering what you'll actually talk about. It depends on how you are planning on utilizing circle time, but I'm going to share with you ways to use Restorative Circles for Social Emotional Learning (SEL), though once you understand that, it will be possible to make the ideas your own. I've divided the conversation topics into categories. I'll be making these into "conversation cards" for my own students. I plan to have them laminated and students can either draw from a deck of questions or choose a category. These are also found on my website, flexibleclass.com, under the "Conversation Cards" tab. I'll be adding more topics throughout the year, so check back. For social distancing purposes, I could also make a Google Classroom and create these as categories, or create an interactive slideshow that students could navigate.

There are times when the whole group simply can't meet. This is when I am going to use "bubbles," as in "break into your bubbles now." These will be smallish circles (five to seven members) that meet to hold a quick conversation about a specific topic. This can be content related or solely SEL, but the bubbles should operate just as the Restorative Circles do. This means that a talking piece is used, someone is facilitating, and the ability to abstain is always there. How is this different from traditional groups? First, it is steeped in the traditions brought into the class via Restorative Circles where the individual is always valued. Secondly, the group will have a facilitator. This means that every student has the potential for leadership, and, thus, ownership over their own learning. The key to the bubbles is going to be that the groups are fluid, constantly intermingling all students. This is very different from strategic groupings that I use for sheerly academic situations. The bubbles will end with my proclamation to "pop" and return to your normal seat. There, I will ask students to turn and talk to others nearby, creating another bubble. Think about when bubbles touch and they bond together—that's what we are going for with this idea.

The World around You

The World Around You category is meant to address both self-awareness and social awareness. These questions are best used to help students think outside their own little world. It will help them think through their place in the world, as well as recognize that their worldview is not the only one. Here are five "cards" to get you started:

The World around You: *Perspective*
Take a close-up picture of something with your phone. Zoom in, resize, and crop until it is very abstract. See if your group members can guess what it is.
Question: How does "zooming in" impact how we see things? How is this true with situations that happen to you? How might we "zoom out" before we judge people?

The World around You: *Heritage*
Take turns describing a food that is a tradition for your family or friends. You can make it sound really yummy or really icky. Give specific details.
Question: How does eating with someone or a group bond people together? Do "traditional" foods hold special meaning? How might we learn more about our friends' or families' traditions?

The World around You: *Alien POV*
Imagine you are an alien. You land in Florida. What do you observe? You land in Montana. What do you observe? You land in Paris. What do you observe? You land in Argentina. What do you observe?
Question: What are similarities amongst all people? What differences did you notice? Can you guess the reason for the differences?

The World around You: *Travel*
Share your favorite way to travel (boat, plane, car, bus, camel, buggy, horse, etc.).
Question: How does traveling together impact a group of people? Why might people choose different methods of travel? What is your favorite thing about travel?

The World around You: *Time Travel*
Imagine you have traveled back in time 100 years. What would be mostly the same? What would be entirely different? What is the most surprising?
Question: If you could live in any era or time period, when would you choose and why?

Heart Check

Heart Check questions are meant to address self-management and relationship skills. These are questions that are about the things that matter the most to our kiddos. We are trying to examine their emotions and help them regulate them. Lots of students don't know how to process the complex feelings they have, and the pandemic likely exacerbated that. These can act as "get to know you" type cards as well.

Heart Check: *A Single Moment*
Think of an important moment. Talk about the drilled down, very specific part. For example, scoring the winning basket vs. a whole game, or seeing a baby giraffe stand up for the first time vs. a whole trip to the zoo.
Question: Are you able to tell what each person is feeling about their moment? How? Could you have a different reaction to the same event?

Heart Check: *Advice*
What advice do you give to friends that you should take yourself?
Question: Do you like to give advice? Get it? When someone shares important personal information, what can we say instead of giving advice?

Heart Check: *Pets and Comfort Items*
Share with the group your pets (or lack of pets). Share with your group if you have a comfort item (blanket, stuffed animal, etc.).
Question: If you could have any pet, what would it be? Do you think animals understand people? What makes a "comfort item" special?

Heart Check: *Being the Best?*
Would you rather be the best player on a bad team or the worst player on a great team? Share.
Question: What do you think your answer tells you about yourself? There isn't a wrong answer.

Heart Check: *Ice Cream Invention*
If you could create an ice cream flavor, what would it be? Think about combining several of your favorites.
Question: After hearing everyone's answer, would you keep yours the same or change it? What does this tell you about brainstorming? If someone uses your idea, how does that feel?

Brain Freeze

Everyone knows what a brain freeze is, right? Usually, you get a brain freeze from eating ice cream or drinking something really cold. These questions are important and good (like ice cream), but they could cause that sharp, jarring feeling. It is important that circle time helps students deal with things that are not fun to discuss. Many of the Brain Freeze questions are about self-management and responsible decision-making.

Brain Freeze: *Sore Spot*

When we know someone will respond badly about a particular subject, we say that it is a "sore spot." Think of a sore spot you have. You may choose to share or simply think of your sore spot.

Question: What are some things we can do if we know a person has a sore spot. How can we make things easier for them? How do you want people to handle your sore spot?

Brain Freeze: *Is There a Dislike Button?*

Isn't it weird that you can dislike something that other people like a whole lot? Share with the group something that most people like or enjoy, but you hate.

Question: How much did you agree with your group members? Are there things that are more important to agree on? What are those?

Brain Freeze: *Sadness*

Every single person feels sad sometimes. Some people are good at hiding it, while others wear their heart on their sleeve. Share something that makes you sad.

Question: What are some things you can do to "cheer yourself up"? Do you have any suggestions for the group?

Brain Freeze: *Help!*

Most people don't like to ask for help. With your group, talk about why this might be.

Question: What is something you need help with? What could you help others with? How could we use this information to help the whole group?

Brain Freeze: *Venter or Volcano*

Everyone gets angry. Some people let off a "little steam" at a time, "venting" their irritation. Other people hold it in until there is an eruption of emotion, like a volcano, causing a lot of damage. Which type are you: a "venter" or a "volcano"?

Question: What are some healthy ways to "let off steam" so that you don't erupt? Is there such a thing as venting too much?

Sunny Stuff

This is a fun category. The entire purpose of these questions is to help communities deepen their ties or to introduce new members. The goal is to have fun with these questions and is great for small bubbles. I plan to use the Sunny Stuff conversation cards during the first several weeks of school.

Sunny Stuff: *Talents*

Everyone has talents. Some of them are traditional, like playing a sport or singing. Others are more unusual, like being able to moonwalk or being double-jointed. What is your talent?

Question: What talent do you wish you had? Is there a way to gain this talent?

Sunny Stuff: *Famous*

Have you ever met anyone famous? What was that like?

Question: Would you like to be famous? For what?

Sunny Stuff: *Humor*

Memes. Vines. Jokes. Cursed images. People have all kinds of humor. Share with the group something you think is funny. Be school appropriate and make sure you are being kind.

Question: What makes something funny? Discuss in your group. See if you can come up with a definition or criteria.

Sunny Stuff: *Imagine*

People sometimes forget that you can "play" with your imagination. Complete these sentences to come up with a new animal: The head of a _____. The body of a _____. The speed of a _____. It can even _____!

Question: With your group, come up with an imagination exercise like the one above and try with your group.

> **Sunny Stuff:** *Music*
>
> Music is so important, right? Share with the group three songs you like.
>
> Question: Why might it be important to stay respectful and not diss someone's music choices? Do you have any guilty pleasure songs that are kind of embarrassing? ("Baby Shark"?!)

I'm clearly a proponent of giving over time to Restorative Circles for SEL, but I'm also a realist. There are districts whose curriculum is scripted, you have to live with accountability over everything else, or you genuinely don't feel comfortable with this type of thing. I'd implore you to do what you are comfortable with and find others who are either interested in trying out more SEL activities or who are already doing them. Trust me, those of us who are really into this way of doing things are looking for allies! If you can't do Restorative Circles, why not use the last five minutes of class to do a whip around on one of these topics? Or, have students answer one of these questions on the way into your class. For example, as students walk in, ask everyone what their favorite song is. Take note of some of them and play them in the coming week.

Recently, at the end of a webinar, one of the participants asked me how to describe SEL to people without getting into programs or CASEL's competencies. I remembered an "elevator speech" I had once prepared for a grant, where the task was to drill down SEL. If you want to strip everything away and get to the essence of SEL it is this: *see every learner.* I hope that you'll try Restorative Circles, but if nothing else, know that every time you give students an opportunity to see each other and interact, you are improving the climate of your classroom, creating emotional connections, and these small intentional moves on your part will improve the lives of students while demonstrably impacting grades, behavior, and learning outcomes.

> **Your Turn**
>
> How are you going to incorporate Restorative Circles?
>
> ★ *I still worry about the curriculum, but I have experienced the power of restorative work, and I implore you to give it a chance.* What level of commitment can you give to restorative work? How much can you implement alongside the curriculum?
>
> ★ *At this point, you are probably thinking about a student who would absolutely not want to participate. Perhaps, you would have been that person. That's OK.* How will you allow students to abstain, but also help them to feel like a part of the class? In what ways can you continue to encourage participation?

★ *Trust me, those of us who are really into this way of doing things are looking for allies!* Who do you already know who is into this way of doing things? Do you have a list of educators to follow on social media who might be helpful? Can you identify a mentor for your foray into Restorative Circles?

Post-Pandemic Principles

As I reflect on how to implement Restorative Circles, I have a nagging feeling about how this idea will be received. I can hear overworked teachers who already have a ton on their plate (topped with all the "leftover" stuff that we didn't get to the year before) wondering why I'm trying to give them another thing to do. I can feel that. I know that I'm nervous myself. However, I've experienced the transformative power of restorative practices, and circles and bubbles are a logical place to start. Even if a teacher isn't able to commit their full time and attention to Restorative Circles, the bubbles may be used on a smaller scale to help students feel that there is a caring community.

Even if it seems daunting, and even if it seems like another thing to add to our list, I think it is crucial that we begin to listen to students. Listen with an open heart and mind. Listen with the intent to be an obstacle-mover. Listen with the notion that you could be the person that saves them from themselves. Be the one who sees, hears, and knows the child who is too quiet or shy to get the obvious attention. Or, be the one who looks past the behaviors that are a cry for help and instead hear what a troubled child needs to say. The Post-Pandemic Principle here is simple: every child needs an advocate, caring adult, and safe space in their school.

Resilience

Just Keep Pedaling

Developed by Collaborative for Academic, Social, and Emotional Learning and used with permission.

The dominant theme of all my writing about the Covid-19 pandemic has been one of grace. I've said quite a bit about giving grace to families because they don't know how to juggle this chaos, and they certainly didn't sign up to be a co-teacher. Much like those teachers who had to teach kiddos at home and those at school simultaneously, so many families had a caregiver who was working from home while simultaneously trying to make sure their child was on the right call or doing their work. As teachers, we know how

DOI: 10.4324/9781003230311-8

helpless this type of pandemic teaching made us feel, so I preached that we should be tolerant of pandemic parenting as well. I know that at my house our "pandemic parenting" involved letting my son skip homework that was worth two points because we were just sick of talking about it. I know that we let my daughter work more hours at a local restaurant than we would if she were in school full time. I don't want to be judged by my pandemic parenting, so I made a point of giving a tremendous amount of grace to the families.

As for my students, I felt horrible for them. They were suddenly expected to manage their time like college freshmen and exhibit adult-like discipline. So many students just couldn't do what was expected of them, and they felt terrible about that. Others struggled and weren't even successful after putting in their best effort. Grace was the name of the game for me. For some of the year, Wednesdays in my district were for "office hours," which meant that my students could join a Google Meet at a particular time to get extra help, remediation, or simply chat for a bit. I took this time to also schedule parent meetings, preferring to do them in a Meet, so that we could see one another.

One particular Wednesday, right around Thanksgiving, I had a memorable call. I was perched in my armchair, coffee at the ready, my composition book on my lap, ready to take notes about each student. Many no-shows, a few emails, and then I had a call that was live with "Joey's" mom. Joey was an athlete, polite, and a good-natured kiddo, and he and I had connected in the first days of school over a shared love of *The Office*. I had reached out to Joey's mom because he'd gone from an "A" average in the first quarter to failing miserably in the second. He'd stopped showing up to calls, didn't turn in work, and he had ignored my emails. Our conversation was a revelation to me. Here's how it went:

Me: Hi! I just wanted to let you know that I'm very concerned about Joey. As I mentioned in my email, I'm not sure what to do to help him. He's really tuned out. He's a great kiddo, and I know he can do the work.

Mom: Well, we are in complete agreement. He is a great kiddo. He is really tuned out. I know he can do the work too. I also don't know what to do to help him. I'm very concerned too. The problem is, I'm at work, and he's at home. He's 13, and he isn't responsible enough for this. I probably babied him in 7th grade, but I didn't know that he was going to have to be completely independent in the 8th grade.

Me: Absolutely. I hear you. I have my own 7th grader at home, and if someone were not here, he would never be able to do this. It is a lot of responsibility, for sure.

Mom: How about this: I won't blame you when he fails because I know that you care about my son, and you won't blame me because I can do absolutely nothing to make my son get out of bed when I'm not there, and I deeply care about how he does. There's no one to blame. I'm not a bad mom. You aren't a bad teacher. He isn't a bad kid.

The relief that I felt, hearing that this woman wasn't going to blame me, was almost too much to bear at that moment. I carried the burden of each student, always assuming that I could figure something out to reach them. The extra effort worked, usually, but when I couldn't reel students back in, I beat myself up.

As you may have already guessed, I was good at giving everyone else grace, but I held myself to a superhero standard. This chapter is the last one because I've put it off. I've had a rough year personally, with my dad, brother, and brother-in-law all passing away within six months, as well as my husband having to find a new job after being furloughed. The pandemic caused my already-anxious children to struggle in ways that I am yet to fully comprehend. I know that historically, when I think of those who lived through the Great Depression or went to war or experienced some act of God that forever changed their lives, I think of the resilience those people exhibited as they kept putting one foot in front of another. That is what I've tried to do. I think that is what we have all attempted, and frankly, we are doing a better job than I would have ever guessed.

I've struggled with a definition of *resilience* that works for me. It is the ability to keep going, of course, but it is also about attitude. As for me, and my family, I'm not sure that we were consciously "doing" anything as we experienced so much loss, but I do know that there is some hope that with resilience we will "come out the other side" of this pandemic intact. The definition I've settled on is from the author Sharon Salzberg, a New York Times bestselling author and teacher of Buddhist meditation practices in the West. She says, "Resilience is based on compassion for ourselves as well as compassion for others."

Sneak Peek

In this chapter, we will

★ think about ways our students have had "pandemic gains"
★ determine a course of action for "learning loss" in our classrooms
★ explore how we can help our students to recognize and celebrate their own narratives as stories of resilience

Pandemic Gains

At the height of pandemic teaching, when we were attempting to do it all: my students were hybrid on an A/B schedule, except for Wednesdays, which were alternating weeks, with asynchronous work and their electives on their day at home, where they also joined Google Meet to do things like phys ed, technology, home and careers, and art virtually. On top of that, many teachers still gave "homework." Oh yeah, since teachers were scrambling to provide asynchronous work (or worse yet, for some, teaching simultaneously), most of us introduced new platforms. I alone used CommonLit, Edpuzzle, and Quizizz to provide previews or reinforcements for my students.

If your head is spinning, imagine being 12 years old, where, prior to the pandemic, your mom checked your agenda every night. Now, your mom is at work or working from the bedroom or bathroom or back porch, and you are somehow expected to know what to do! Or, you're 6 years old, with a daycare provider logging you into classes as best he can. Almost every day of the week a different adult is "in charge" of you, but many of them don't know how to use the platforms either. Or, you're 16 years old and suddenly you are in high demand at your part-time job, and the need for money outweighs your desire to sit in on a class of 30 students, most of them with their cameras off, while your desperate teacher is trying to engage students, but not seeing how that is possible.

In my estimation, students had to learn at least a dozen new skills to even participate in classes, all while living with the harsh realities of the pandemic. Some got sick. Many were quarantined. Some watched family members lose their jobs. Everyone was learning phrases like "flatten the curve" and "comorbidity." We watched as the political climate disrupted their entire families, as masking, vaccinations, and racial tensions erupted, often dividing relatives into distinct camps. The adults around them were struggling with issues that permeated all aspects of life. Some students lost family members to the disease. It was surreal, and I'm "the grown-up." I truly can't imagine what being a student during this time was like. I don't think we'll know for years the impact of the isolation, loss, fear, and anxiety.

However, as educators, we have an obligation to have compassion for ourselves and our students, recognizing and celebrating the massive obstacles that we've all overcome just to "come out the other side" of this experience. I personally plan to take every opportunity to praise students for their gains. When we use the many new platforms, I'm going to make sure they know that this is a skill they have learned. The primary way I'm going to help students process what has happened is to help them to see that they are resilient, that they are able to do hard things, and that we must recognize the growth that has happened. Posted on my door is a reminder: "So far, you have survived 100% of your worst days. You are doing great!" It is a reminder for them, but it will be a reminder to me as well.

Learning Loss

I'm going to be brutally honest here. Every single year, my students are all over the place—some are reading at a 10th-grade level and could ace the SATs. Others are several grade levels below in reading, comprehension, and even struggling with phonics. The "learning loss" that is being discussed ad nauseum is something that happens *every* year. Some students learn easily, but others have not kept up for whatever reason. Sometimes they needed more remediation, other times they were suffering some sort of trauma, and other times inequities are widening the gap. The fact is, the pandemic may have laid bare those inequities in a way that suddenly everyone is willing to acknowledge. When everyone was talking about students not having devices or internet connectivity, or support at home, I felt like screaming into that void: "They never have, yet they have been assigned homework and expected to do research at home, and any number of completely ridiculous tasks that only *some* students could ever do, not just during the pandemic. *This is not new.* It has never been fair."

Instead of making blanket statements about learning loss, the best thing to do at this moment on the classroom level is to use assessments to identify strengths, weaknesses, and areas that need remediation. It has always been the best thing to do from the classroom level. I do *not* mean to use standardized testing, as I strongly doubt that the assessments students took last year are effective measures of much of anything. Instead, here's how I've been using assessments, and I'm going to double down on this going forward. Of all the things that I write or say, the following paragraphs probably have the strongest reaction (both positively and negatively), so get ready!

An Atmosphere Where Learning Is the Goal

Students must believe that the reason you are there is to help them learn. Not for one test. Not for one year. They need to believe that everything is a learning process. If you consider how most schools do things, you'll soon realize that the atmosphere is usually one of preparation, not one of learning. If your class is racing toward a test, cramming for review, revisiting for an end-of-year assessment, there is a better way. What if you look at everything as a learning opportunity? What if when a student didn't complete an assignment you asked what was wrong, what pitfalls had they encountered, how can you help? Believe it or not, students often have very real reasons that they didn't do an assignment but have not shared it because they haven't learned how to do so. We've created a culture of compliance that casts students in such a negative light if they don't comply that they stop trying, and they certainly stop communicating with us if we lecture them on responsibility or make comparisons to others. *Students want to learn; we all do.* However, when there are obstacles that prevent them from learning, we can, and should, help move those obstacles.

Once you establish a classroom of learning, students will come forth in surprising ways and tell you the truth. Some students will admit that they've shut down, given up, or you'll find out that your class is not a priority. It is our job to help students understand how what we are teaching will help them or why it is necessary. Think about how irritating it is when we are forced to attend a training or a staff development without context of why we are learning it or how it will ever be applicable. I'd venture to say that most of us in those situations couldn't pass an assessment on the non-essential information that we've been forced to listen to. If you create an atmosphere where learning is the goal, and you remind yourself of that, you'll soon see that every situation is an opportunity to help students learn about themselves and how to be successful. This approach helps me prioritize what it is that I actually want them to learn vs. all the things that there are to learn. We have to decide what we think is essential, and we must make a way for all students to learn it.

Pre-assessments

I don't waste time doing a huge pre-assessment, other than the one that is required in my district. Instead, before each unit, I prepare a quick pre-assessment or one that is embedded in something fun that we are doing. For example, in the beginning of the year, every year, I must teach students how to write complete sentences in the first quarter. Second quarter, I always teach them how to create complex sentences. Third quarter, we work on making their writing more sophisticated, and finally in the fourth quarter they are expected to write using a variety of sentences.

Each quarter, I give a pre-assessment, almost always one that doubles as a get-to-know you or an Social Emotional Learning (SEL) activity. The playlist assignment in the next section asks students to write five paragraphs (one per slide). I don't have to tell students that I'm using those paragraphs to assess their abilities to write complete sentences, but each year, I record a number that is *not* a part of their grade that gives me their baseline writing score that I will use to build upon. It is the best type of assessment because it is used to inform my instruction, and I can measure the students' growth across assignments. They are writing authentically, and it isn't a separate assignment. I use what information they give me without preparing them for it, as that is the only thing that really matters in the end. If students only use complete sentences on the Complete Sentences Test, they haven't really mastered complete sentences.

Formative Assessments

I give lots of grades. That sounds counter to what else I do, but I explain to students that I'm just giving them grades as a barometer of how they are doing. They may redo anything that is given as a graded assignment, so grades are really just a check-in. People always ask me, "How many students do you have? How can you do all that grading?" I have between 120 and 140 students each year. I do "all that grading" by utilizing a wide variety of resources. Let's pretend I graded an assignment on how well students wrote in complete sentences. Assume that 20% of my students didn't do well. They know that they are not meeting the standard of writing in complete sentences. I don't force them to redo the assignment, as we will continually be assessing this skill all year. However, if they want to, I can assign anything I want to check the skill again. Last year, Tom was a NASCAR fanatic. I asked Tom to write ten complete sentences explaining NASCAR to me. Tom did this four times before he got a 100 on the sentences, but he was willing to do it because I kept telling him he had to learn how to write complete sentences, but I didn't tell him what he had to write them about. He had some choice, and he really loved talking about NASCAR.

If I need to, I go to the internet to provide instruction or remediation on the skill students are struggling with. I assign an Edpuzzle video, a Khan Academy video, and I make videos of skills my students commonly struggle with, like commas. I tell them they need to go watch the videos, or practice on Quizlet, Quizizz, or Kahoot and send me a screenshot of their practice. Once they have practiced, I'll give them an alternate assignment that will replace the low grade. It isn't averaged because I want them to understand that it just might have taken them a little longer and a bit more practice, but they can achieve mastery. Mastery is not a 75 because you got a 50 on the first assessment and eventually got a 100. Mastery is that it took you a while, but with hard work and perseverance, you earned a 100. This builds resilience, and many students learn how to study the first time around.

Summative Assessments

I break my summative assessments into parts that I count as separate grades. For example, my students will do a WebQuest to help them learn about the setting and background to the novel *The Outsiders*. I give three grades. They will have a grammar/mechanics grade where I'm measuring their mastery of complex sentences, and they are required to use a specific number of sentences with specific constructions. They will have a research skills grade where I'm measuring their ability to find the accurate answers. They will have a technology grade where I'm measuring their ability to insert the links into the document. Students, and their families, can easily see where their strengths are and what they are still learning. They can then do more practice, and replace their grade in the area where they struggled, but they have reason to be proud of themselves and celebrate as they see what they have mastered.

This past year, I had a student who was very creative and quite bright, but she never took the time to learn how to use complex sentences. Around the third quarter, it finally sunk in that if she would learn complex sentences her grades would be awesome. In a parent conference, I was able to reference her strengths, and give her ways to practice and work on complex sentences. For the rest of the third quarter and into the fourth, she began doing her "revisions" (which is what I call all the retakes). She finally learned the material and her grades improved, but most important, she realized that she always had had that opportunity, but she just had not taken it. My goal is for students to see the value in pushing themselves and always trying to improve.

Resilience in academics is achieved when students are able to take the feedback we give them, in the form of grades, and do something about it. It isn't just studying more next time, but instead it is taking charge of their own learning by doing the work to learn what they have missed right now. If we can help students understand that every time they "work on themselves" after a struggle, they are growing stronger and more able to weather the next storm or problem, then we are helping them to be resilient, successful, independent learners.

Teaching Identity and Resilience with Disney's *Cruella*

I'm a big fan of origin stories, prequels, and perspective-shifting stories like *Wicked*, *Maleficent*, and *The True Story of the Three Little Pigs*. When I saw the trailer for *Cruella*, I was intrigued by the snippet of Emma Stone's raspy, "I was born brilliant. Born bad. And a little bit mad." I love this type of movie, and I could tell from the previews that there would be an excellent character arc, which is what really pulls me in. The Chandlers were ready to return to one of our favorite places, the movies, but I was a little nervous with this choice. My husband and I have seen hundreds of movies together, and he can be a tough critic, but he does share my love for Emma Stone, so I felt a bit better. My 13-year-old son, Oliver, is interested in cinematography and "movie magic" over storyline, and I wasn't sure he'd want to sit through the 2 hours and 14 minutes, after the previews. Zoey, my 16-year-old, was the least of my worries because she takes a blanket with her to the movies and simply takes a nap if she's not interested. If you haven't guessed, I was the most excited.

Then the movie started. Every Chandler was mesmerized within the first three minutes. It's that good. The storyline is familiar, but reimagined and fresh. The music is amazingly appropriate to each scene, and I found myself comparing the situation on the screen to the lyrics. For example, when Estella lands her dream job, Nina Simone's sweet "It's a new dawn / It's a new day / It's a new life for me" from "Feeling Good," was flawlessly interwoven. The fashion and sets made me wish I'd been born earlier. Then *it* happened.

It happens occasionally, and once it does, the movie changes for me. *It* is that moment when I lean over to one of my kiddos and say, "I'm going to teach this." I immediately want to pull out a pen and start jotting things down, but I force myself to enjoy the experience, knowing that I will purchase the movie and watch it another half a dozen times before I share it with my students. *It* has happened to me many times, most notably when I watched *Zootopia*. This *it* moment felt the same way: *there's so much I need to talk with my students about!*

First, let me clear up a few things. Most important, the weird dog-fur-coat thing from *101 Dalmatians*, which is incidentally super scary, is not a part of this movie. Within the first five minutes, we learn that Estella/Cruella finds a dog in the dumpster, names him Buddy, and he is her shadow for the rest of the movie. Another dog, Wink, is introduced, and he is another member of the friends-who-become-family of this story. The dalmatians do have their role, but they are never seriously considered for fur coats, though Cruella lets her archenemy think so. Second, there's nothing that seriously suggests that Cruella is the devil him-/herself as I'd heard someone mention. Instead, there's some word play around DeVil (a getaway car) and devil, with Horace pointing out that it may be spelled devil, but it is pronounced DeVil. "Hellman Hall," the Baroness's mansion, becomes Hell Hall, but that is one of many brilliant homages to the previous movies and book. There's a whole bunch of references/allusions/Easter eggs that you can read about in the "*Cruella* Pre-Viewing Guide." Students love these kinds of connections, so I will share those before diving into the movie itself.

The approach I'm taking to teaching this movie is to frame it as an identity story. Yes, it is an origin story of sorts, a prequel with a whole lot of creative license, and a shift-in-perspective piece as well. It is now told from Estella/Cruella's perspective with a human protagonist, instead of animal protagonists from the original book. Despite these compelling classifications, I could not let this opportunity pass without utilizing this movie to get my students talking about all kinds of important things that lead to social and emotional learning around the idea of identity. The main questions can be found in the "*Cruella* Rotating Chair," which is a student-led discussion that will occur after watching the movie. These types of questions help students with self-awareness, while also developing social awareness and building class community and relationship skills (all a part of CASEL's SEL Competencies), and all a part of their own identification and development of their own identity.

I found myself whacking my daughter when Arty, who introduces himself as "Art. As in, work of," describes the abuse he takes for his chosen self-expression via his clothes. Estella asks, "How's that play on the street?" referring to his red velvet, makeup, and bold attire. He replies, "Some abuse and insults, but I like to say that 'normal' is the cruelest insult of all, and at least I never get that" to which Estella replies, "I couldn't agree more." In our current climate, I am excited to make a safe space for my students to express themselves in whatever way they feel best. Though clothes and costumes are at the center of this story, there are other interesting paths to follow as well.

Questions of nature vs. nurture, what makes a family, how does socio-economic status impact people, and identity are abundant. The movie is long, and I know that this mini-unit will take about two weeks. Here's how I plan to approach this, with 40-minute classes:

Days 1 and 2: "*Cruella* Pre-Viewing Sheet"

Days 3, 4, 5, 6: Watching *Cruella* with stop/start (focus on SEL)

Days 7 and 8: "*Cruella* Rotating Chair" student-led discussion

Days 9 and 10: Teacher-led debrief from notes I'll take throughout, with a focus on the literary terms we can address (allusion, characterization, plot structure, theme, etc.), all leading to a slideshow students will create with five pieces of media that is their "playlist"

While this may seem like a long time to spend on a movie, that would be missing the point. I'm double-dipping, even triple-dipping. I'll be teaching using English language arts (ELA) standards of speaking and listening, in addition to reviewing literary elements. I'll be getting to know my students through our discussion, as well as laying the groundwork for our future work together in Restorative Circles. The "Playlist" activity is something that students will create using Google Slideshow, and each entry of their playlist has an accompanying paragraph, which is the pre-assessment I mentioned earlier. The underlying message of this unit, and all of the others I'll teach for the next few years is going to be simple: resilience. We must have compassion for ourselves and each other, and this interweaving of the academic, social, and emotional with high-interest pop culture is a methodology I plan to utilize all year as we are all emerging from the alienation, isolation, and trauma of the pandemic. This, I believe, is the best way to teach, and from my experience, perhaps it always has been.

Pre-Viewing:

Cruella

Before we view the movie, let's think about some of the topics we'll discuss.

1) What do you think the color white symbolizes? Black? Red?
2) What qualities are girls TRADITIONALLY supposed to have? Is this fair? Why or why not?
3) What qualities are boys TRADITIONALLY supposed to have? Is this fair? Why or why not?
4) What do you think of when you hear the word "home"?
5) Can people who aren't related to you by blood be considered family? Give some examples.

People are a combination of "nature" (their genetics) and "nurture" (how they are treated in life). Brainstorm some characteristics you believe are "nature," some that are "nurture," and some that are both. One example is done for you below.

Nature	Nurture	Both
David's dad is 6 feet tall. David Jr. is also 6 feet tall.	David Jr is very shy, but his mom makes a point of teaching him conversation starters to make meeting new people easier.	David Jr's mom and dad are great dancers. David has liked to dance since he was little. His parents always praised him and he took lessons. David is a confident dancer.

Figure 8.1 *Cruella* Pre-Viewing Sheet

Most everyone knows the story of *101 Dalmatians*. This movie is the prequel--in essence, the backstory. It has also been called an origin story, which means that it tells how something or someone was created. This movie is dramatically different in many ways, but one of the fun things the directors do is pay homage to the original *101 Dalmatians* movie and book. Paying homage is like giving a shout out. Here are some "look fors" as you watch. Sometimes these allusions are called "Easter Eggs" because they are hidden in the story.

Cruella	101 Dalmatians
Hellman Hall	Hell Hall
Horace and Jasper are her good friends (their clothes and sizes are very much like the book)	Horace and Jasper are her henchmen
Anita Darling is Estella's childhood friend and reporter. Gifted Perdita. *Darling could be a Peter Pan reference	Anita is the human protagonist. Perdita is her dog.
Roger is the Baroness' lawyer and in the end is pursuing music. (his office at the end is nearly identical to Roger in the book)	Roger is the human protagonist. Pongo is his dog.
Horace comments that people look like their dogs.	The opening of *101 Dalmatians* has this exact scene.
Horace watched tv with the stolen dalmatians.	Roger watched tv with the dalmatians.
Artie's intro says, "If you can dream it, you can dress it." This is an allusion to Disney's "If you can dream it, you can do it."	Artie is not in the original.
Cruella is a horrible driver, pointing out that she never learned since she was an orphan.	Cruella is a dangerous driver with no regard for anyone on the road.
When Cruella is looking out the window, the television is playing a Tallulah Bankhead movie.	Tallulah Bankhead was the original inspiration for Cruella in terms of her mannerisms.

Figure 8.1 Continued

Student Viewing Guide:

Cruella

Below are some "look fors" to pay attention to during the movie. I'll pause so you can jot down your ideas. Save these notes because you'll use them later to think about how the directors shaped the viewers interpretation of the story.

½ Black and ½ White hair:	Example:	Example:
The Necklace:	Example:	Example:
Trash:	Example:	Example:
Stories about Cruella:	Example:	Example:
Hats:	Example:	Example:
Costumes:	Example:	Example:

Figure 8.2 *Cruella* Student Viewing Guide

Teacher Viewing Guide:

Cruella

Below are times to stop the movie and point out the incredible details that help this movie get its point across--some subtle and some more obvious. Students should discuss how they feel and what they think about each.

½ **Black and ½ White hair:** Estella is born with ½ black and ½ white hair. Her mother, the Baroness, is evil and her father is kind/good.	**Example:** **:46** "From the very beginning, I've always made a statement. Not everyone appreciated that... but I wasn't for everyone."	**Example:** **14:33** Estella knows she must dye her hair in order to hide in London. Jasper says, "I don't know. I quite like it." This is the first instance of Estella being accepted as she is, unconditionally.
The Necklace: The Necklace symbolizes Estella's history, as it is called a "family heirloom." It plays a large role throughout as Estella searches for who she is and belongs to.	**Example:** **9:48** "I had killed my mother. And in that moment, the best I could think to do is run." (drops the necklace)	**Example:** **40:39** *Estella:* "Your necklace." *Baroness:* "Family heirloom. Funny story actually. An employee once stole it." *Estella:* "No she did not."
Trash: "Trash" is equated with being useless, but it is also reappropriated by Cruella later in the story when she creates her dress from trash and upstages the very rich and posh Baroness. When there's trash, it signals to the viewer that Estella is doubting herself.	**Example:** **2:49** When the school boys push her into the trash, she finds her dog Buddy. This is when she feels the worst about herself. **23:53** When things are going poorly at work, the trash bag breaks and she's covered with trash. This is immediately before meeting the Baroness.	**Example:** **1:11** Cruella brings a dumpster of trash and dumps it at the Baroness' feet. Cruella is wearing a dress made of trash. This is reappropriating the meaning of trash because the newspapers report that "Cruella" has arrived, and the Baroness' dresses were a part of the trash.

Figure 8.3 *Cruella* Teacher Viewing Guide

Stories about Cruella: Estella and Cruella both address the narratives that are told about them. In both cases, they control that story, which gives them power. Students should consider how they shape their own narrative.	**Example:** **3:30** Estella's mom withdraws her from the school just as the headmaster is trying to expel her, pointing out that this "can't be on her record." In this way, the mom controls the narrative about the past.	**Example:** **1:01** Cruella approaches Anita, her childhood friend and journalist. *Anita:* "You have that glint in your eye. You have a bit of an extreme side." *Cruella:* "Now I want you to tell them who I am." She controls the story.
Hats: Estella's mother tries to get her to cover her full personality, calling the spunky, unique, and tomboy side "Cruella." The hat symbolizes her mom's desire for her to fit in and for her to be like everyone else.	**Example:** **1:46** *Mom:* "Wear the hat" *Estella:* "I don't need the hat." Also her mom: "Be polite. And good. And friendly."	**Example:** **8:03** *Mom:* "Keep the hat on before anyone sees that." The viewer later learns that this is to protect Estella, but the impact is the same.
Costumes: Costumes are used throughout the movie with an interesting twist. Typically, we think of costumes as clothing that hides our true identity, but in the movie, it is when the truest identity of characters is revealed. Estella turns her drab uniform into a costume, and she's happy, but others aren't. The same is true for Arty. Costumes are the characters' true selves.	**Example:** **7:35** "For the first time in my life, I felt like I belonged." Estella says this at the ball, fortelling her passion for fashion design, but in this case it is a costume party. Costumes are a way Estella wants to express herself, but at school her unique clothing only brings her trouble.	**Example:** **34:56** *Estella:* "How's that look go on the street?" (referring to Arty, the flamboyant thrift store owner who dresses in costumes) *Arty:* "Some abuse and insults, but I like to say that 'normal' is the cruelest insult of all, and at least I never get that." *Estella:* "I couldn't agree more."

Figure 8.3 Continued

Rotating Chair Questions:

Cruella

A rotating chair is a student led discussion in which students call upon each other after answering a question. The person who is called upon should consider what the first person said and respond with:

"I agree with . . ."
"I disagree with . . ."
"I agree with . . . however, . . ."
"I disagree with . . . but I can see that . . ."

This helps students actually listen to the students who speak before them. Students should use their *"Cruella* Pre-Viewing" sheet, as well as their *"Cruella* Student Viewing Guide" to use specific details from our initial conversation and from the movie itself.

The first student who asks the questions moderates, and once they feel that the conversation is complete, then they summarize what the participants have said, ending with a statement of their own.

1) What do you think the directors are trying to say about "nature vs. nurture"?
2) What characteristics about Estella make her "not for everyone"? Do you think she'd have an easy time fitting in now? Why or why not?
3) Do we wear "costumes" in our lives? Does it matter what kind of clothes we wear? Is it true that you "can't judge a book by its cover"?
4) How would you feel if we were required to wear uniforms?
5) Does everyone have a "good side" and "bad side"?
6) What is the theme of the movie?

Figure 8.4 *Cruella* Rotating Chair Questions

Playlist Assignment

"The Story of Your Life"

This assignment is designed for you to be reflective about your life so far. Who has influenced you? What events have shaped you? Are there important places that make you, you? **Instead of just telling us this, you are going to share some forms of media that demonstrate it.** For example, your grandma may have always sang you a special song, or your BFF and you have all the words to a certain movie memorized from hundreds of viewings. Here's what you will do:

1) Choose 5 "media" that you'd like to share because it reminds you of an important person, memory, event, belief, period of time, etc.
2) Create a slideshow. You should have a title slide with your name, period you have ELA, and "The Story of My Life" on it. Then, you will have ONE slide for each media. You will include a picture, a video, or an MP3 on the slide, as well as a 5-8 sentence paragraph explaining why you chose it.
3) When you have finished the five slides, you will have a Gratitude slide. This is the list of people you appreciate.
4) Finally, you will create a Table of Contents. That slide will be your second slide, so you will need to move it up into that spot.

You will present "The Story of Your Life" as told through your Playlist. Don't limit yourself with what you include on your playlist. Here's some ideas:

◆ Movies
◆ YouTubers
◆ TikToks
◆ Songs

We are all on a journey through life. I bet you will be surprised how many things you have in common with each other. We depend on each other, so make sure that you are respectful while viewing these personal details!

Figure 8.5 *Playlist* Assignment

Name: _____   Cohort
Playlist Paragraphs TEST GRADE   PLAYLIST PRESENTATION QUIZ GRADE

#1: 1 2 3 4 5 6 7 8 9 10	Loud, clear, enthusiastic 1 2 3 4 5 6 7 8 9 10
#2 1 2 3 4 5 6 7 8 9 10	Presented on day asked 10 → yes; 5 → no; 1 → more than one day late
#3 1 2 3 4 5 6 7 8 9 10	Slides are easy to read 1 2 3 4 5 6 7 8 9 10
#4 1 2 3 4 5 6 7 8 9 10	Links work 1 2 3 4 5 6 7 8 9 10
#5 1 2 3 4 5 6 7 8 9 10	Material is school appropriate 1 2 3 4 5 6 7 8 9 10
TOTAL: X 2 = _____	TOTAL: X2 = _____

Paragraphs should: Comments:

- ❏ Be 6-10 sentences
- ❏ Correctly punctuated
- ❏ Correct grammar
- ❏ No blue or red underlines
- ❏ No lowercase i's
- ❏ Use specific details to explain the Playlist choice.
- ❏ Playlist choice is school appropriate

Figure 8.6 Playlist Rubric

Your Turn

How are you going to help your students become resilient?

★ *As you may have already guessed, I was good at giving everyone else grace, but I held myself to a superhero standard.* In what ways are you holding yourself to a superhero standard? What is a specific situation where you can give yourself grace?

★ *Instead of making blanket statements about learning loss, the best thing to do at this moment on the classroom level is to use assessments to identify strengths, weaknesses, and areas that need remediation.* How will you identify strengths, weaknesses, and areas that need remediation? In what ways can you "double-dip" and incorporate SEL?

★ *I do "all that grading" by utilizing a wide variety of resources.* Identify all the tools that you can use in your class to give students multiple opportunities to practice, learn, and retake. Check to see what your district has to help you, and explore options like Quizlet, Quizizz, Edpuzzle, CommonLit, and Kahoot.

★ *While this may seem like a long time to spend on a movie, that would be missing the point.* Could you use *Cruella* or some other movie to help students consider their identity or SEL competencies?

Post-Pandemic Principles

Personally and professionally, until two years ago, I would easily have told you that I have never had to be particularly resilient. I'm happily married, have two healthy kiddos, am healthy myself, and I've enjoyed success in my career. I haven't wanted for much. Then, on Good Friday—the Easter break that we never returned from because Covid hit in full force—my dad went into the hospital and only left to go to hospice. He passed away in June. My brother passed away in August. My brother-in-law died suddenly and unexpectedly of a "heart event" in December, leaving my sister devastated. My mom, who had lost her husband and son, began to experience more dementia. My own son began struggling with mental health issues. My husband was furloughed. I was in two car accidents in three months. It just kept going and going. One. Thing. After. Another.

I'm a very private person when it comes to my emotions. I don't cry. I certainly don't complain. "Buck up buttercup" is my personal motto. Instead, I take drives. I immerse myself in work. I paint. I write. I turn the music up. However, all of my normal coping mechanisms weren't enough. I was just trying to survive day to day. The thing that I noticed though was this: everywhere I looked, there were others who were experiencing new strains, new problems, and we were all doing it in isolation and without our normal routines. People were hurting. Everywhere, it seemed, peoples' lives were falling apart, just like mine. The adults were struggling, and eventually it occurred to me that "wow, we really all need to check on the children. They are probably not OK either." When I started looking outside of myself, I found the wreckage was everywhere. So much trauma all around me.

As time passed, things improved for me, and the worst of the worst seems to be over. However, I've come to see that the Post-Pandemic Principle here is really simple: we truly don't know what others are going through, and we don't know how much more they can handle. If we can lighten someone else's load, if we can give each other an abundance of grace, then we will be doing our part. If we can give ourselves that abundance of grace, and if we can recognize the resilience we've all demonstrated just by surviving this disaster, we will move toward healing.

Afterword

This past summer, I was a participant in the New York State United Teachers' Future Forward Taskforce. Our goal was to gather many voices and perspectives to discuss a way forward—through and post-pandemic. I'd been asked to participate due to my background and passion for Social Emotional Learning (SEL). Every few weeks we'd have an hour-and-a-half conversation about topics like poverty, technology, and community schools. Finally, the day came when Social Emotional Learning was on the agenda. I could hardly wait! What happened next has left me a bit bewildered, while also, I think, seeing more clearly than I have before the complexities of implementing SEL.

The first hour was chock-full of good ideas, stories of tried-and-true programming, and inspiring stories of connections and successes. As we moved into the second hour though, an important issue came up that I think is well-worth exploring and clarifying: *how do we measure SEL?* I have to admit that my heart was pounding when I shared my thoughts about measuring SEL. Even as I type this, I expect pushback, and I'm getting all fired up, but here it goes:

We cannot standardize SEL. There cannot be a bubble sheet or a Scantron, and God forbid our students are given a grade or a number to equate with their human experience. We cannot "teach" SEL. We cannot outsource it. We cannot do that to well-meaning teachers, and we certainly can't do that to children. If Social Emotional Learning is to be reduced to the most basic of principles it is this: *see every learner.* If we see every learner, truly see them, we will know that standardizing is the exact opposite of what we need to do. Instead, we need radical differentiation, a "plan" for every student, a way forward for everyone. This way forward must be about relationships, connections, and flexibly meeting the needs of students.

Sure, I've heard the adage too—"What gets tested, gets taught." I hate that adage. I don't care what gets taught; I care what gets learned, experienced, and internalized for future use. As soon as we see SEL as "another thing" or a mandate or a top-down directive, we're going to lose our power. You'll have to excuse the union leader in me, but the facts are simple: as educators *we have the power* to make or break a student's school experience. We have to use that power, right here, right now. We should not wait for a program, but instead find ways to do the work ourselves. Find others who want to reach kiddos first, and teach content second, and build momentum together.

I've been the teacher in both kinds of classroom: the content delivery room and the caring community. For years, we drilled for standardized tests; I perfected lessons to maximize the number of power standards I taught. My students did well. I led professional development on Danielson's Domains, and I felt pretty good about what I was doing. However, there was always a nagging feeling that I was missing something. I certainly didn't remember my great content-deliverers, nor did I really remember what I'd supposedly learned in their classrooms.

Instead, I went into teaching because of Miss Neely, who wrote a note to the tooth fairy when I lost my tooth on the playground. Or, Mrs. Fletcher, my volleyball coach and 8th grade teacher, who helped me learn to quit apologizing all the time. And of course there was Mr. Burger, our Key Club adviser, who always made sure that students from my small town high school had "big city" experiences with awesome field trips and taught me how to introduce myself with confidence. In college, Dr. Benert taught me about social justice in her garden, since she invited all of her students to lunch at her house, a few at a time, so we wouldn't be too homesick. I wanted to be inspiring, just like those who inspired me.

So, I did it. I decided I'd have a grand experiment. I'd do everything in my power to help every student feel seen, heard, known, and noticed, which is what those teachers had done for me. I'd build a community. We'd do giant, fun projects. That was the year I let a rowdy group of boys build a volcano to celebrate the fact that all five of them had actually read the survival book they did for a book club (and liked it). We all learned to juggle, just because we could. (I never was good, but a surprising number of middle school students were.) I invited families in and asked for guest speakers, and I'd take risks that the content deliverer wouldn't have time for. The first year was a wild ride, as I felt like a new teacher all over again. I'll admit it, as I waited to have my postconference with my principal and talk about state test scores, I was sweating. Then it happened: my test scores came back, and my students did just as well, *without any of the drilling, lecturing, or rote memorization*. More important, I didn't have behavior management issues anymore, attendance was up, and I loved what I was doing. My students were thriving and they were a part of a special community: our classroom.

The most magical moments and milestones can't be measured in a way that would satisfy a rubric. I can flip through my scrapbooks and tell you stories about my own children, tracing their development, but it is hard to pinpoint when my timid little girl turned into a confident young woman, learning two languages, saving money for a ten-day trip to France next summer. *There aren't numbers for this. There are stories.* We always joke about my son because he is either "on" or "off," and he seemingly learns things overnight.

He went from barely speaking to complete sentences. He didn't learn to tie his shoes until he really wanted a pair of Converse, no matter how much we made him practice, and then one day, he just did it. He taught himself how to solve a Rubik's Cube, but will become visibly distressed when made to do a word search. The fact is, every kiddo is different, and they are all dazzling when we learn to see them as people, not people-in-the-making.

So, I encourage you to measure SEL by the lives you touch, the families you help, and the inspiration that you can provide. The world is a very scary place—now, more than ever in my lifetime—but your classroom can be the caring kind, a world within a world, where students can become the best versions of themselves. They will love your caring classroom, and the best part is, so will you.

Works Cited

Britton, Dan, Jimmy Page, and Jon Gordon. *One Word That Will Change Your Life*. Hoboken, NJ: John Wiley & Sons, 2013. Print.

CASEL. "Competency Wheel." Web. 01 Jan. 2017.

CASEL. "Policy Recommendations." Web. 01 Jan. 2017.

CASEL. "What Is SEL?" Web. 02 Dec. 2016.

Castillo, Stephanie. "Fishing for Compliments is Actually a Power Move." *Medical Daily*. 13 Oct. 2015. Web. 18 June 2017.

Dweck, Carol S. *Mindset: The New Psychology of Success*. New York: Random House, 2006. Print.

Elmore, Tim. "The Five Greatest Predictors of Student Success." *Growing Leaders*. 11 Jan. 2013. Web. 23 Nov. 2016.

Emba, Christine. "Confirmed: Echo Chambers Exist on Social Media. So What Do We Do About Them?" *The Washington Post*. 14 July 2016. Web. 18 Feb. 2017.

Glatter, Hayley. "A Cartoon Gateway to Real-World Issues." *The Atlantic*. 29 Dec. 2016. Web. 16 Feb. 2017.

Heitner, Devorah. *Screenwise: Helping Kids Thrive (and Survive) in Their Digital World*. Brookline, MA: Bibliomotion, 2016. Print.

Kinlan, Carol A. "Failure to Launch and the Disorganized Teenager." *The MGH Clay Center for Young Healthy Minds*. 03 Mar. 2016. Web. 23 Nov. 2016.

Loehr, Peter. "Intentionally Creating a Consistent School Culture Focused on Principles of High Achievement." Manuscript draft, developing version, Jan. 2010.

National Education Association. "Indicators of Success: GPA and Noncognitive Skills." *Backgrounder*. Web.

National Middle School Association. *This We Believe: Keys to Educating Young Adolescents*. Westerville, OH: National Middle School Association, 2010. Print.

Pink, Daniel H. *Drive: The Surprising Truth About What Motivates Us*. New: Riverhead, 2009. Print.

"Social Justice Standards: The Teaching Tolerance Anti-bias Framework." *Learning for Justice – Diversity, Equity and Justice*. N.p., n.d. Web. 23 Oct. 2021.

Staff Picks: What We're Watching | *Learning for Justice – Diversity, Equity and Justice*. N.p., n.d. Web. 23 Oct. 2021.

Teaching Tolerance. "Social Justice Standards: The Teaching Tolerance Anti-Bias Framework." Web. 17 Feb. 2017.

TheRSAorg. "Brené Brown on Empathy." YouTube. 10 Dec. 2013. Web. 17 July 2017.

Wesson, Kenneth. "Learning & Memory: How Do We Remember and Why Do We Often Forget?" *Brain World Magazine.* 01 Mar. 2012. Web. 15 Feb. 2017.

Wiseman, Rosalind. *Queen Bees and Wannabes: Helping Your Daughter Survive Cliques, Gossip, Boyfriends, and Other Realities of Her Life.* New York: Three Rivers Press, 2009. Print.

Wright, Shelley. "Academic Teaching Doesn't Prepare Students for Life." *Powerful Learning Practice.* 07 Nov. 2013. Web. 23 Nov. 2016.

muscle

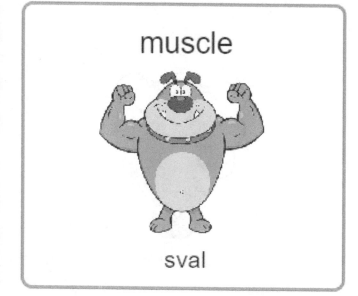

sval

evil

zlo

working

pracovní

gifts

dárek

ballon

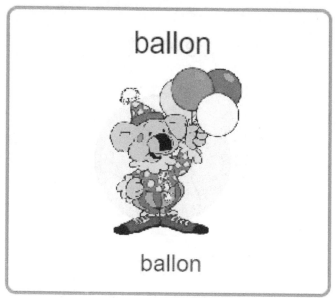

ballon

teeth

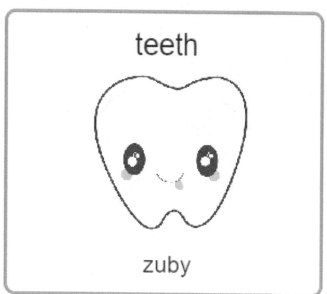

zuby

cow

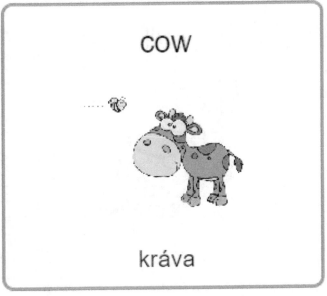

kráva

doll

panenka

mat

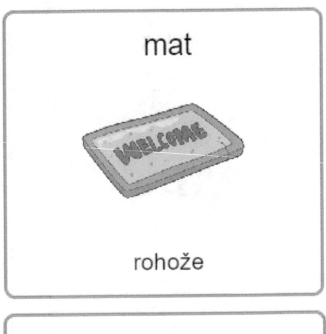

rohože

wheat

pšenice

good

dobrý

peanut

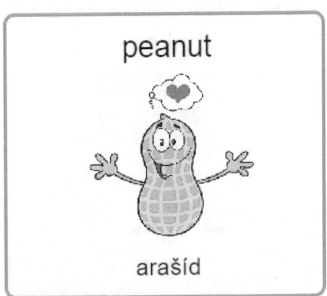

arašíd

throwing

házení

arm

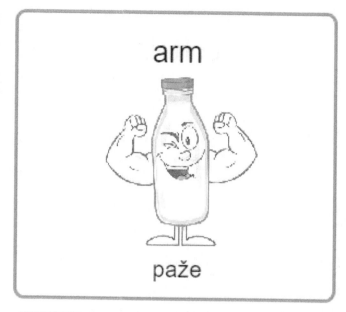

paže

volcano

sopka

wolf

vlk

massage

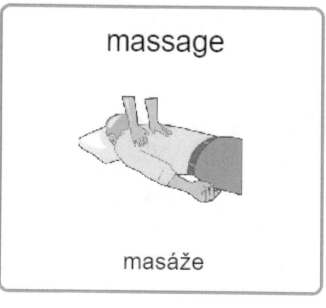

masáže

nap

zdřímnutí

curtain

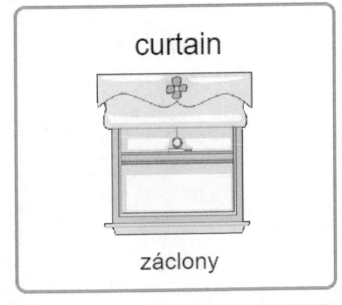

záclony

van

dodávka

dust

prach

rocks

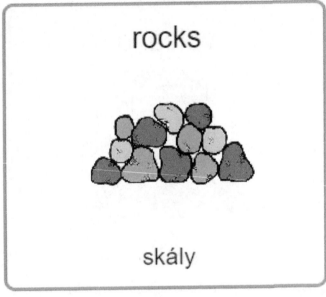

skály

shopping

nakupování

lemon

citrón

sinking

potopení

smile

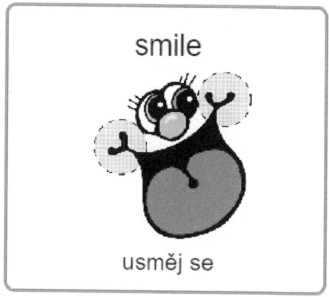

usměj se

grapefruit

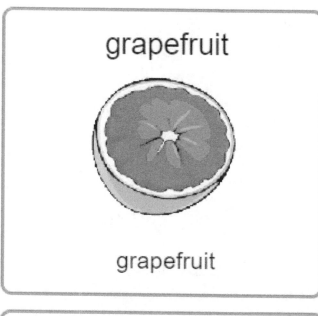

grapefruit

maid

služka

bread

chléb

bite

kousat

peach

broskev

yak

yak

puppy

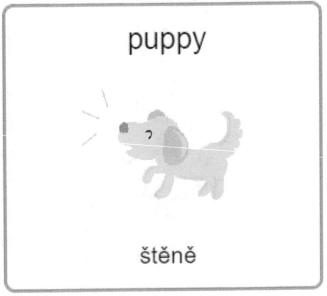

štěně

help

pomoc

rocket

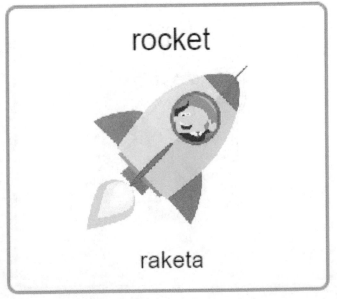

raketa

package

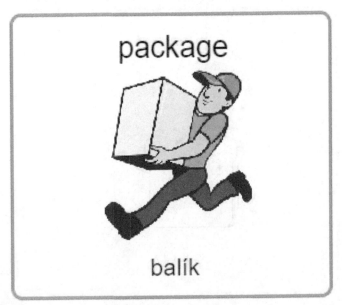

balík

hen

slepice

bell
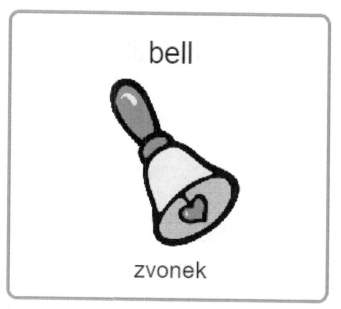
zvonek

jam
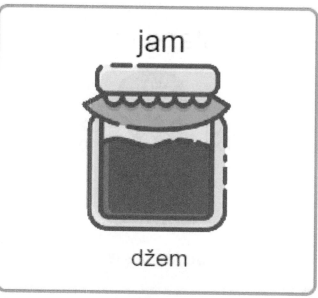
džem

play

hrát si

lion

lev

oven

trouba

windmill

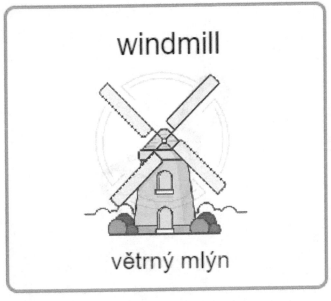

větrný mlýn

basketball

basketball

sailboat

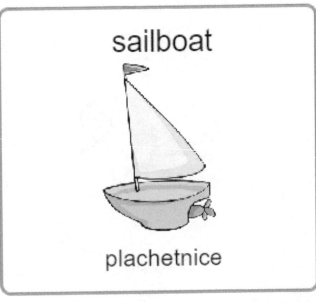

plachetnice

stand up

postav se

pair

párů

boots

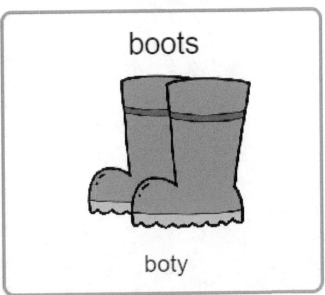

boty

fall

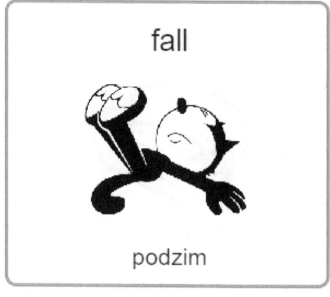

podzim

penguin

tučňák

three

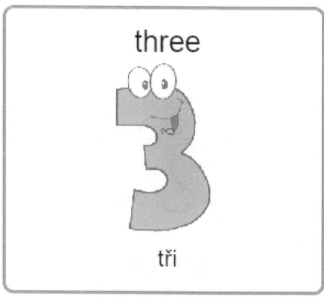

tři

quiz

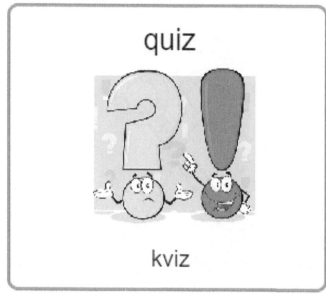

kviz

skunk

skunks

banana

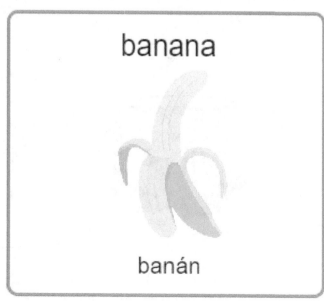

banán

quiet

klid

sofa

gauč

scissors

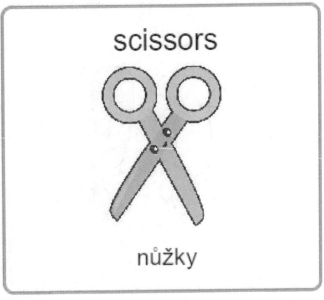

nůžky

wag

šprýmař

cup

pohár

elephant

slon

pelican
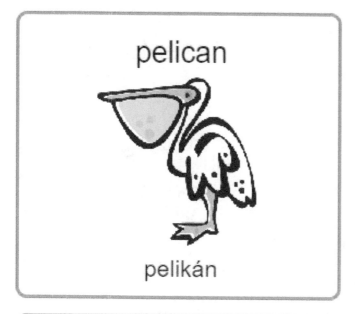
pelikán

broom
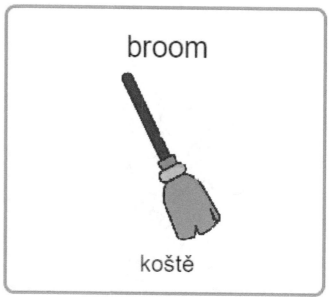
koště

vase
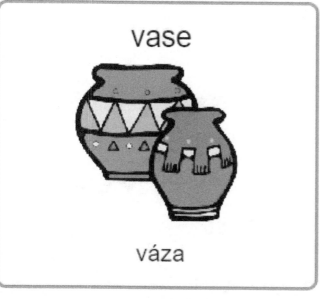
váza

diamond
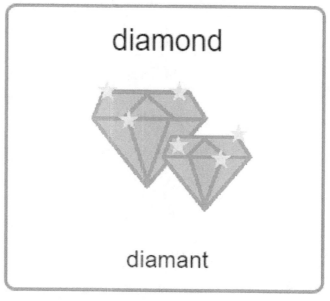
diamant

fitness

zdatnost

wash

praní

parrot

papoušek

presents

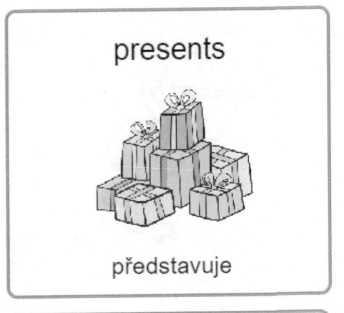

představuje

girl

dívka

point

bodů

hug

objetí

church

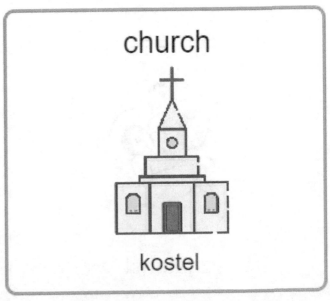

kostel

wet

mokré

monster

netvor

grape

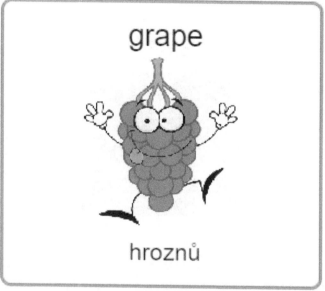

hroznů

serving

porce

knife

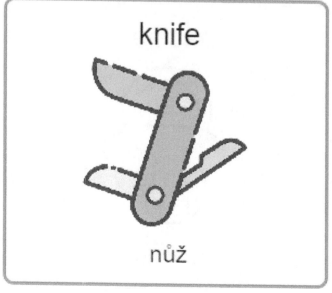

nůž

soccer

fotbal

lid

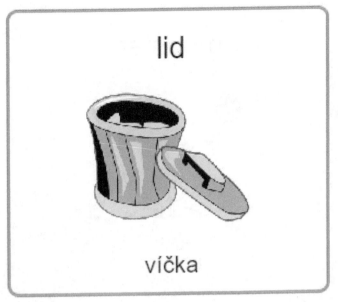

víčka

fence

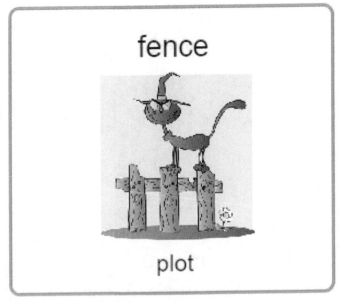

plot

bottle

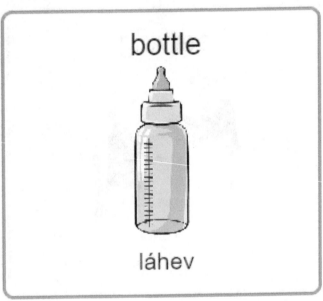

láhev

fireplace

krb

street

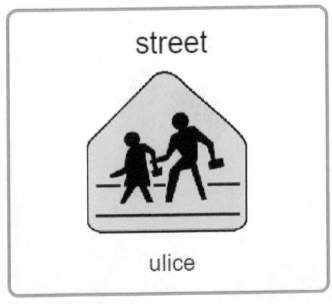

ulice

pacifier

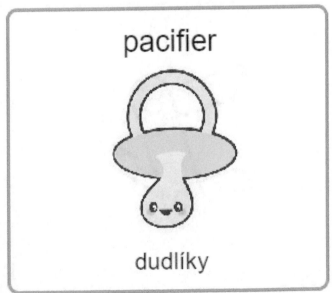

dudlíky

slicing

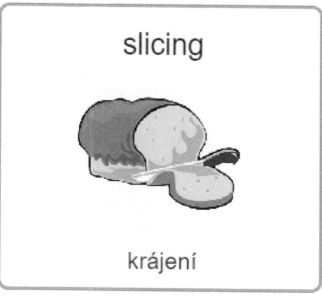

krájení

eight

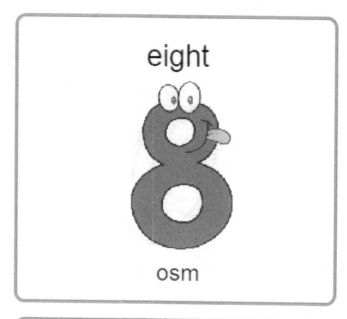

osm

fresh

čerstvý

pulling

tahání

bug

chyba

sleeping

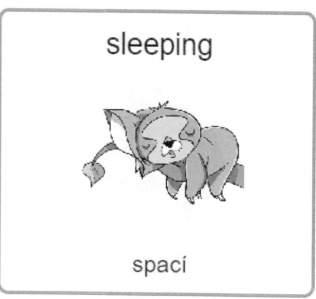

spací

nibble

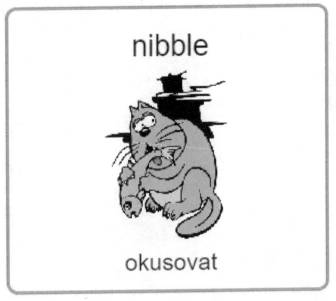

okusovat

koala

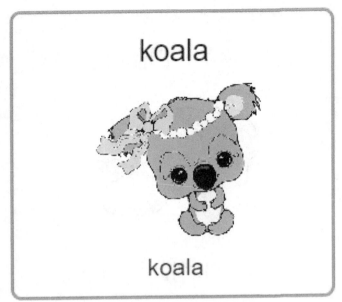

koala

mirror

zrcadlo

water

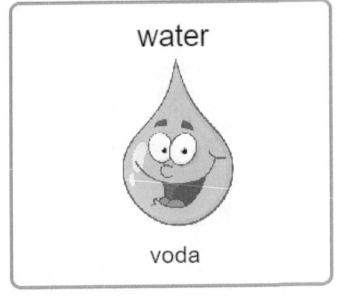

voda

raspberry

malina

red

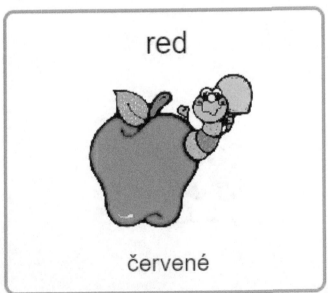

červené

gun

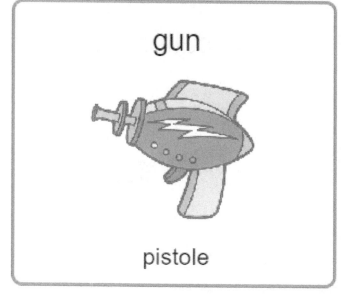

pistole

one

jeden

duck

kachna

baker

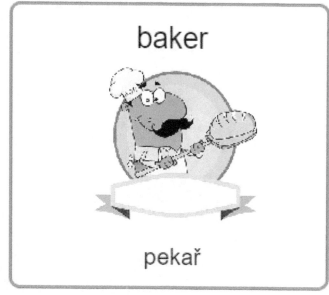

pekař

delivery

dodávka

loud

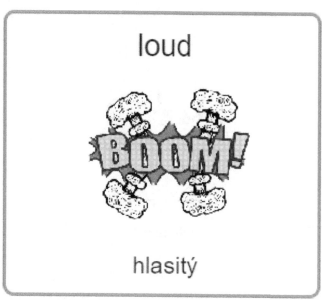

hlasitý

vulture

sup

cutter

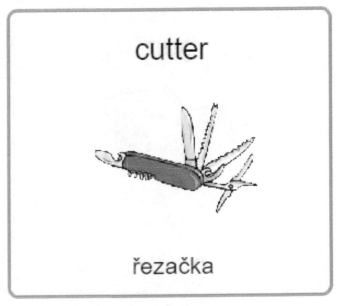

řezačka

pear

hrušky

apple

jablko

rooster

kohout

carrot

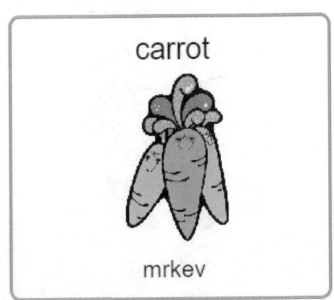

mrkev

piano

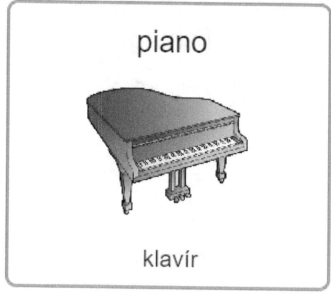

klavír

donut

koblihy

showering

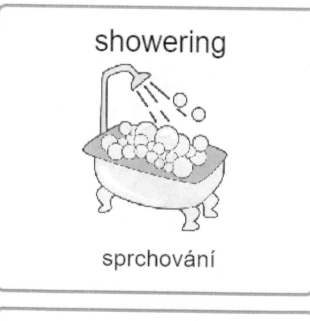

sprchování

guitar

kytara

bean

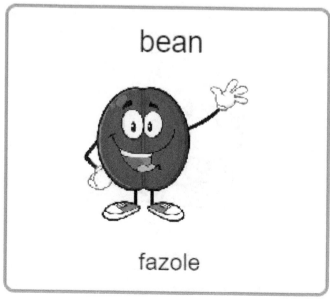

fazole

lantern

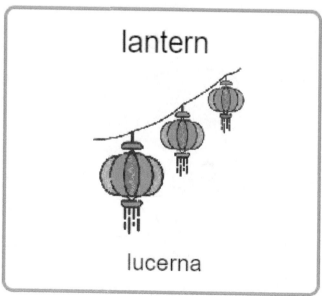

lucerna

cub

mládě

fishing

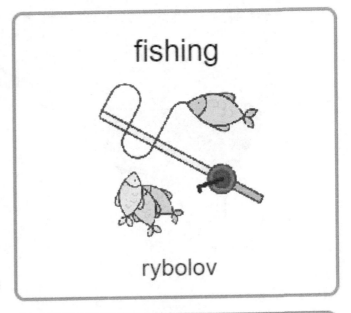

rybolov

gasoline

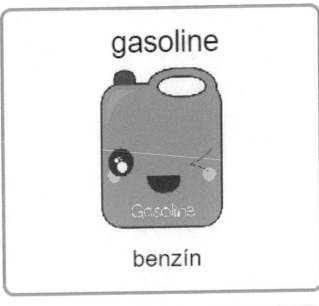

benzín

tiger

tygr

jug

džbán

frog

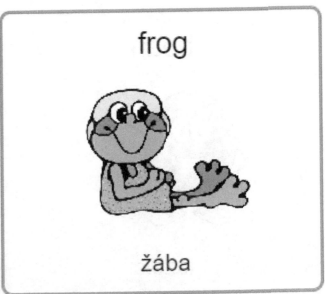

žába

wind

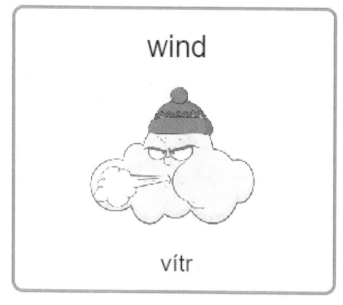

vítr

computer

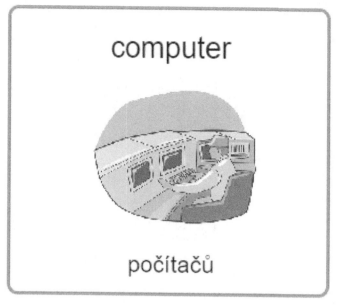

počítačů

gorilla

gorila

jump

skok

goodbye

ahoj

bored

znuděný

shirt

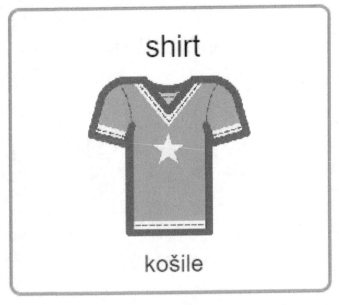

košile

fat

tlustý

star

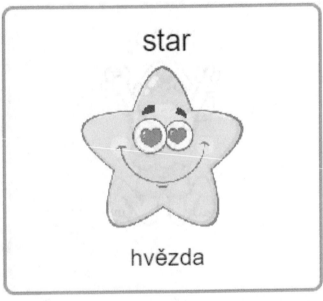

hvězda

cactus

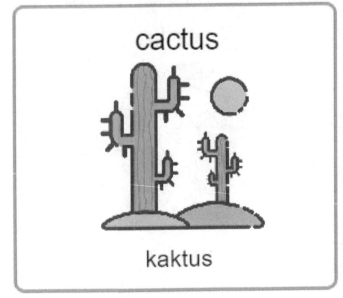

kaktus

turban

turban

glue

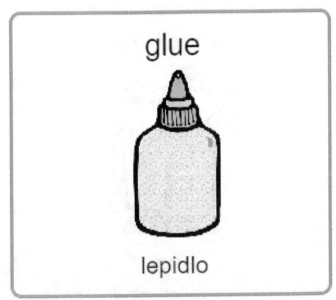

lepidlo

22

groundhog

groundhog

oyster

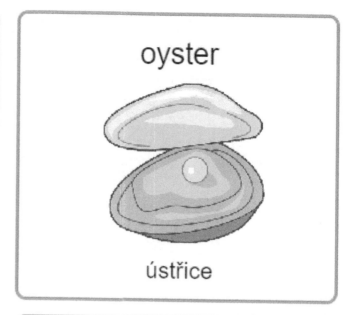

ústřice

father

otec

tombstone

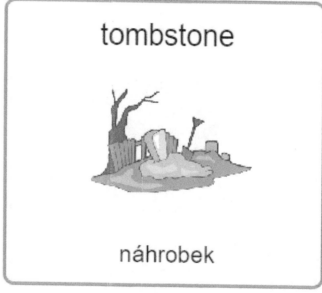

náhrobek

mermaid

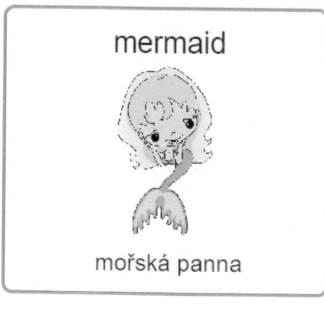

mořská panna

pirate

pirát

cheese

sýr

turnip

vodnice

museum

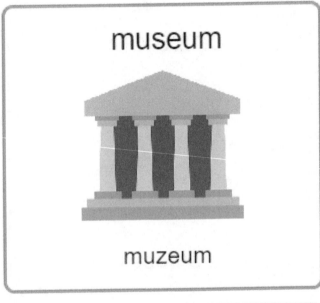

muzeum

handkerchief

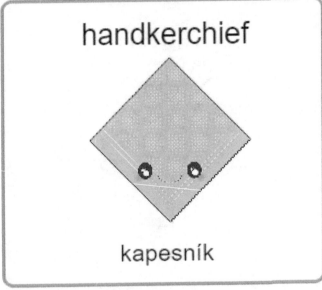

kapesník

arrow

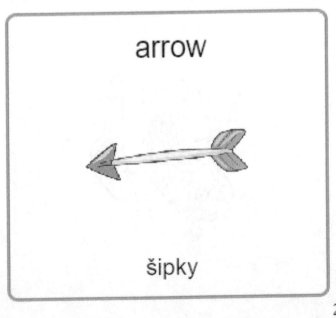

šipky

knitting

pletení

animals

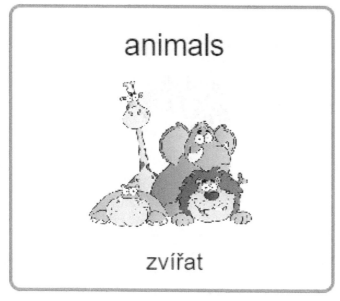

zvířat

spider

pavouk

avocado

avokádo

bird

pták

ears

uši

pig

prase

whale

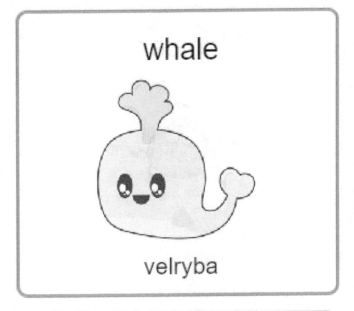

velryba

beach

pláž

pomegranate

granátové jablko

factory

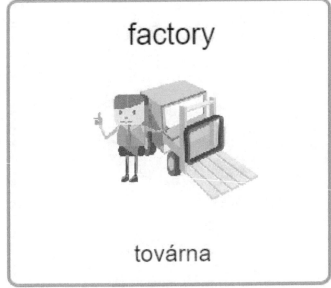

továrna

rat

krysa

ice

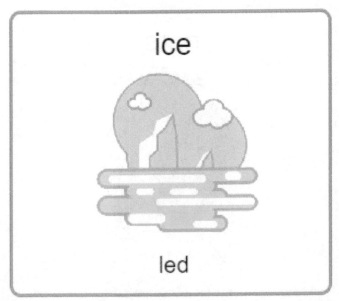

led

suitcase

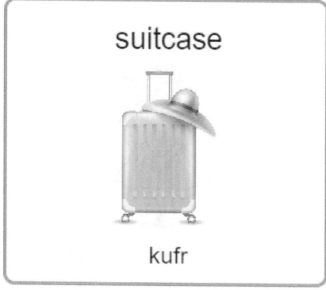

kufr

seven

sedm

scooter

skútry

pencil

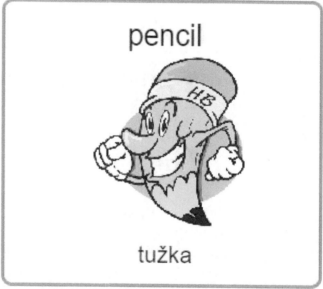

tužka

body

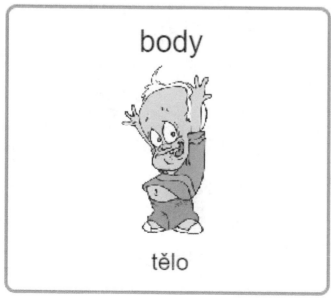

tělo

chair

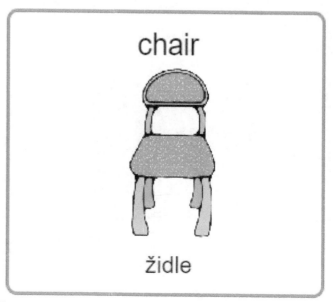

židle

cooking

vaření

dress

šaty

boxing

box

hexagon

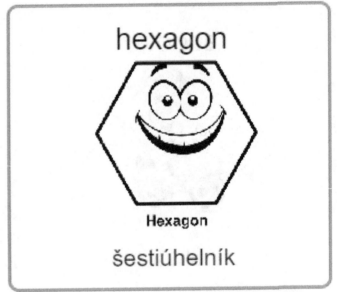

Hexagon

šestiúhelník

door

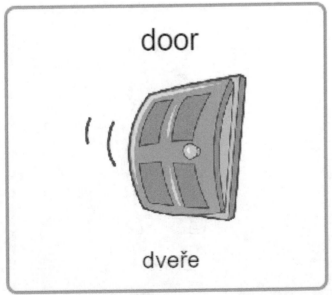

dveře

ink

inkousty

sweater

svetry

race

závod

trash

odpadky

sketch

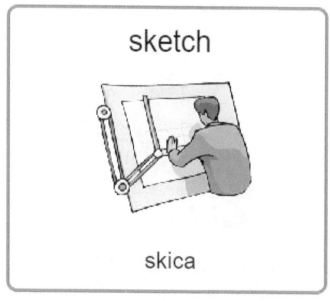

skica

aggressive

agresivní

baseball

baseball

head

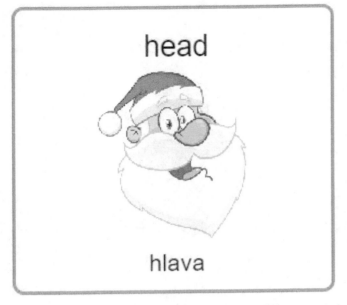

hlava

chimney

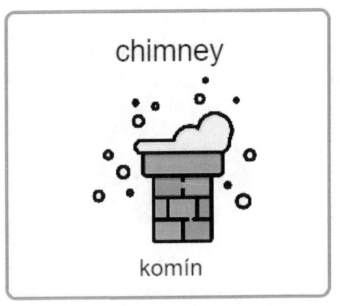

komín

tire

pneumatika

watermelon

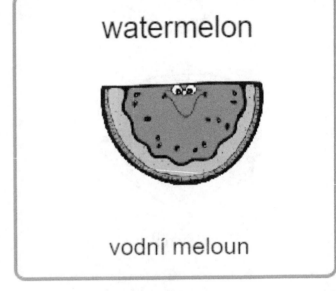

vodní meloun

desk

stoly

book

rezervovat

cookie

cookie

pillow

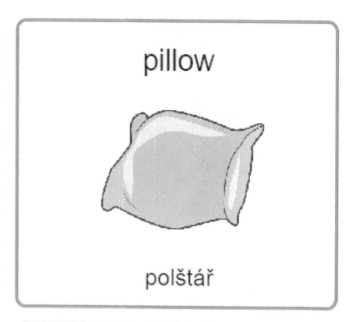

polštář

dance

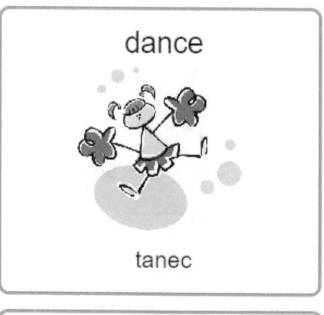

tanec

night

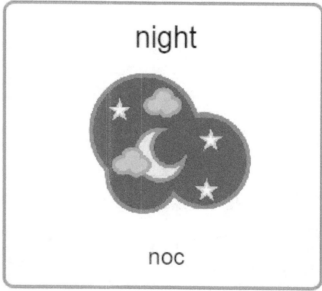

noc

paintbrush

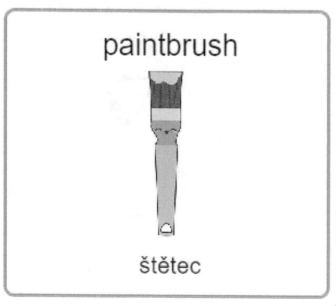

štětec

reindeer

sob

friend

příteli

signature

podpis

boat

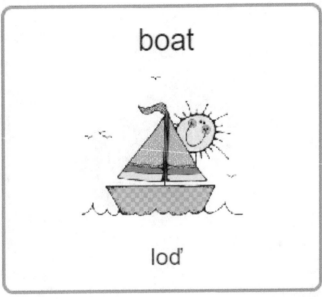

loď

plum

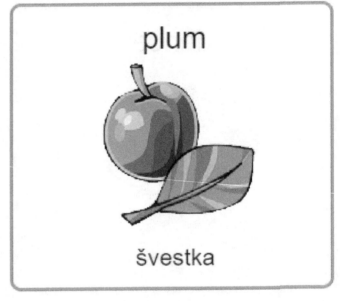

švestka

nut

ořechy

feeding

krmení

rabbit

králičí

insect

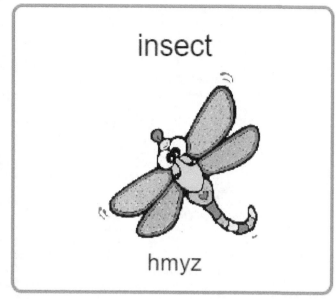

hmyz

christmas

vánoce

alphabet

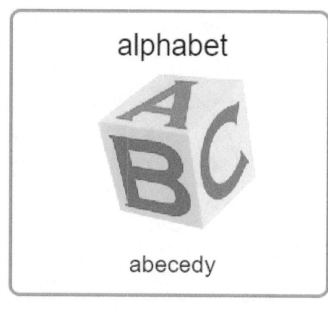

abecedy

bedroom

ložnice

podium

pódium

pizza

pizza

lamp

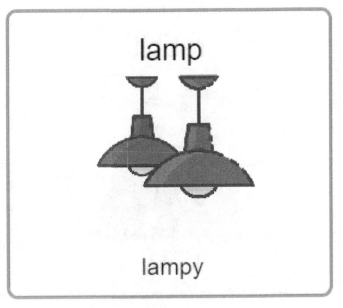

lampy

onion

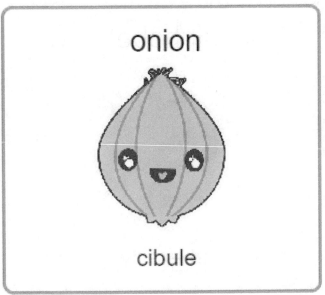

cibule

monkey

opice

cheetah

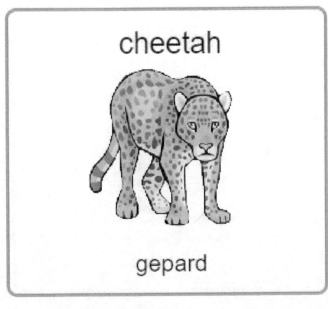

gepard

window

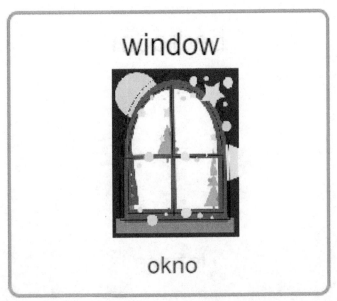

okno

mice

myši

tongue

jazyk

tray

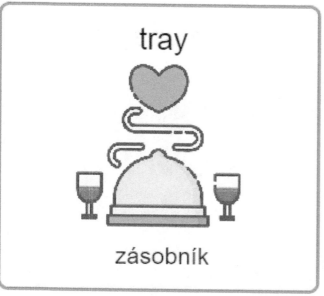

zásobník

children

děti

pan

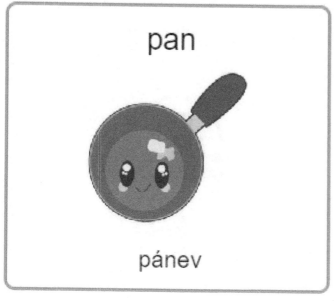

pánev

toy

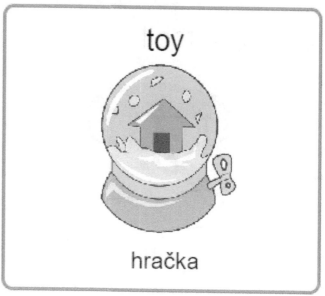

hračka

bone

kost

nine

devět

corn

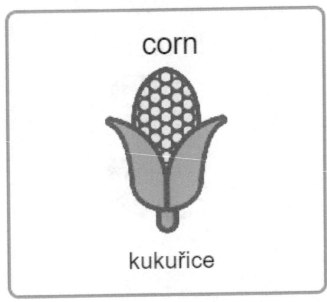

kukuřice

money

peníze

tooth

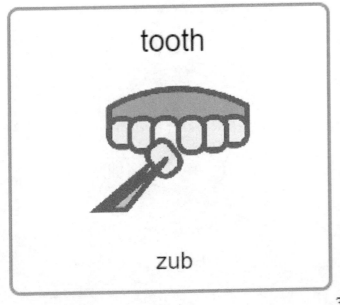

zub

driving

řízení

eyes

oko

queen

královna

coat

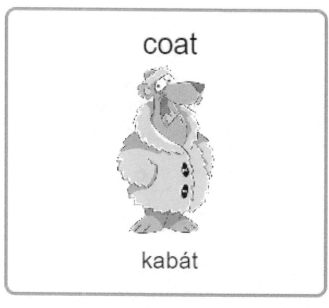

kabát

radio

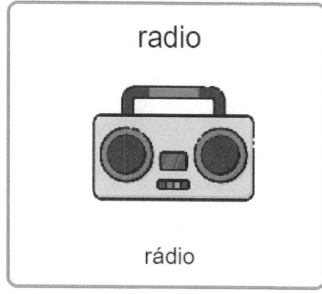

rádio

sick

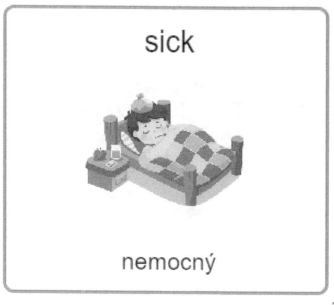

nemocný

artist

umělec

manager

manažer

cucumber

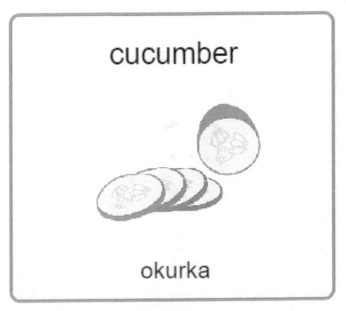

okurka

walrus

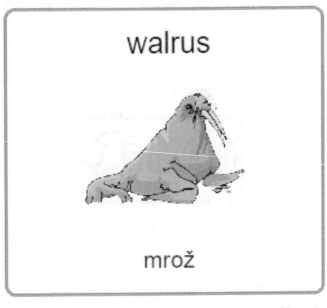

mrož

bib

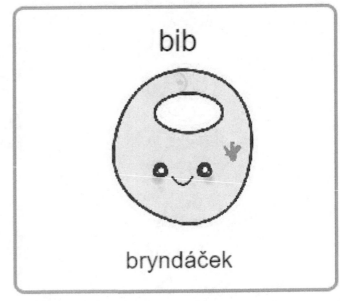

bryndáček

yarn

příze

team

tým

snake

had

hedgehog

ježek

backpack

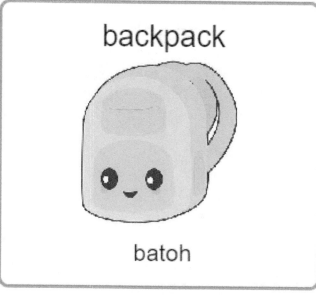

batoh

game

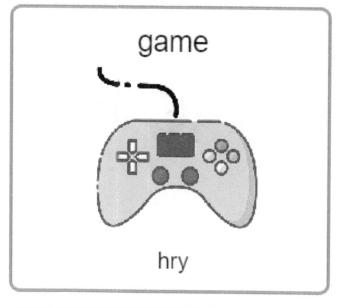

hry

ruler

pravítko

message

zpráva

rain

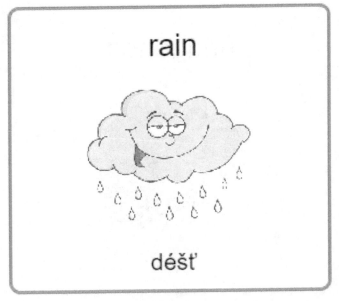

déšť

picture

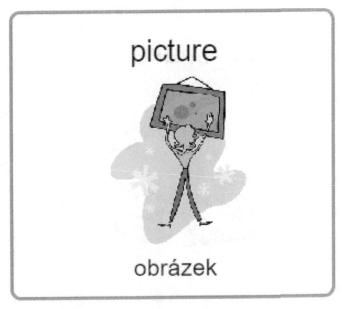

obrázek

juice

šťáva

teach

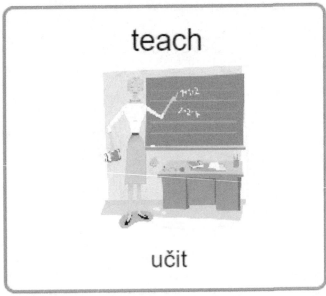

učit

witch

čarodějnice

ostrich

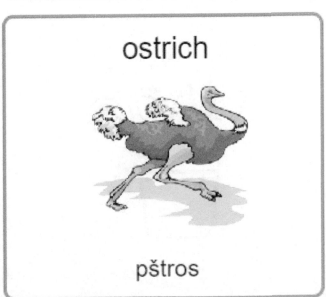

pštros

lipstick

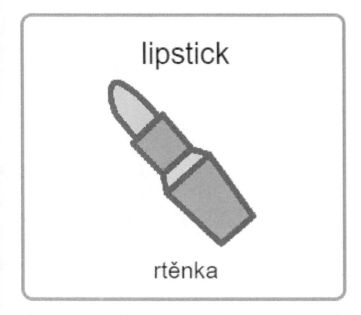

rtěnka

pot

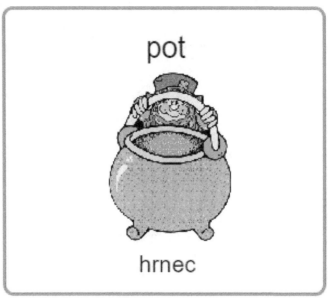

hrnec

pigeon

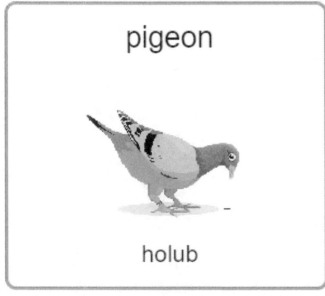

holub

chalkboard

tabule

carpenter

tesař

yogurt

jogurt

41

cowboy

kovboj

wallet

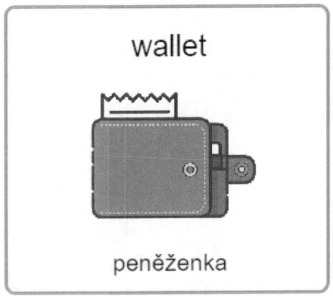

peněženka

run

běh

racket

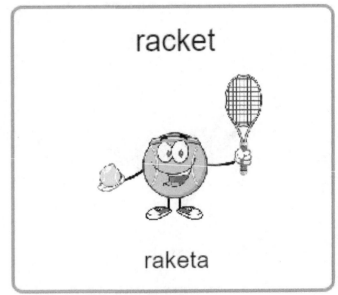

raketa

magician

kouzelník

bucket

kbelík

butterfly

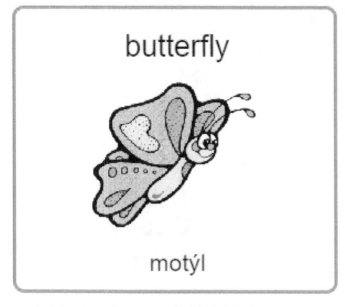

motýl

music

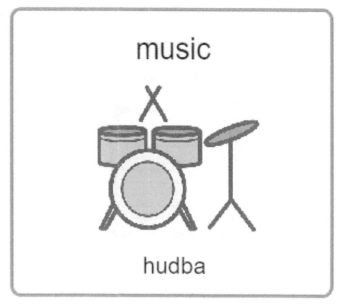

hudba

mare

kobyla

photographer

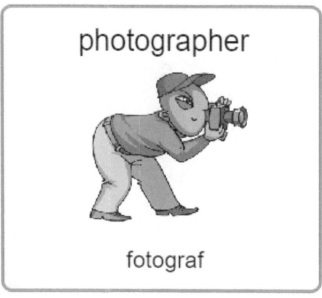

fotograf

pen

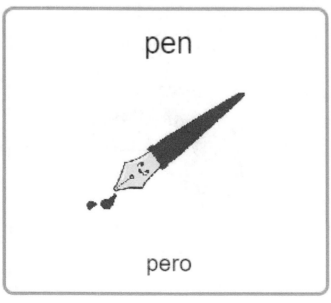

pero

candle

svíčky

paper

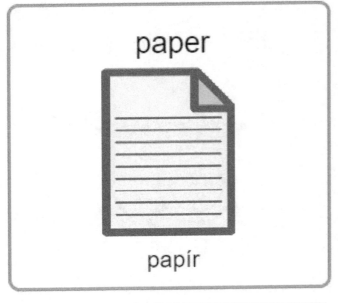

papír

paint

malovat

dig

kopat

shy

plachý

pearls

perly

rainbow

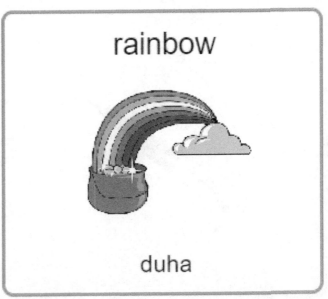

duha

laugh

smát se

oval

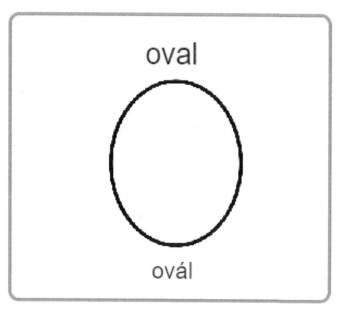

ovál

teacup

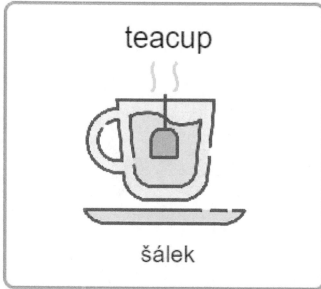

šálek

hand

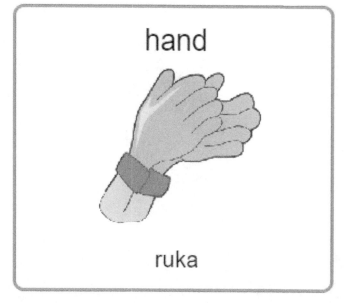

ruka

ground

přízemní

leaf

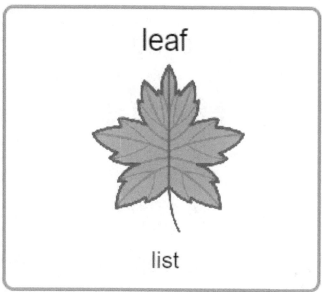

list

happy

šťastný

bicycle

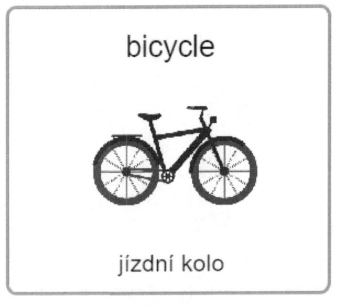

jízdní kolo

mole

krtek

barrow

kolečko

song

píseň

hurt

zranit

ladder

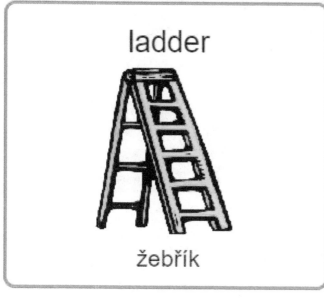

žebřík

meat

maso

musician

hudebník

island

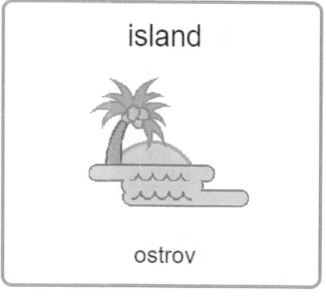

ostrov

turtle

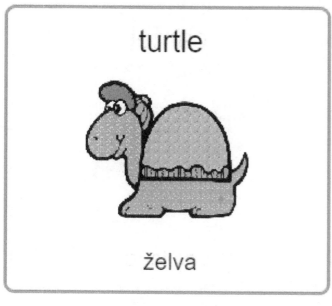

želva

truck

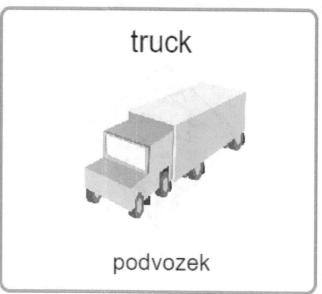

podvozek

jeep

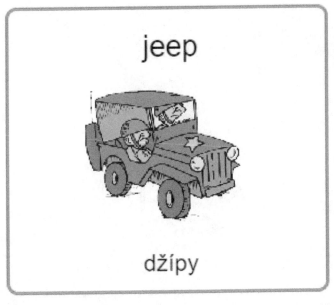

džípy

coffee

káva

microscope

mikroskop

sound

zvuk

kite

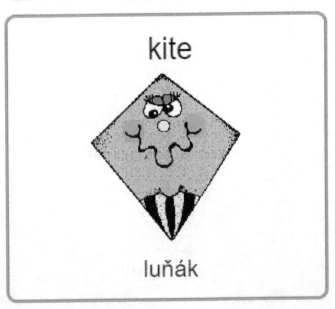

luňák

camel

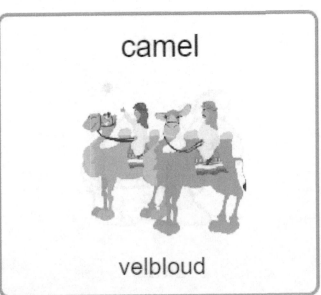

velbloud

castle

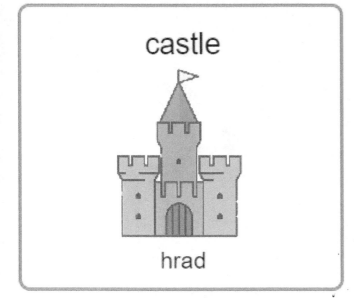

hrad

impress

zapůsobit

bowl

miska

stockings

punčochy

stinky

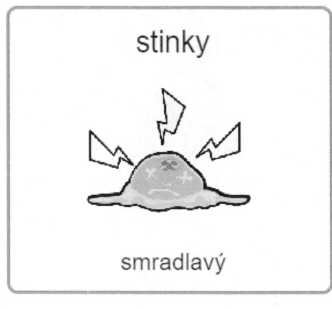

smradlavý

giraffe

žirafa

honey

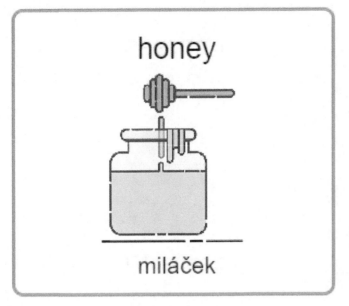

miláček

deer

jelen

violin

housle

tea

čaj

pudding

pudink

ketchup

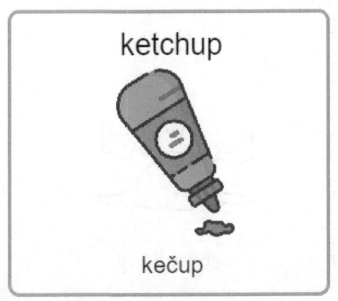

kečup

turkey

krocan

spatula

špachtle

golf

golf

shovel

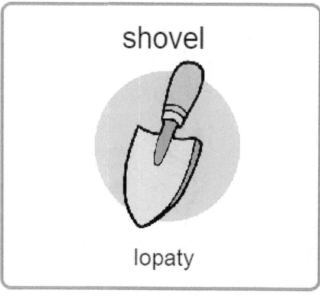

lopaty

pagoda

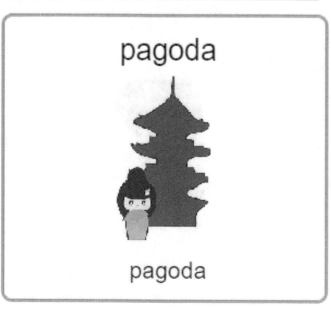

pagoda

pie

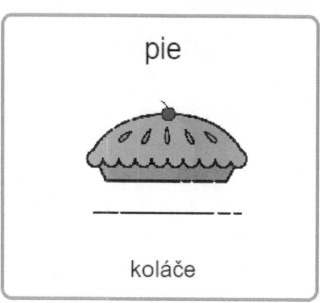

koláče

bag

taška

man

muž

sit

sedět

farmer

zemědělec

question

otázka

cry

plakat

kitten

kotě

seeds

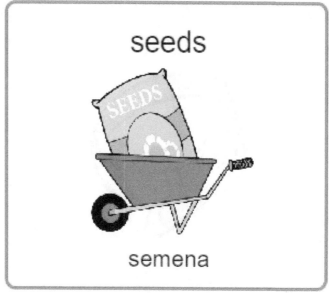

semena

bike

kolo

steak

steak

face

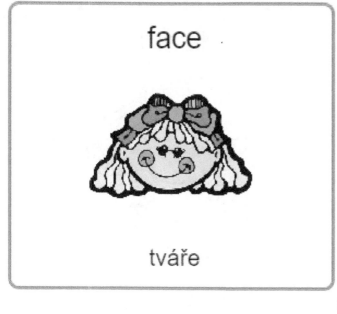

tváře

dice

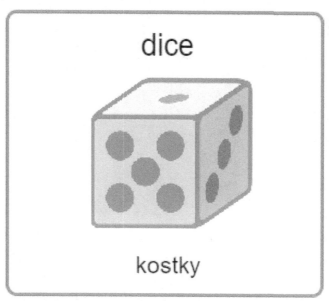

kostky

belt

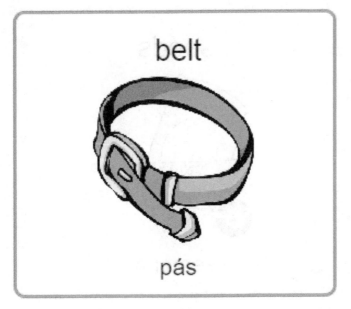

pás

kitchen

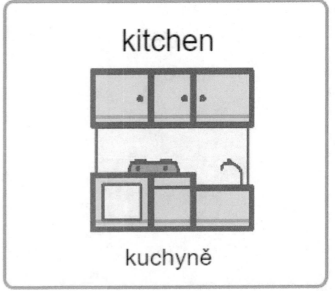

kuchyně

camera

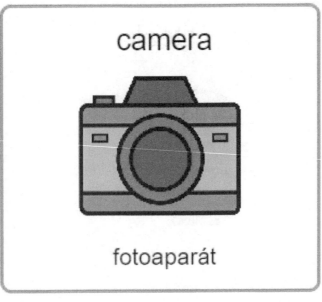

fotoaparát

sack

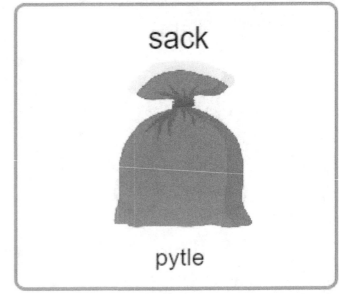

pytle

snail

hlemýžď

lizard

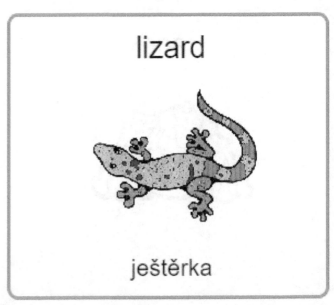

ještěrka

clam

škeble

plants

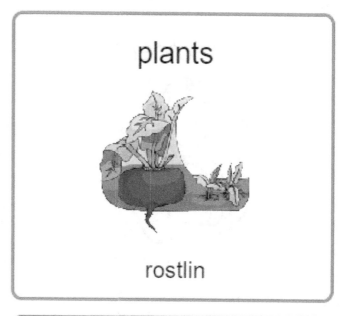

rostlin

baby

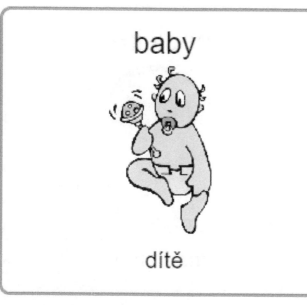

dítě

cafe

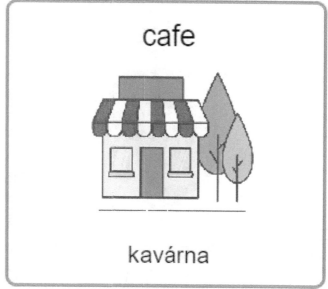

kavárna

vaccine

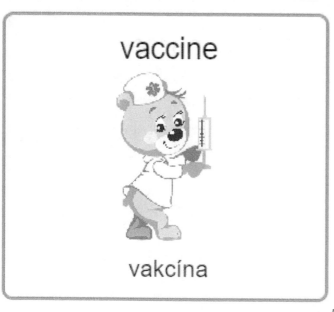

vakcína

shorts

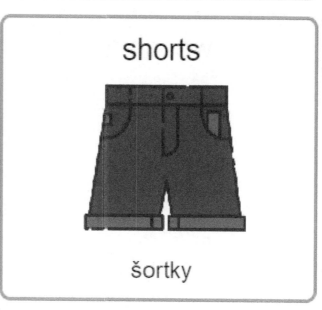

šortky

mother

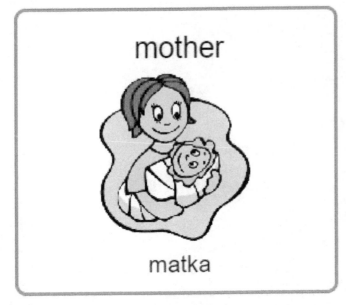

matka

alligator

aligátor

glass

brýle

medicine

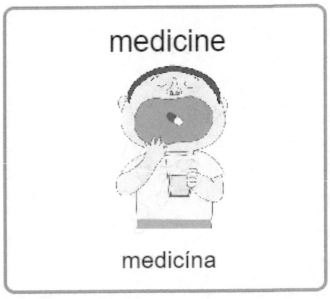

medicína

wedding

svatba

nurse

chůva

soup

polévka

rake

hrábě

prize

ceny

reading

čtení

joyful

rozradostněný

briefcase

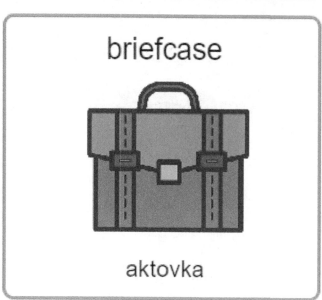

aktovka

brain

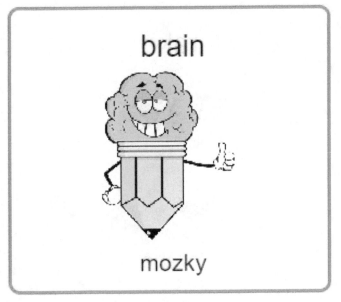

mozky

respect

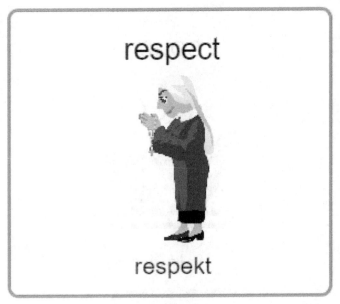

respekt

hippopotamus

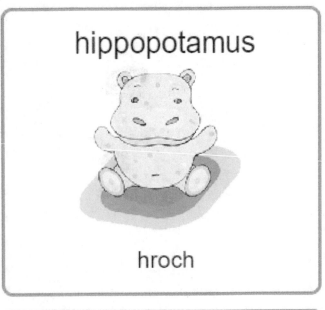

hroch

soil

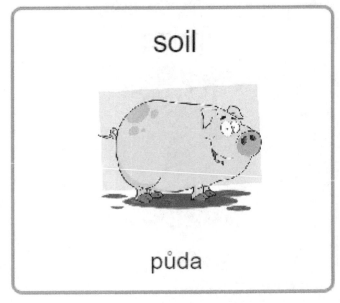

půda

tangerine

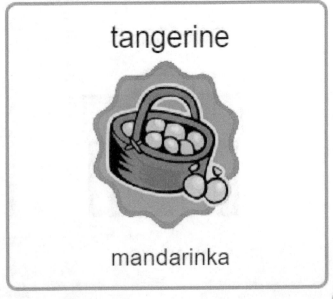

mandarinka

toad

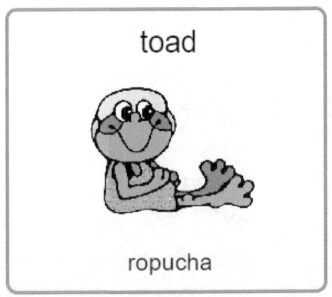

ropucha

ring

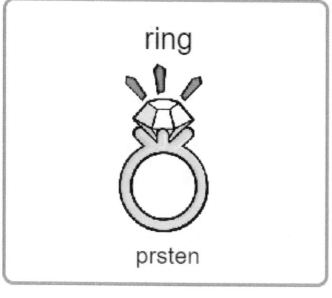

prsten

dock

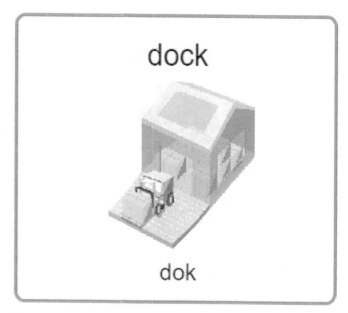

dok

map

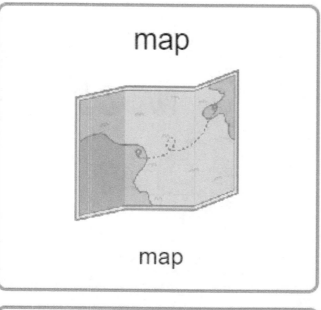

map

stove

kamna

hotel

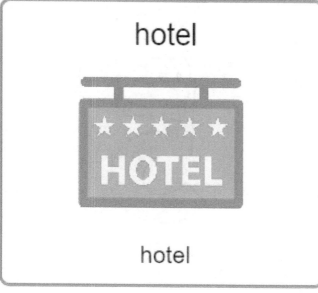

hotel

unicorn

jednorožec

ironing

žehlení

crab

krab

snowflake

sněhová vločka

ghost

duchové

mom

maminka

five

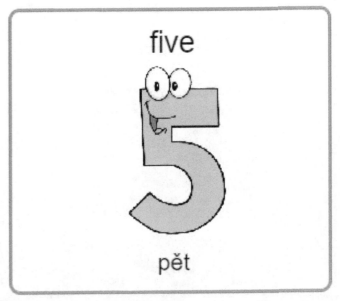

pět

telescope

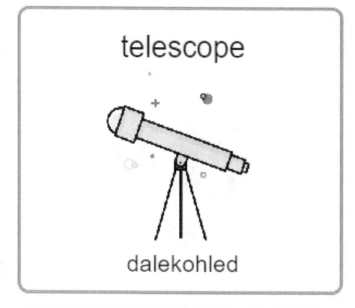

dalekohled

policeman

policista

mask

maska

drink

napít se

tomato

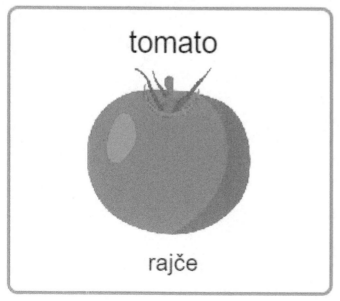

rajče

bathtub

vana

snow

sníh

bee

včela

kiwi

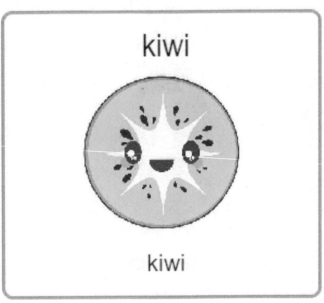

kiwi

strong

silný

love

milovat

syringe

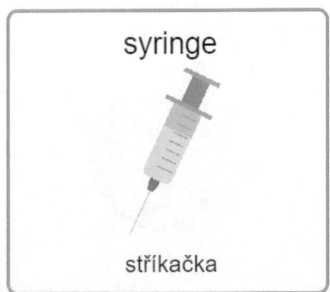

stříkačka

shoes

obuv

tail

ocas

leader

vedení

jacket

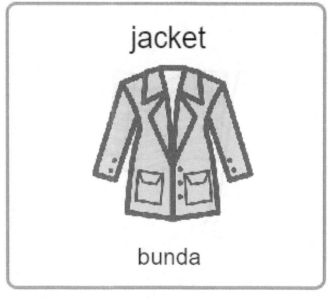

bunda

nose

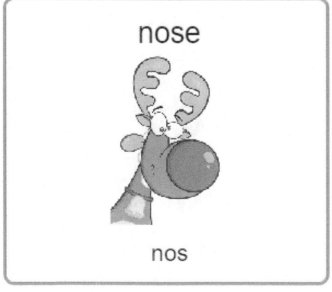

nos

mad

šílený

school

škola

bad

špatný

flag

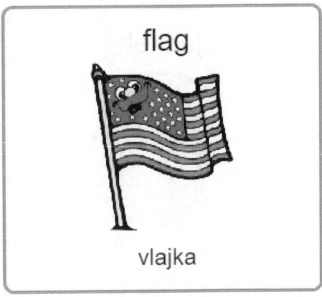

vlajka

fox

liška

bin

zásobník

ant

mravenec

neck

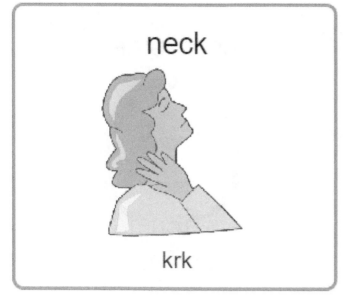

krk

hair

vlasy

tugging

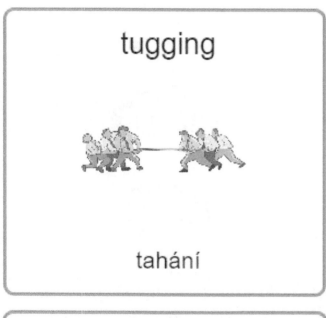

tahání

hopping

poskakování

grass

tráva

tame

krotit

wig

paruka

porcupine

dikobraz

celebrate

slavit

blender

mixér

peg

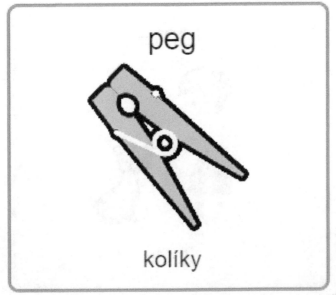

kolíky

dumbbells

činky

two

dva

eggplant

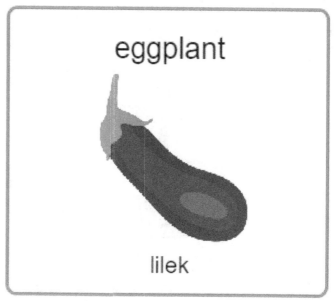

lilek

sheep

ovce

puddle

louže

leg

nohy

ham

šunka

beg

žebrat

looking

hledá

kneeling

klečící

science

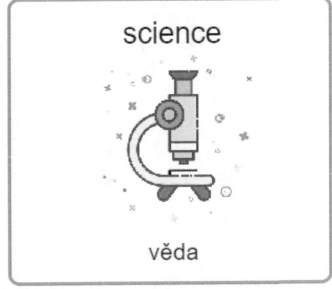

věda

powerful

silný

garden

zahrada

earth

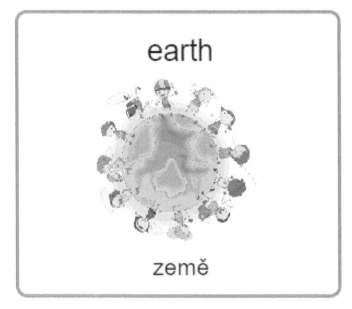

země

under

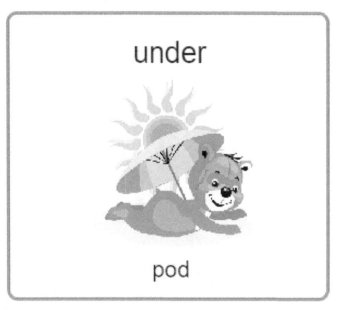

pod

barrel

hlaveň

squirrel

veverky

hill

kopec

crayons

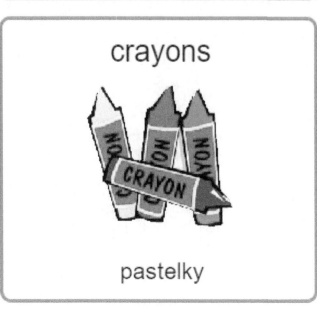

pastelky

riding

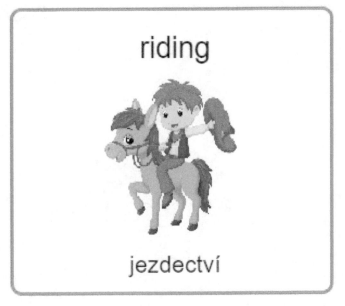

jezdectví

finger

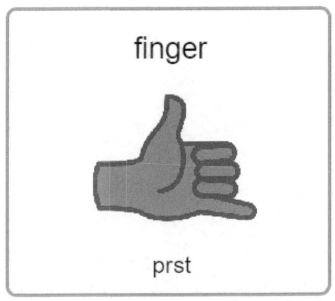

prst

sausage

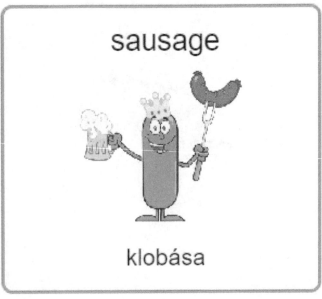

klobása

angel

anděl

knight

rytíř

hospital

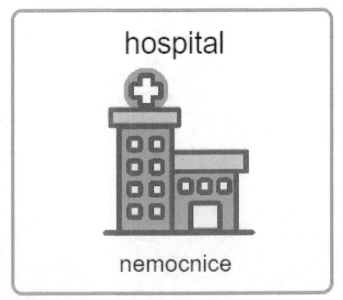

nemocnice

stylish

stylový

slippers

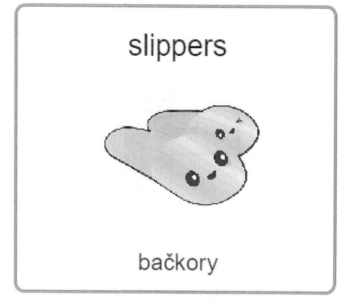

bačkory

hide

skrýt

rob

okrást

thumb

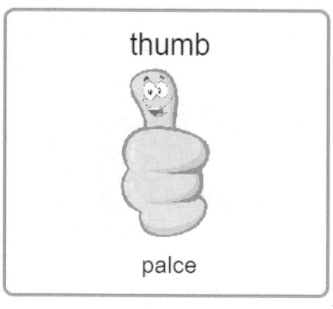

palce

pretty

pěkný

four

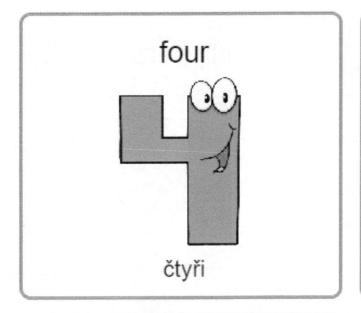

čtyři

zero

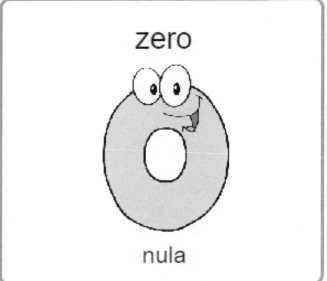

nula

engine

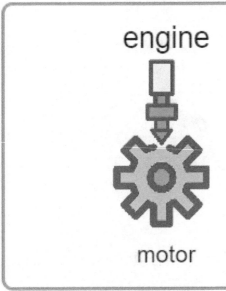

motor

dinner

večeře

calculator

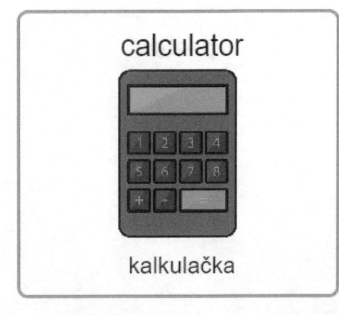

kalkulačka

mop

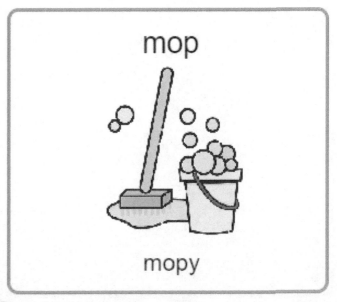

mopy

umbrella

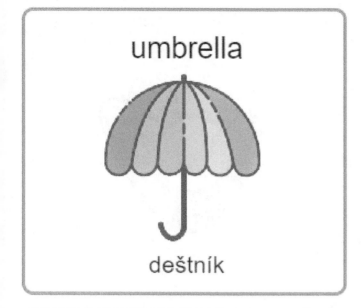

deštník

socks

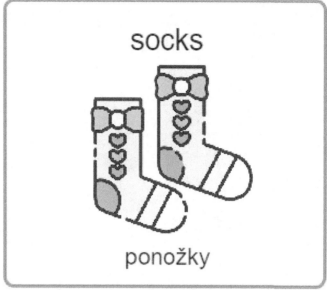

ponožky

boy

chlapec

medication

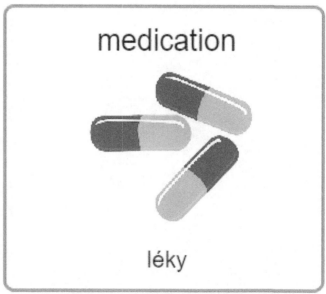

léky

collar

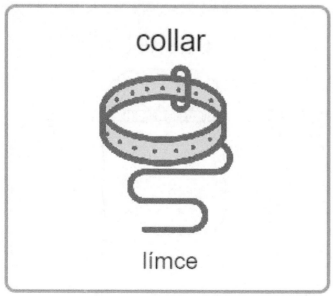

límce

whiskey

whisky

king

král

glove

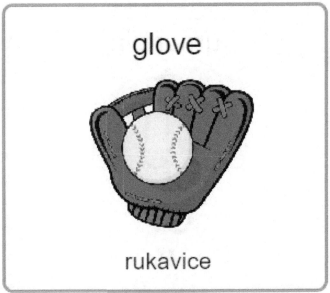

rukavice

box

box

mug

hrnky

acorn

žaludy

basket

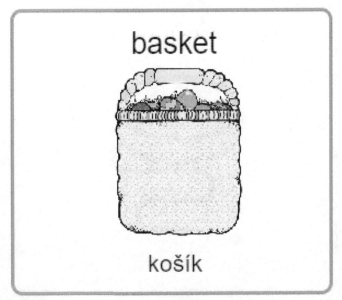

košík

tent

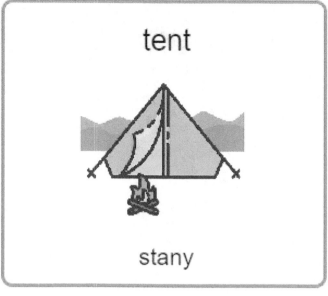

stany

chicken

kuře

smelling

vonící

day

den

goat

koza

chin

brada

meet

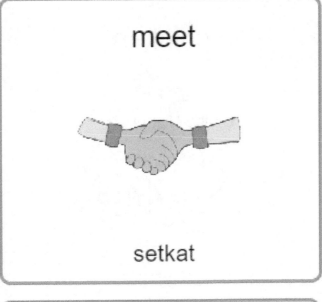

setkat

stop

stop

sleepy

ospalý

soda

soda

number

čísla

cat

kočka

kangaroo

klokan

fin

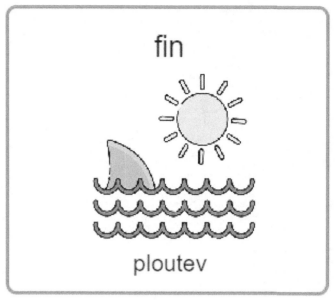

ploutev

microphone

mikrofon

bed

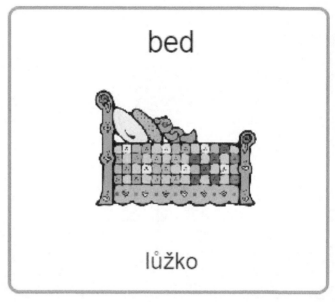

lůžko

hot

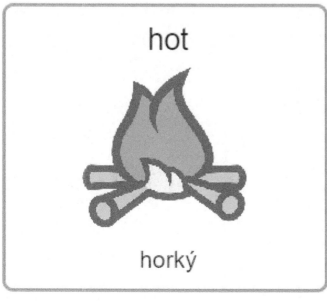

horký

zipper

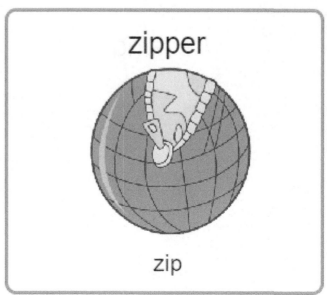

zip

toilet

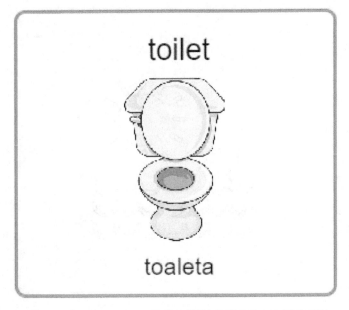

toaleta

win

vyhrát

wood

dřevo

hit

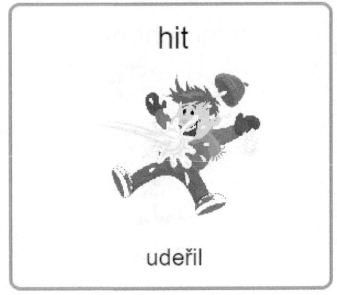

udeřil

dressing

obvaz

airplane

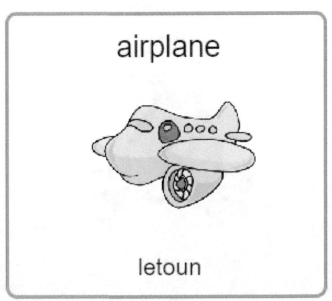

letoun

dad

táto

tree

strom

scary

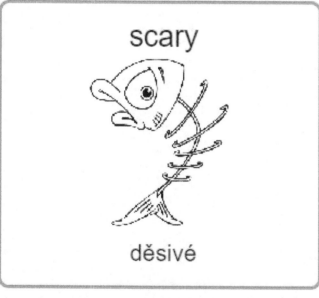

děsivé

zebra

zebra

shark

žralok

farm

hospodařit

mouth

pusa

carpet

koberec

couch

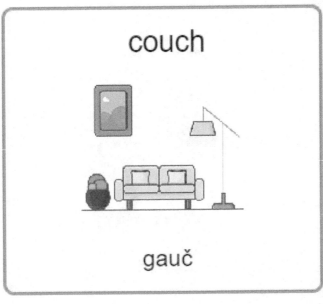

gauč

towel

ručník

name

název

salad

salát

shelter

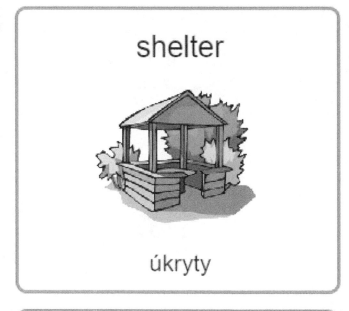

úkryty

ice cream

zmrzlina

swan

labuť

iguana

leguán

eat

jíst

dirt

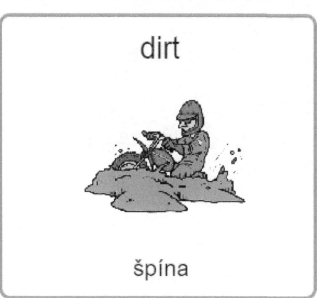

špína

proud

hrdý

palm

dlaň

news

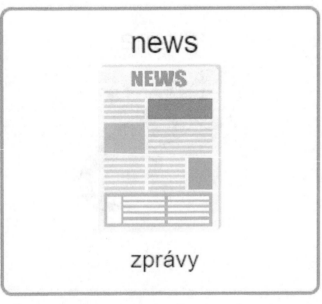

zprávy

barber

holič

plane

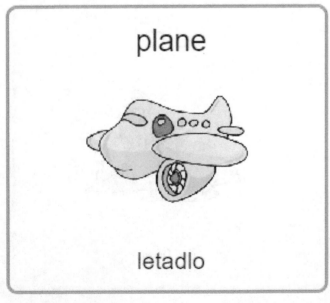

letadlo

drawing

výkres

strawberry

jahoda

hockey

hokej

decrease

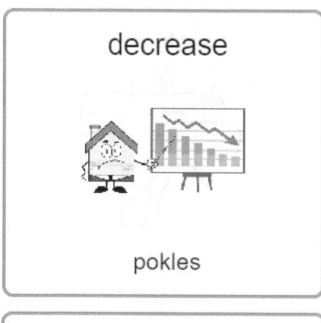

pokles

ten

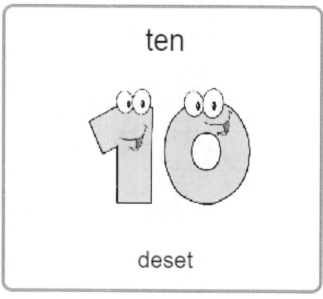

deset

fire

oheň

bridge

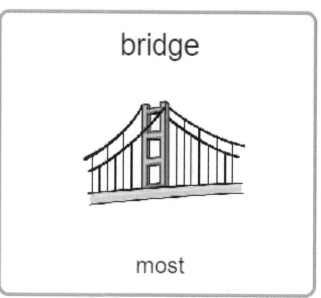

most

mushroom

houba

potato

brambor

lightbulb

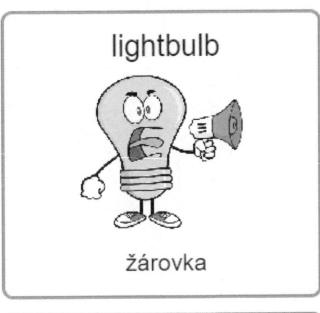

žárovka

letter

dopis

chef

šéfkuchař

rug

koberce

unhappy

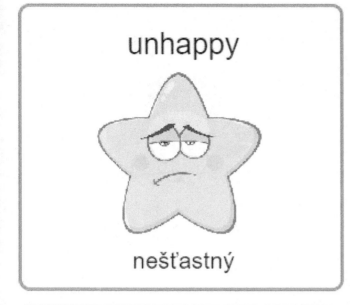

nešťastný

singing

zpěv

cherry

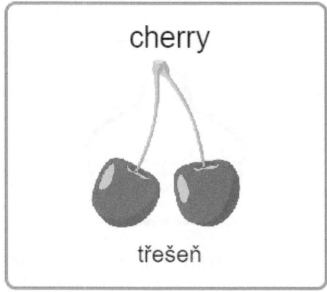

třešeň

sun

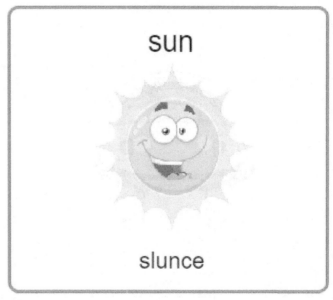

slunce

igloo

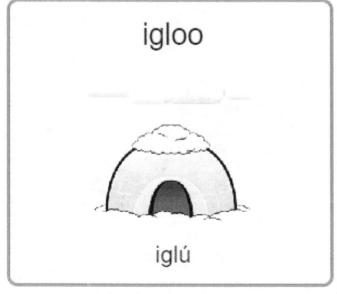

iglú

flower

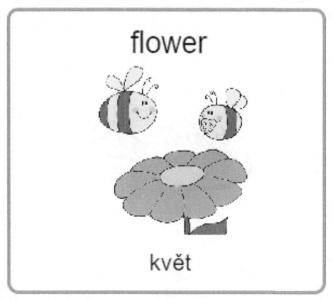

květ

wake up

vzbudit

broccoli

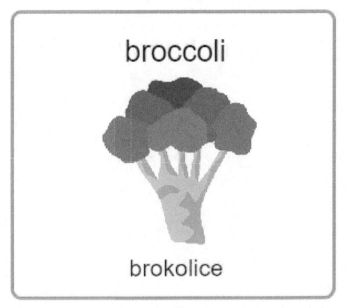

brokolice

car

auto

necklace

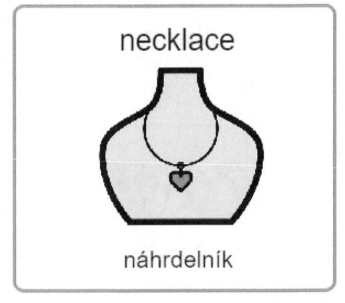

náhrdelník

comb

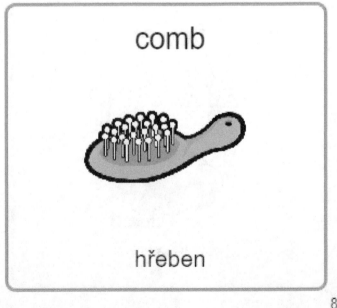

hřeben

walk

procházka

thunder

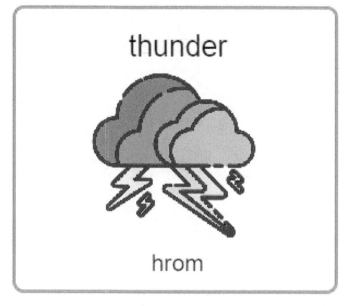

hrom

cot

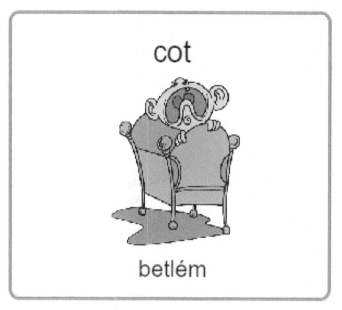

betlém

compass

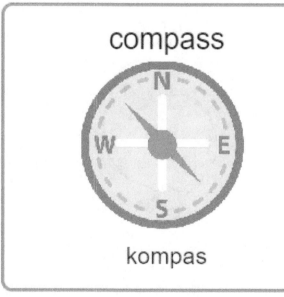

kompas

nest

hnízdo

waiter

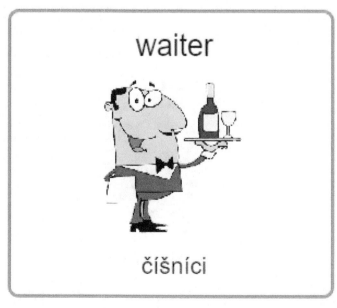

číšníci

friendly

přátelský

quail

křepelka

pajamas

pyžama

hat

čepice

chick

kuřat

fly

mouchy

angry

rozzlobený

peas

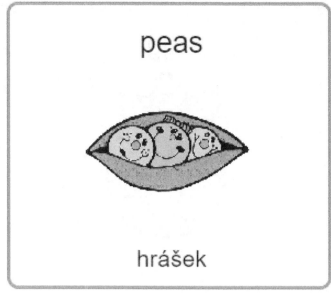

hrášek

delicious

lahodné

teapot

konvice na čaj

dog

pes

kids

děti

clean

čistý

him

mu

egg
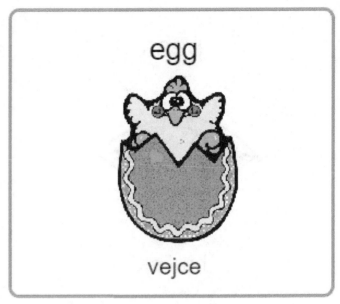
vejce

beard
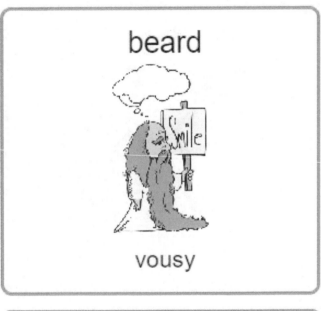
vousy

vest
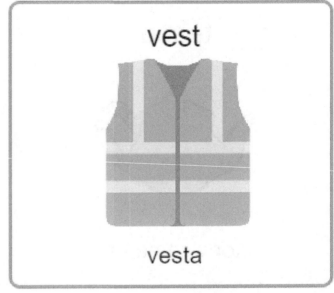
vesta

party

večírek

studying

studovat

eagle

orel

quilt

deky

politician

politik

jogging

běhání

wreath

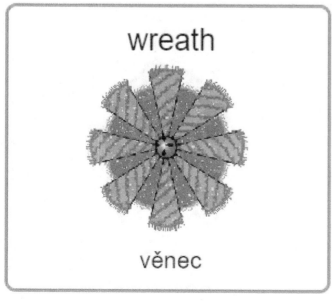

věnec

forbid

zakázat

noodles

nudle

ax

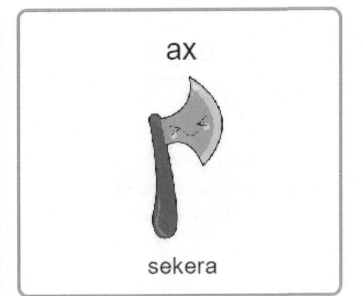

sekera

worm

červ

cute

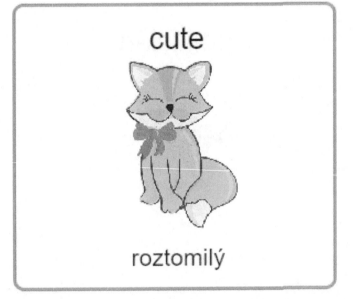

roztomilý

house

dům

clap

tleskat

open

otevřeno

hip

kyčle

octopus

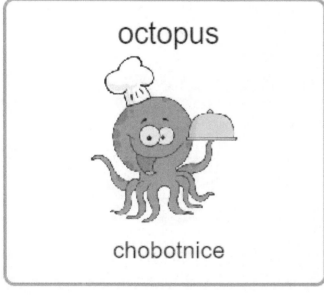

chobotnice

blood

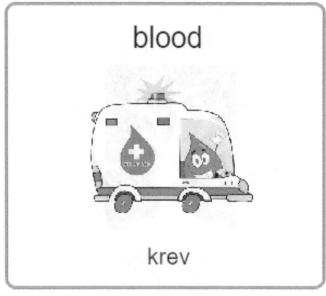

krev

boar

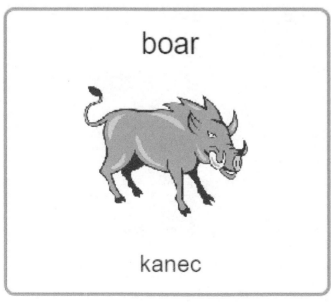

kanec

math

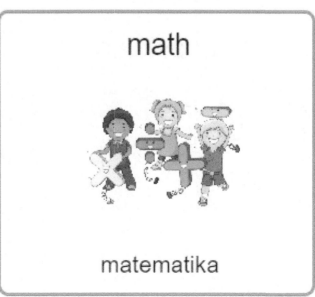

matematika

skirt

sukně

pineapple

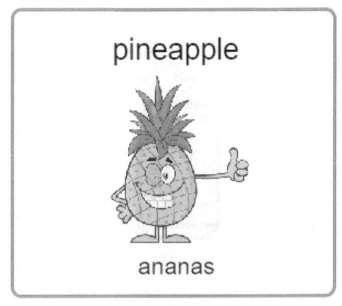

ananas

autumn

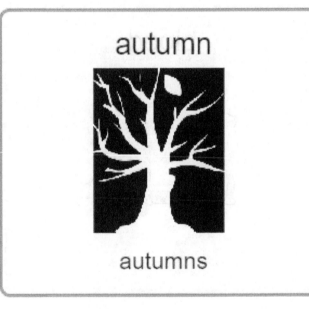

autumns

six

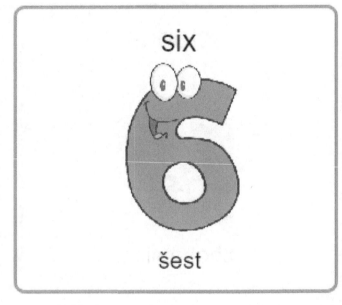

šest

popsicles

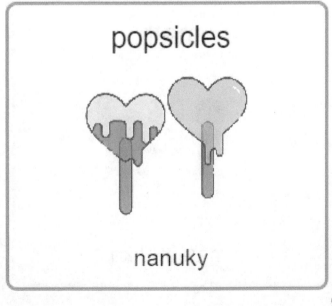

nanuky

bear

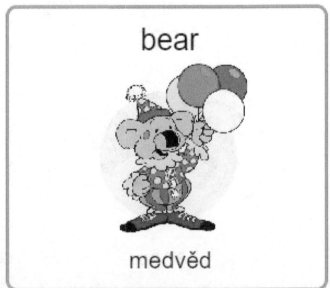

medvěd

moon

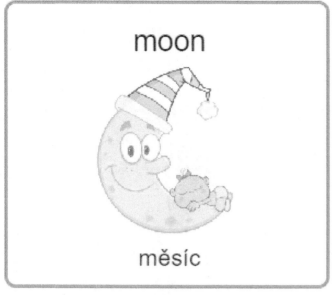

měsíc

family

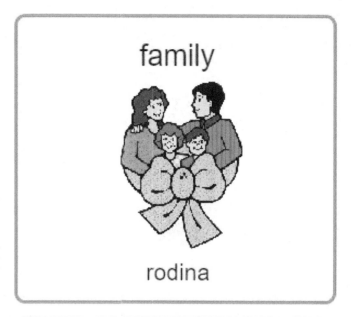

rodina

wiping

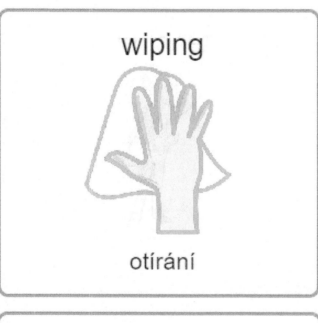

otírání

cage

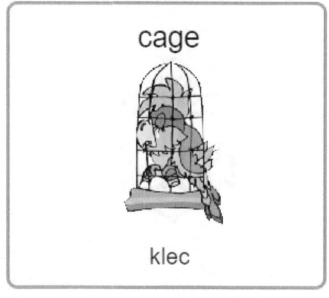

klec

cake

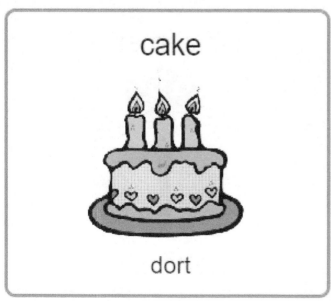

dort

chocolate

čokoláda

butcher

řezník

chili

chilli

anchor

kotva

teacher

učitel

ball

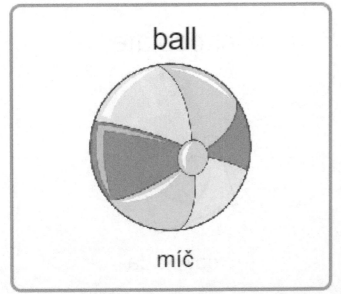

míč

hammer

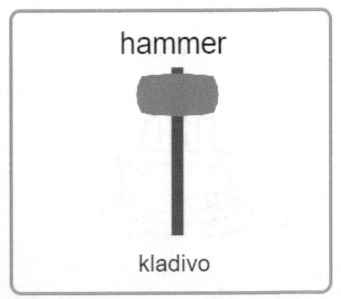

kladivo

summer

letní

helmet

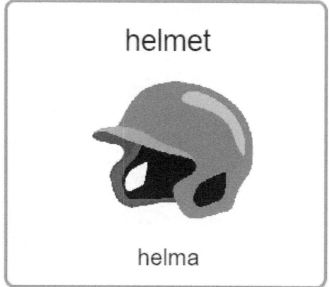

helma

clock

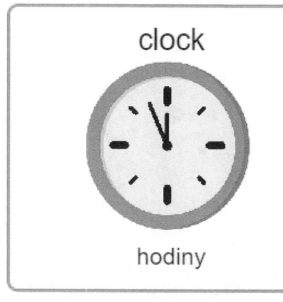

hodiny

owl

sova

torch

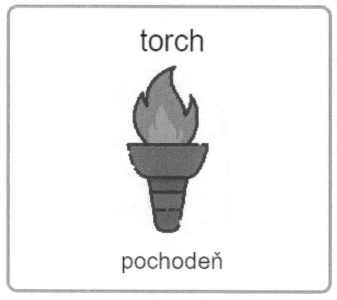

pochodeň

coconut

kokos

doctor

doktor

stick

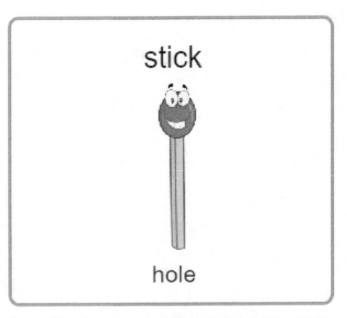

hole

utensils

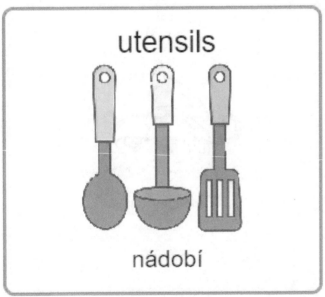

nádobí

orange

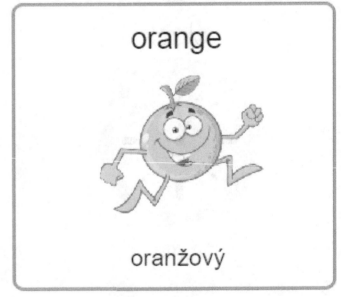

oranžový

sandwich

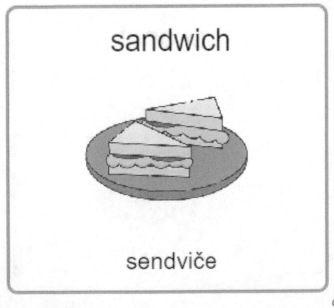

sendviče

big

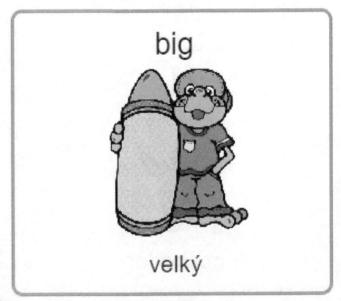

velký

candy

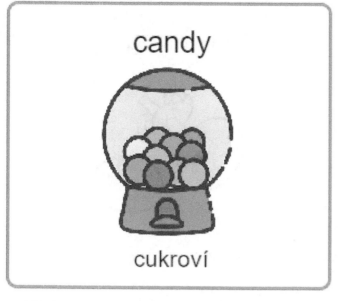

cukroví

pin

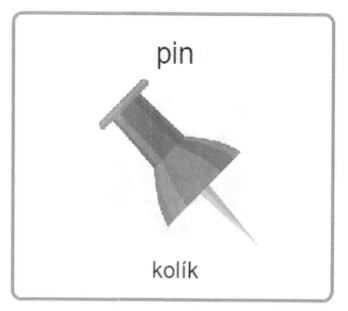

kolík

shoulder

rameno

rose

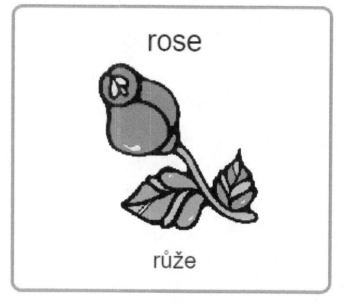

růže

brick

cihlový

vegetable

zelenina

panda

panda

earring

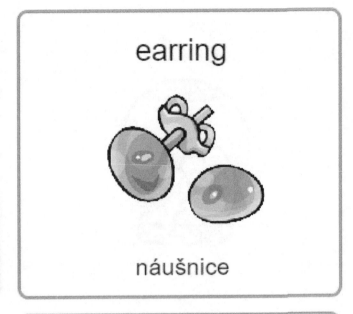

náušnice

morning

ráno

bomb

bomby

up

nahoru

tuxedo

smoking

hello

ahoj

enjoy

užívat si

dolphin

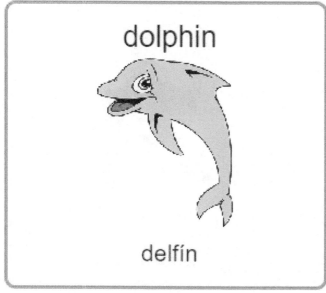

delfín

elbow

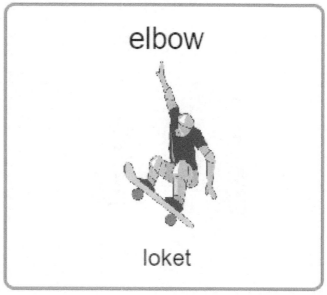

loket

cab

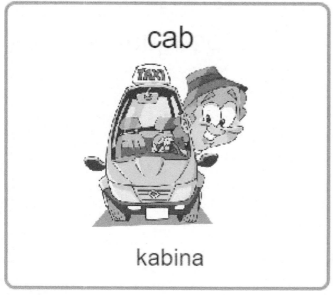

kabina

lotus

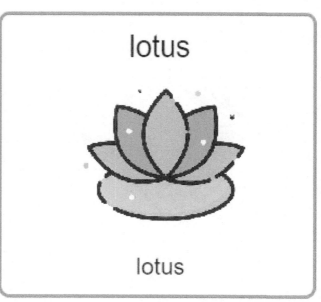

lotus

circle

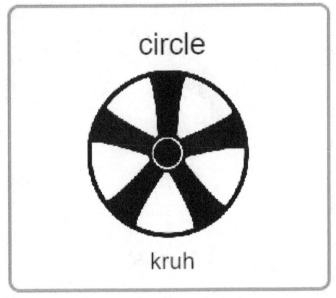

kruh

milk

mléko

bookshelf

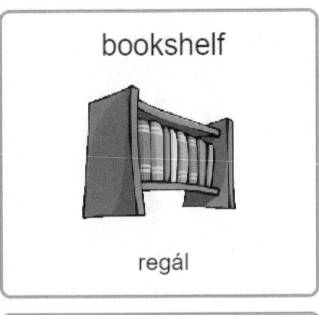

regál

writing

psaní

horse

kůň

bouquet

kytice

swimming

plavání

sad

smutný

mountains

hory

toddler

batolata

fish

ryba

princess

princezna

drum

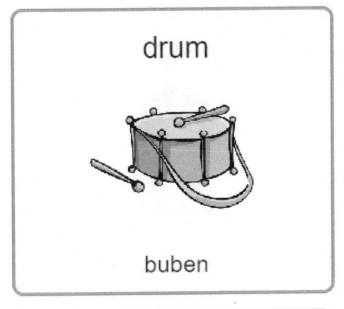

buben

wagon

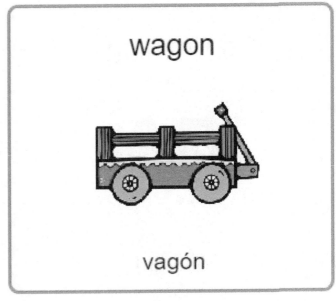

vagón

climbing

lezení

train

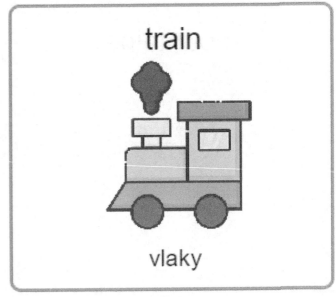

vlaky

parachute

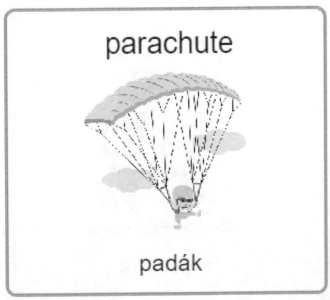

padák

scarf

šátek